Using Netscape IFC

que®

Using Netscape IFC

Written by Arun Rao

Using Netscape IFC

Library of Congress Catalog No.: 97-68572

ISBN: 0-7897-1251-2

99 98 97 6 5 4 3 2 1

Interpretation of the printing code: the rightmost double-digit number is the year of the book's printing; the rightmost single-digit number, the number of the book's printing. For example, a printing code of 97-1 shows that the first printing of the book occurred in 1997.

Screen reproductions in this book were created using Collage Plus from Inner Media, Inc., Hollis, NH.

Contents at a Glance

Table of Contents

Credits

PRESIDENT
Roland Elgey

SENIOR VICE PRESIDENT/PUBLISHING
Don Fowley

PUBLISHER
Stacy Hiquet

PUBLISHING MANAGER
Tim Ryan

GENERAL MANAGER
Joe Muldoon

EDITORIAL SERVICES DIRECTOR
Elizabeth Keaffaber

MANAGING EDITOR
Patrick Kanouse

ACQUISITIONS DIRECTOR
Cheryl D. Willoughby

ACQUISITIONS EDITOR
Stephanie McComb

PRODUCT DIRECTOR
Jon Steever

PRODUCTION EDITOR
Sean Medlock

EDITORS
Sean Dixon, Pat Kinyon, Phil Worthington

STRATEGIC MARKETING MANAGER
Barry Pruett

PRODUCT MARKETING MANAGER
Kourtnaye Sturgeon

ASSISTANT PRODUCT MARKETING MANAGER/ DESIGN
Christy M. Miller

ASSISTANT PRODUCT MARKETING MANAGER/ SALES
Karen Hagen

TECHNICAL EDITOR
Keith Ballinger

MEDIA DEVELOPMENT SPECIALIST
Brandon Penticuff

TECHNICAL SUPPORT SPECIALIST
Nadeem Muhammed

SOFTWARE RELATIONS COORDINATOR
Susan D. Gallagher

EDITORIAL ASSISTANT
Andrea Duvall

BOOK DESIGNER
Ruth Harvey

COVER DESIGNER
Dan Armstrong

PRODUCTION TEAM
Marcia Deboy
Kay Hoskin
Laura Knox

INDEXER
Kevin Fulcher

Composed in *Century Old Style* and *ITC Franklin Gothic* by Que Corporation.

To Namrata, Mom, and Dad

About the Author

Arun Rao is the founder of Digerati Corporation, a networking technology vendor providing Java products and services. Digerati has been on the forefront of pure Java application development using IFC technologies and has released such groupware products as superMail! and Discussor, which were showcased at the JavaOne exhibition at San Francisco in 1997.

After obtaining a degree in computer science, Arun has worked for over 10 years in various software development roles for such organizations as IBM, Lotus, and CommLabs. He has worked on such diverse systems as embedded control systems and Unisys mainframes, and spent the majority of his career developing Object-Oriented systems on Unix and NT platforms.

During his career, Arun has authored three patents relating to Internet and imaging technologies, and has been involved in developing many first-of-a-kind systems. These include one of the first Intranet solutions in 1994, while at IBM.

Arun has embraced Java and IFC since their inception and continues to support them in the business environment.

Arun lives with his wife, Namrata, in Dallas, Texas. His leisure activities include adventure sports and tourism.

Acknowledgments

Writing this book has fulfilled a dream. This would not have been possible without the support of family, friends, and the publisher.

First, I owe many thanks to my wife, Namrata, for her support, understanding, and patience. A big thanks to my parents and Anjana, John, and Arvind.

I would like to thank Vijay Kumar, Vic Moore, and Ujjwal Samel for their support throughout the years.

Thanks to the folks at Que who made this book a reality and did an excellent job in handling this challenging project. Special thanks to Stephanie McComb, Jon Steever, Sean Medlock, Keith Ballinger and the rest of staff at Que. It was a pleasure working with them.

We'd Like to Hear from You!

As part of our continuing effort to produce books of the highest possible quality, Que would like to hear your comments. To stay competitive, we *really* want you, as a computer book reader and user, to let us know what you like or dislike most about this book or other Que products.

You can mail comments, ideas, or suggestions for improving future editions to the address below, or send us a fax at (317) 581-4663. For the online inclined, Macmillan Computer Publishing has a forum on CompuServe (type **GO QUEBOOKS** at any prompt) through which our staff and authors are available for questions and comments. The address of our Internet site is **http://www.quecorp.com** (World Wide Web).

In addition to exploring our forum, please feel free to contact me personally to discuss your opinions of this book: I'm **jsteever@que.mcp.com** on the Internet.

Thanks in advance—your comments will help us to continue publishing the best books available on computer topics in today's market.

Jon Steever
Product Development Specialist
Que Corporation
201 W. 103rd Street
Indianapolis, Indiana 46290
USA

INTRODUCTION

Netscape IFC Introduction and Installation

The Abstract Windowing Toolkit (AWT) has been the de facto standard in building the user interface elements in Java-based applets and applications. For performance reasons, AWT creates peer objects on the native platform, so that the Java Virtual Machine (JVM) does not have to interpret those commands. This creates inconsistencies in the look and feel of various platforms because the native implementations differ. Another drawback of the AWT has been the event mechanism, which is cumbersome and heavyweight.

The Internet Foundation Classes (IFC) addresses some of the above issues and provides a complete set of user interface elements that are built on top of AWT. In addition, IFC provides frameworks for animation, object persistence, and drag-and-drop, among other things. (See Figure I.1.)

FIG. I.1
Sample IFC Application.

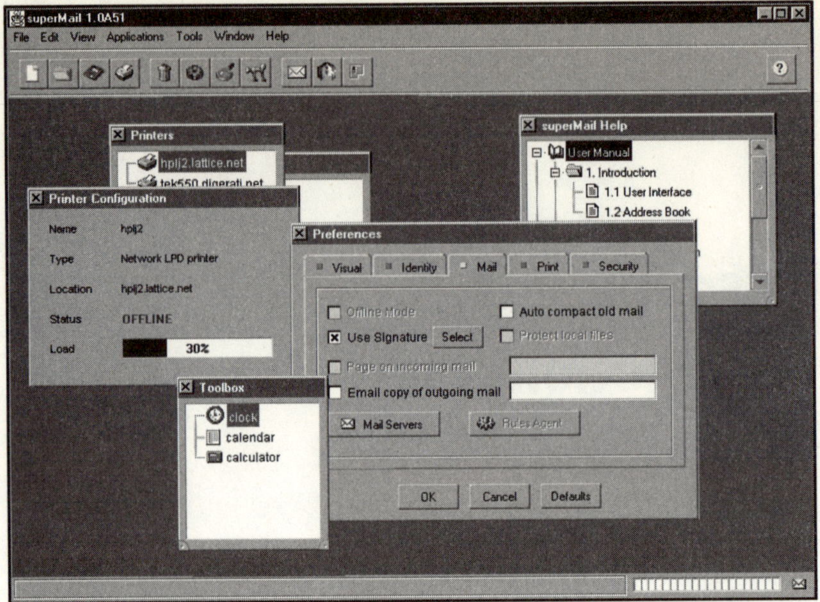

Some of the significant features and functions provided by IFC are:

- Powerful drawing and event framework
- Windowing system
- Advanced user-interface elements
- Animation framework
- Drag-and-drop framework
- Multi-font text support
- Persistent store/object archive system

We will be covering most aspects of IFC in subsequent chapters in the book. ■

History

In August 1995, Jayson Adams realized that writing serious Java applications using the existing user interface system was difficult. At that time, Java was evolving and was being used mainly to spice up Web pages with applets. For full-fledged applications to be written, reliable and extensible frameworks needed to be built. Javasoft had not yet released AWT, and there were many vendors working on user interface toolkits at that time. Adams created a view-based drawing/event framework later that year and founded Netcode Corporation along with Scott Love.

Meanwhile, Netscape encountered the same problems with writing Java-based applications and were looking for solutions. They started talking to Netcode in early 1996 and acquired them soon thereafter.

The Internet Foundation Classes (IFC) was born in early spring 1996 and showcased at the 1996 Netscape Internet Developers Conference.

The Netcode team was hired to continue work on the fledgling IFC, with Jayson Adams as the lead developer. After a few beta releases, IFC 1.0 was released in December 1996.

The IFC runtime classes are bundled with Netscape Communicator. Consequently, IFC applications will load faster in it because it will not download those classes.

Obtaining IFC

Netscape has a well-supported developer program called DevEdgeTM, which is at this URL:

http://developer.netscape.com

IFC is available as part of the NetscapeOne initiative, which is a collection of technologies to create an open network environment. The official IFC home page is at:

http://developer.netscape.com/library/ifc/index.html

The latest version of IFC is available there. (See Figure I.2.)

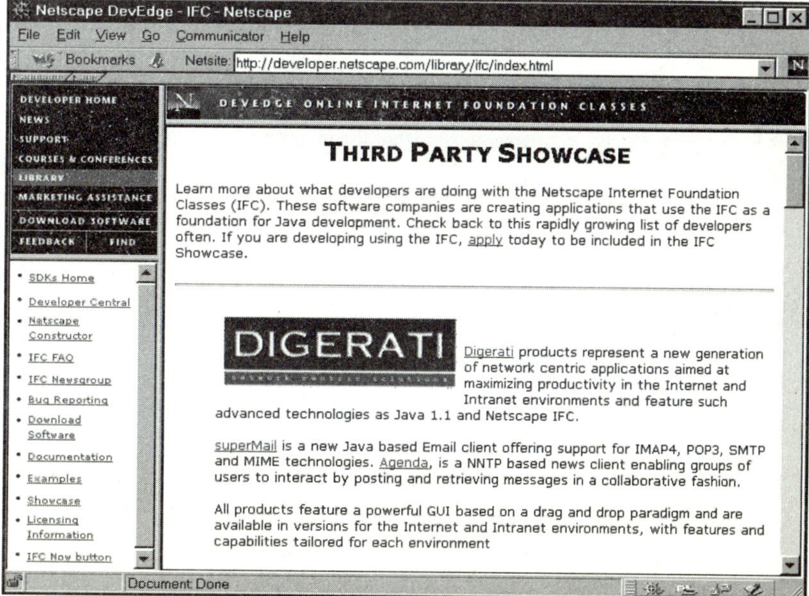

FIG. I.2
IFC Home Page.

The IFC runtime, which is the collection of classes required to run IFC applications, is available at:

http://home.netscape.com/eng/ifc/download.html

The IFC Software Development Kit (SDK), which we as developers are concerned about, is packaged in different formats for easy downloading and installation on various platforms. Source code versions of the IFC SDK are also available from this site.

NOTE IFC is subject to the Netscape ONE SDK license. Please read the license agreement before downloading.

We have included the latest versions available at the time of publication on the CD accompanying the book.

NOTE For simplicity, we will refer to the IFC SDK as IFC.

Developers are also encouraged to subscribe to the IFC news mailing list to receive important information regarding IFC.

The IFC package contains various files that are categorized by subdirectories into the following types:

- Classes—The Java classes that make up the `netscape.util`, `netscape.application`, and `netscape.constructor` packages.
- Examples—Example applications built using the IFC.
- Documentation—`javadoc`-generated HTML files that document the IFC.

Because you will frequently access the documentation files, it's a good idea to bookmark them in your browser.

IFC Installation

The SDK is packaged in zip and tar.gz formats.

NOTE The `zip` package contains files with long names. An unzip tool that restores long filenames, such as the infozip package available from **www.download.com**, should be used to unzip it.

IFC requires Java 1.0.2 or higher support. The Java SDK, or JDK, comes with all the tools necessary to develop Java programs. The Java compiler, called `javac`, is a command-line tool that uses environment variables to figure out the location of the runtime libraries.

The simplest IFC installation uses the JDK environment, with the associated CLASSPATH environment properly configured.

NOTE Macintosh installations, which do not use environment variables, are explained later in this chapter.

The basic procedure in the following platforms is to place the IFC class files in the CLASSPATH or a location where the Java compiler can find them.

Win32 (Win95, NT4.0) Installation

1. Using an unzip tool that restores long filenames, uncompress the IFC distribution file into a suitable location. For purposes of this example, it's assumed that this was the root directory of drive C. This will create a directory tree `C:\ifc10`.
2. Now append the classes subdirectory, `C:\ifc10\classes`, to the CLASSPATH environment variable as follows:

   ```
   SET CLASSPATH= %CLASSPATH%;C:\ifc10\classes;
   ```

3. To make these changes permanent, append the preceding line to your AUTOEXEC.BAT and reboot your machine.

NOTE An OS/2 installation is quite similar to the Win32 installation.

UNIX Installation

1. Uncompress the IFC distribution file into a suitable location. For purposes of this example, it is assumed that this was `~/lib`. This will create a directory tree `~/lib/ifc10` containing the directories discussed previously.
2. Now edit the CLASSPATH environment variable to include `ifc10/classes`.

   ```
   setenv CLASSPATH=~/lib/ifc10/classes
   ```

3. To make these changes permanent, append the above line to your `.profile` and restart your session.

Macintosh Installation

You cannot specify a CLASSPATH environment variable on the Macintosh. To use the IFC class library, you must make sure that it resides in the proper location:

1. Create the following folder within the System folder:

   `Preferences¦Netscape¦Java¦netscape-classes`

2. Copy the contents of the decompressed `ifc10¦classes` folder into the folder you created.

When you're finished, the `netscape-classes` folder should contain the `netscape¦application` and `netscape¦util` folders.

Using IDE Platforms with IFC

Development tool manufacturers like Symantec and Microsoft have Integrated Development Environments (IDE) available that are quite popular among professional programmers. The following section discusses IFC installation for three of the most widely used ones.

Visual Café

The path to IFC class files is specified in the Project Settings dialog box, which is available from the Project menu. You can append the path of your IFC files, `C:\ifc10\classes`, to the existing class path.

Visual J++

In Microsoft Visual J++, you can specify the path to the IFC class files in the `Tools¦Options¦Directories` fields (see Figure I.3).

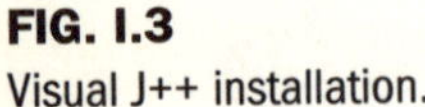

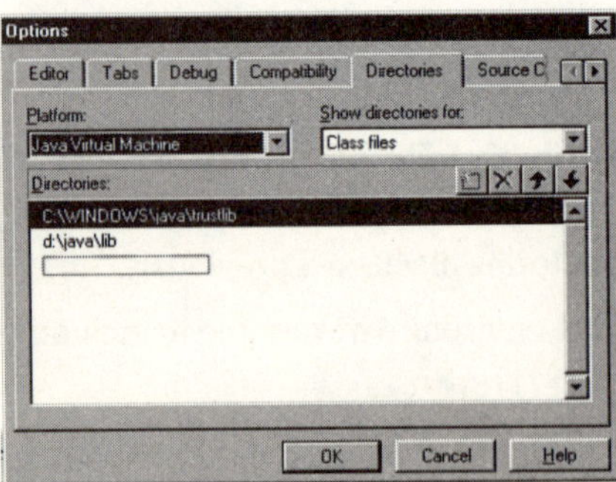

FIG. I.3
Visual J++ installation.

Java Workshop

Java Workshop from Sun Microsystems allows you to specify the path of extra class files in the `Project¦Edit` menu selection. You can append the path to the IFC class files in the Additional classpaths field (see Figure I.4).

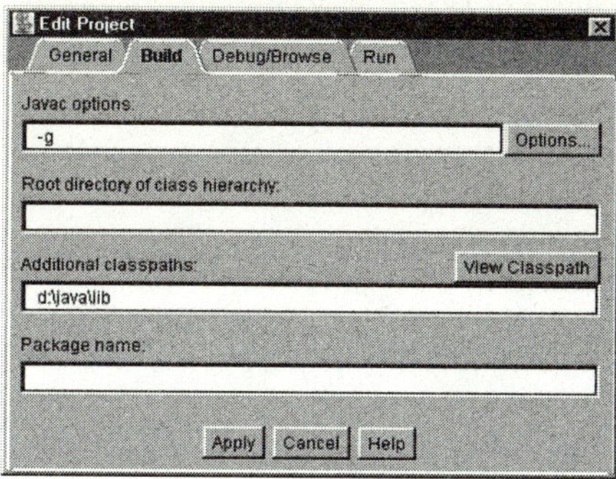

FIG. I.4
Java Workshop settings.

Testing Your Installation

Most common IFC installation problems are caused by incorrect classpath settings. A common compile time error message looks like this:

```
Package netscape.application not found in import
```

And runtime exceptions look like this:

```
java.io.FileNotFoundException:
➥\test\Simple\netscape\application\FoundationApplet.class
```

You can check the value of your current classpath variable by issuing the `set` command on Win32 platforms and the `set` or `showenv` commands on Unix platforms.

Another common error is encountered when using unzip tools that do not support long filenames. This causes all the filenames to be mangled and sometimes the subdirectories are not created.

If you're using an IDE for development, you might encounter similar messages. Please see your IDE software documentation for hints.

Besides the classpath problems, installing and running IFC should be quite easy. ●

PART I

Getting Started

CHAPTER 1

Getting Started

The big picture

Explore what IFC is all about and the various modules and frameworks that constitute IFC. Briefly look into some of the important subsystems and modules.

Create your first IFC program

Start writing our first IFC applet. We see the essentials of IFC programs and get a feel for some of the components which are available.

Write stand-alone IFC applications

Extend our first applet program to make it a stand-alone Java application.

Using foundation classes has been a popular practice among object-oriented programmers in recent times. Frameworks such as MacApp and Microsoft Foundation Classes (MFC) have enabled programmers to develop applications rapidly.

The IFC library is a collection of frameworks to help you write full-fledged applications in Java. These programs, which can run as applets or as applications, incorporate one or more of these frameworks. For example, most IFC applications have some sort of graphical interface, and include the drawing framework along with the event framework.

We will use the term "IFC application" to denote an IFC program irrespective of whether it's running as an applet or an application. ■

We touched upon some of these frameworks in the Introduction. Let's revisit them and see how they fit into the big picture. They're covered in depth in subsequent chapters of the book, as noted.

Some of the most common IFC frameworks are shown in the following list:

- Event framework

  The IFC event framework, also called the Target/Command framework, provides a generic mechanism for connecting objects and forms an integral part of most IFC programs. It lets IFC objects communicate with each other without knowing anything about the object. This framework is explored in Chapter 3, "Events."

- Drawing framework

  The IFC drawing framework provides a consistent component-based mechanism that delegates drawing to each of the components. The containerized structure of these components allows them to hold other components. IFC provides a rich set of ready-to-use components, called *Views*, and also provides an extensible architecture so you can create your own. Views are discussed in Chapter 2, "Foundations."

  The framework also provides features like offscreen buffering and mouse event coalescing. The drawing framework is explored in Chapter 2, "Foundations," mouse control in Chapter 4, "Keyboard and Mouse, " and views in Chapter 5, "Widgets."

- Windowing framework

  The IFC windowing system provides an advanced windowing system that comes in two varieties: external and internal. External windows are implemented natively and provide a platform-dependent look and feel. Features specific to that platform, like menu handling, are mapped natively. On the other hand, internal windows exist only within the frame of the application and can be customized to a great extent. Windowing is discussed in Chapter 6, "Windows."

- Drag-and-drop framework

  The IFC drag-and-drop framework enables IFC programs to implement familiar and intuitive drag-and-drop operations. It also provides a certain number of standard utilities, called *Choosers,* that are used to select entities such as colors and fonts. Choosers are based on a drag-and-drop paradigm and may be integrated into IFC applications with ease. This is discussed in Chapter 8, "Drag and Drop."

- Timers & animation

  Timers send messages to objects at predefined times and are used to build an extensible sequence framework. The generic sequence framework handles any sequence of tasks, including frame animation, in a repetitive or nonrepetitive manner. Timers and animation are discussed in Chapter 10, "Utilities."

- Multifont text

  The TextView object in IFC provides powerful multifont text-processing abilities, along with basic HTML handling abilities. Multifont text handling is discussed in Chapter 5, "Widgets."

- Persistence

  The IFC persistence system lets applications archive objects in their current state. These can be transported through a stream, which can include a network connection, a disk file, or a custom stream. The archived object can be restored with all its information and methods intact. Persistence is discussed in Chapter 9, "Persistence."

There are other systems and frameworks not listed here that are discussed in different sections of this book.

First IFC Program

Let's begin writing our first IFC program. We will attempt an extremely simple program that does nothing useful but illustrates some basic concepts about IFC.

firstApplet Example

The `firstApplet` example runs as an applet and displays a button with an "OK" label. It does little else. The program is shown in Listing 1.1.

Listing 1.1 ***firstApplet.java*: *firstApplet* Example**

```
import netscape.application.*;

public class firstApplet extends Application {

        public void init() {
                super.init();

                //.. create a Button component and set its label
                Button b = new Button(10,10,50,25);
                b.setTitle("OK");

                //.. add this button component to the background
                mainRootView().addSubview(b);
        }
}
```

Let's examine this program in detail:

```
import netscape.application.*;
```

The `import` statement imports the `netscape.application` package, which contains most of the classes required to build IFC programs. Unless you're using some explicit Java package, there's no need to import any Java packages.

NOTE Some IFC class names, such as `netscape.util.Vector`, clash with their Java counterparts, such as `java.util.Vector`. In such cases, you must explicitly refer to the classes by their fully qualified names. ■

Next, we write our application by subclassing the `netscape.application.Application` class:

```
public class firstApplet extends Application {
```

The `Application` class represents a complete IFC application, whether running as an applet or as a stand-alone Application. It handles most of the event processing and interfacing to the AWT, and manages resources on a application-wide basis among other functions. We will examine the Application class in greater detail in Chapter 11, "Advanced Topics."

NOTE All IFC programs must subclass the Application class. ■

The `init()` routine of the Application class initializes the Application, and in this example, we do most of our work here. We start up calling the `init()` method of the base class:

```
public void init() {
      super.init();
```

We then create a Button component and set its label:

```
Button b = new Button(10,10,50,25);
b.setTitle("OK");
```

The `Button` component is one of the many widgets that are part of IFC. The statement constructs a `Button` component at the pixel coordinates (10,10) with a width of 50 pixels and a height of 25 pixels. The IFC coordinate system is based on the familiar Cartesian coordinate system, with X representing the horizontal axis and Y the vertical axis. The origin (0,0) is always the top-left corner of the coordinate system. This is illustrated in Figure 1.1.

FIG. 1.1
IFC coordinate system.

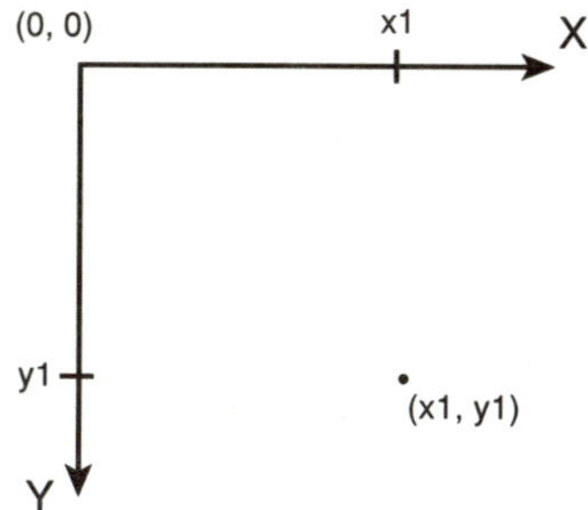

NOTE By default, IFC does not use any layout managers, and uses absolute positioning to lay out components.

We then set the label on the Button to "OK" using the `setTitle()` method of the `Button` component.

```
mainRootView().addSubview(b);
```

Lastly, we add the component to the RootView. The `mainRootView()` method of the `Application` class returns the parent background panel, which holds all other views for the application. The `addSubview()` method adds another view to this background panel.

Next, we implement the HTML file that uses this applet.

firstApplet HTML File

The HTML file that uses `firstApplet` example is shown in Listing 1.2.

Listing 1.2 *firstApplet.html*: *firstApplet* HTML File

```
<HTML>
<APPLET NAME="firstApplet" CODE="NetscapeApplet" WIDTH=70 HEIGHT=45>
<PARAM NAME="ApplicationClass" VALUE="firstApplet">
You need a Java enabled browser to use this document.
</APPLET>
</HTML>
```

Notice that our applet is passed as a parameter called `ApplicationClass` to the main `NetscapeApplet` class. This is due to the architecture of IFC, which must perform system-level functions for your application. The NetscapeApplet class, along with a more detailed explanation, is explored in the section titled "NetscapeApplet Class" at the end of the chapter.

Running the JDK `appletviewer` program with `firstApplet.html` JDK brings up the screen shown in Figure 1.2.

FIG. 1.2
firstApplet output.

Loading the HTML file inside a browser shows similar results.

NOTE Most IFC programs running as applets will have an HTML file similar to the one in Listing 1.2. Each IFC program would specify its main class name with the `ApplicationClass` parameter.

Stand-Alone IFC Applications

IFC programs running as stand-alone applications in the Java environment require some additional handling, as compared to their applet versions. This handling involves explicitly setting up the drawing environment and initializing the event-processing mechanism. Let's look into this by building the `firstApp` example.

firstApp Example

The `firstApp` example takes the `firstApplet` example previously discussed and enhances it to run as a stand-alone application. The program is shown in Listing 1.3.

Listing 1.3 *firstApp.java*: *firstApp* IFC Application

```
import netscape.application.*;

public class firstApp extends Application {

       public void init() {
              super.init();

              //.. create a Button component and set its label
              Button b = new Button(10,10,50,25); b.setTitle("OK");

              //.. add this button component to the background
              mainRootView().addSubview(b);
       }

       public static void main(String args[]) {

              //.. create an instance of our application
              firstApp app = new firstApp();

              //.. create an ExternalWindow to hold it
              ExternalWindow win = new ExternalWindow();
              //.. specify the window's background as the main background
              app.setMainRootView(win.rootView());
              //.. resize the window
              Size sz = win.windowSizeForContentSize(70,45);
              win.sizeTo(sz.width, sz.height);
              //.. show it
              win.show();

              //.. start event processing
              app.run();
       }
}
```

As you can see, the initial part of the example remains unchanged from the `firstApplet` version. The additional code is in the static `main()` method. As you know, when running as stand-alone applications, all java programs execute the `main()` method first:

```
public static void main(String args[]) {

       //.. create an instance of our application
       firstApp app = new firstApp();
```

The `main()` method starts off by creating an instance of our `firstApp` application:

```
//.. create an ExternalWindow to hold it
ExternalWindow win = new ExternalWindow();
//.. specify the window's background as the main background
app.setMainRootView(win.rootView());
```

Next we create an `ExternalWindow` component, which can be compared to the `java.awt.Frame` component. The `ExternalWindow` component is discussed in detail in Chapter 6, "Windows." Each `ExternalWindow` object has its own Rootview instance, which forms the background for that window. We then explicitly set our application's main RootView to this `ExternalWindow`'s RootView. Now our application has a place to draw:

```
//.. resize the window
Size sz = win.windowSizeForContentSize(70,45);
win.sizeTo(sz.width, sz.height);
//.. show it
        win.show();
```

Since the `ExternalWindow` has a size of (0,0) by default, we need to resize it to our desired size. Rather than directly resize it using absolute values, we find out the actual size of the `ExternalWindow` for our desired content size (70,45) by using its `windowSizeForContentSize` method. This ensures that the `ExternalWindow` takes into account its own drawing features, if applicable, when calculating its real size. These drawing features could include menu bars, etc.

The `ExternalWindow` is resized using the `sizeTo()` method and displayed using the `show()` method.

```
//.. start event processing
app.run();
}
```

Lastly, we start event processing in our IFC application by calling the `Application.run()` method for our program.

The application displays the screen shown in Figure 1.3.

NOTE Most stand-alone IFC programs will have a very similar `main()` routine

These are the essentials of stand-alone IFC applications. To summarize, stand-alone IFC applications require the following steps:

- Instantiate application object
- Create, size, and place an `ExternalWindow`
- Assign the `ExternalWindow`'s rootview as the application's rootview
- Start application event processing

FIG. 1.3
firstApp.java output.

NetscapeApplet Class

The IFC Application class, along with its associated foundation classes, encapsulates the operating environment of IFC applications. IFC foundation classes, which do basic interaction with AWT and the JVM, are installed as system classes. The standard Java API does not provide a mechanism for system classes to look up an applet's name by using the static `Class.ForName()` method. This method returns the `ClassLoader` associated with the caller's method block, which in this case would be `null`.

Hence, IFC programs running as applets must provide their own name explicitly to IFC. This is done by subclassing the `FoundationApplet` class and overriding the `classForName` method. This ensures that the IFC foundation can refer to the class name correctly.

The `NetscapeApplet` class is shown in Listing 1.4 and consists of a single method, `classForName()`.

Listing 1.4 *NetscapeApplet.java*: *NetscapeApplet* Class Definition

```
import netscape.application.*;

public class NetscapeApplet extends FoundationApplet {
        public Class classForName(String className) throws ClassNotFoundException
➥{
                return Class.forName(className);
        }
}
```

You can find a more technical explanation in the IFC documentation for `netscape.application.FoundationApplet`.

IFC programs running as stand-alone applications don't have this caveat because we explicitly control the program flow.

Here's what upcoming chapters will cover:

- Chapter 2, "Foundations," describes some of the core modules and concepts that form the basis of most IFC programs.
- Chapter 3, "Events," explores the IFC event mechanism, one of the fundamental building blocks of IFC applications.
- Chapter 4, "Keyboard and Mouse," covers events relating to the keyboard and mouse and shows you how to control them in the IFC environment.

CHAPTER 2

Foundations

IFC, which provides a set of useful frameworks for accomplishing many important tasks required in applications, has made writing robust applications in Java considerably easier. The drawing and event framework that IFC provides (one of its most powerful offerings) forms the basis of many other IFC systems and subsystems, such as the drag-and-drop framework. The basic building block of the drag-and-drop framework is the View component, which represents a visual component capable of reacting to events. To build IFC applications, Views are laid out and linked to each other using events.

One of main goals of IFC is to give Java applications the same appearance across different platforms. This is in contrast to the AWT approach, which maps visual components to the closest ones on the native platform.

Consistency across platforms in IFC is achieved by the View class hierarchy, which also provides a rich set of ready-to-use components with a uniform look and feel. The view framework also allows new components to be built with minimal effort. ■

Learn about the View class

Discusses the fundamental aspects of the IFC component system, which is built using the View class as a key building block.

Explore the *RootView*

Explores the special View subclass, which forms the backdrop of IFC applications.

Discover the View layout

Covers the subject of laying out components and discusses layout managers.

Look into Utility classes

Touches on many of the basic utility classes that IFC uses, such as Rect, Font, and Color.

View Class

The View class forms the basis of all GUI components in IFC. Besides handling drawing operations, it also acts as the receptor of events that control its behavior. It forms the base class of most IFC widgets, windows, and other drawable objects in the IFC framework.

IFC GUI applications are built by arranging one or more View objects and using events to connect them together. The event handling itself usually is processed as part of the main application.

The drawing system maintains a list of View objects arranged in a tree-like hierarchy, with each view having zero or more subviews, called *descendants*. This hierarchy also determines the sequence of each of the View objects in the application. This sequence, along with the View's visibility properties, decides what actually displays. There may be one or more views which are not visible at any given time, but which handle events and perform their other functions.

Views may contain one of more subviews and may themselves be contained in another view. The `addSubview()` and `removeSubview()` methods serve to add and delete subviews, while the `superview()` method returns the parent view.

A single View object is the parent of all other views in an IFC GUI application and forms the top level of the IFC view hierarchy. It's a special View type and is a `RootView` instance. (The next section examines `RootView` instances.)

Figure 2.1 illustrates the View hierarchy.

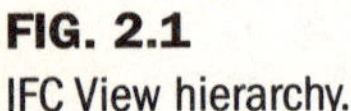
FIG. 2.1
IFC View hierarchy.

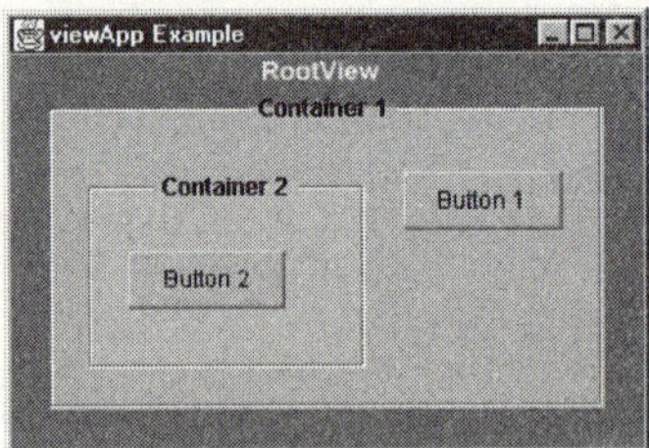

As the figure shows, the IFC application has a `RootView` instance that forms the backdrop of the application. It is accessible via the `Application.mainRootView()` method. The main `RootView` contains the `Container 1` object, which in turn contains `Button 1` and `Container 2`. `Container 2` also contains `Button 2`.

The code for the example depicted in Figure 2.1 is given in Listing 2.1. It shows how you can arrange views in an IFC application. Chapter 5, "Widgets," explores other View objects, such as `ContainerView` and `Button`.

Listing 2.1 viewApp.java: *viewApp* Example

```
import netscape.application.*;

public class viewApp extends Application {

      public void init() {
            super.init();

            //.. add Container 1 to the background
            ContainerView c1,c2;
            mainRootView().addSubview(c1 = new ContainerView(20,20,280,160));
            c1.setTitle("Container 1");

            //.. add Container 1 to Container 2
            c1.addSubview(c2 = new ContainerView(20,40,140,100));
            c2.setTitle("Container 2");
            c2.setBackgroundColor(Color.pink);

            //.. add Button 1 to Container 1
            Button b1;
            c1.addSubview(b1 = new Button(180,40,80,30));
            b1.setTitle("Button 1");

            //.. add Button 2 to Container 2
            c2.addSubview(b1 = new Button(20,40,80,30));
            b1.setTitle("Button 2");
      }

      /**
      *     standard GUI application main() routine
      */
      public static void main(String args[]) {

            viewApp app = new viewApp();
            ExternalWindow win = new ExternalWindow();
            app.setMainRootView(win.rootView());

            Size size = win.windowSizeForContentSize(320,200);
            win.sizeTo(size.width, size.height);
            win.setTitle("viewApp Example");
            win.show();

            app.run();
      }
}
```

Event processing for a view does not begin until after it is placed (using the parent view's `addSubview()` method) in the View hierarchy. Consequently, detached views are not passed any events by IFC, further improving performance.

Views essentially are rectangular in shape and are represented with an origin and size parameters. The origin is relative to its *ancestor*, or *superview*. As expected, the origin is the upper-left corner of the view and has the location of (0,0) in its own coordinate system. The width and height are measured in the X-axis to the right and Y-axis down, respectively. The rectangular region of the view is defined by the `bounds` variable and managed by using the `bounds()` and `setBounds()` methods.

Listing 2.2 gives the View class definition, which is quite powerful and extensive.

Listing 2.2 View Class

```
public class View  implements Codable {

      /* Fields
       */
      public final static int ARROW_CURSOR;                    //.. cursors
      public final static int CROSSHAIR_CURSOR;
      public final static int HAND_CURSOR;
      public final static int MOVE_CURSOR;
      public final static int TEXT_CURSOR;
      public final static int WAIT_CURSOR;
      public final static int NE_RESIZE_CURSOR;
      public final static int NW_RESIZE_CURSOR;
      public final static int SE_RESIZE_CURSOR;
      public final static int SW_RESIZE_CURSOR;
      public final static int N_RESIZE_CURSOR;
      public final static int S_RESIZE_CURSOR;
      public final static int E_RESIZE_CURSOR;
      public final static int W_RESIZE_CURSOR;

      public final static int LEFT_MARGIN_CAN_CHANGE;          //.. relative layout
      public final static int RIGHT_MARGIN_CAN_CHANGE;
      public final static int TOP_MARGIN_CAN_CHANGE;
      public final static int BOTTOM_MARGIN_CAN_CHANGE;
      public final static int WIDTH_CAN_CHANGE;
      public final static int HEIGHT_CAN_CHANGE;

      public final static int CENTER_HORIZ;                    //..layout
      public final static int CENTER_VERT;


      public final static int ALWAYS;                        //..misc
      public final static int WHEN_IN_MAIN_WINDOW;
      public final static int WHEN_SELECTED;

      public Rect bounds;      //.. bounding rectangle

      /* Constructors
       */
      public View();
      public View(Rect);
        public View(int, int, int, int);

      /* Methods
       */
```

```
public DragDestination acceptsDrag(DragSession, int, int);
public void addDirtyRect(Rect);
public void addSubview(View);
protected void ancestorWasAddedToViewHierarchy(View);
protected void ancestorWillRemoveFromViewHierarchy(View);
public Rect bounds();
public boolean canBecomeSelectedView();
public boolean canDraw();
public void computeVisibleRect(Rect);
public boolean containsPoint(int, int);
public boolean containsPointInVisibleRect(int, int);
public MouseEvent convertEventToView(View, MouseEvent);
public void convertPointToView(View, Point, Point);
public Point convertPointToView(View, Point);
public void convertRectToView(View, Rect, Rect);
public Rect convertRectToView(View, Rect);
public void convertToView(View, int, int, Point);
public Point convertToView(View, int, int);
protected Bitmap createBuffer();
public Graphics createGraphics();
public int cursorForPoint(int, int);
public void decode(Decoder);
public boolean descendsFrom(View);
public void describeClassInfo(ClassInfo);
public void didMoveBy(int, int);
public void didSizeBy(int, int);
public void disableDrawing();
public boolean doesAutoResizeSubviews();
public void draw(Graphics, Rect);
public void draw(Rect);
public void draw();
public void drawSubviews(Graphics);
public void drawView(Graphics);
public Bitmap drawingBuffer();
public void encode(Encoder);
public void finishDecoding();
public int graphicsDebugOptions();
public int height();
public boolean hidesSubviewsFromKeyboard();
public int horizResizeInstruction();
public void invalidateKeyboardSelectionOrder();
public boolean isBuffered();
public boolean isDirty();
public boolean isDrawingEnabled();
public boolean isInViewHierarchy();
public boolean isTransparent();
public void keyDown(KeyEvent);
public void keyUp(KeyEvent);
public Rect keyboardRect();
public LayoutManager layoutManager();
public void layoutView(int, int);
public Rect localBounds();
public Size minSize();
public boolean mouseDown(MouseEvent);
```

continues

Listing 2.2 Continued

```
        public void mouseDragged(MouseEvent);
        public void mouseEntered(MouseEvent);
        public void mouseExited(MouseEvent);
        public void mouseMoved(MouseEvent);
        public void mouseUp(MouseEvent);
        public void moveBy(int, int);
        public void moveTo(int, int);
        public View nextSelectableView();
        public void pauseFocus();
        public void resumeFocus();
        public View previousSelectableView();
        public void reenableDrawing();
        public void removeAllCommandsForKeys();
        public void removeCommandForKey(int);
        public void removeFromSuperview();
        protected void removeSubview(View);
        public RootView rootView();
        public void scrollRectToVisible(Rect);
        public void setAutoResizeSubviews(boolean);
        public void setBounds(Rect);
        public void setBounds(int, int, int, int);
        public void setBuffered(boolean);
        public void setCommandForKey(String, Object, int, int, int);
        public void setCommandForKey(String, int, int);
        public void setDirty(boolean);
        public void setFocusedView();
          public void setGraphicsDebugOptions(int);
          public void setHorizResizeInstruction(int);
        public void setLayoutManager(LayoutManager);
        public void setMinSize(int, int);
        public void setVertResizeInstruction(int);
        public void sizeBy(int, int);
        public void sizeTo(int, int);
        public void sizeToMinSize();
        public void startFocus();
        public void stopFocus();
        public void subviewDidMove(View);
        public void subviewDidResize(View);
        public Vector subviews();
        public View superview();
        public String toString();
        public int vertResizeInstruction();
        public View viewForMouse(int, int);
        public boolean wantsAutoscrollEvents();
        public boolean wantsMouseEventCoalescing();
        public int width();
        public void willBecomeSelected();
        public void willBecomeUnselected();
        public InternalWindow window();
        public int x();
        public int y();
}
```

The View class does many things; hence, its extensive API. Various parts of the book cover many of the methods shown in Listing 2.2, and the book refers to them from time to time. The `acceptsDrag()` method, for example, is used in the drag-and-drop framework, covered in Chapter 8, "Drag and Drop."

Drawing is accomplished in the `drawView()` method, which draws itself and its subview in the same order as represented in the view hierarchy default, by default. View subclasses implement custom drawing by overriding the `drawView()` method.

Clipping occurs at the view's boundary and a view may not draw outside its `bounds()`. All references to drawing coordinates are with respect to their own origins. Another key feature of the View class is the availability of off-screen buffering, which decreases *flicker* in drawing-intensive operations at the cost of a small amount of memory.

NOTE Offscreen (or double) buffering refers to the technique of creating a memory buffer on which all drawing takes place. This buffer is drawn at once onto the actual screen, providing flicker-free graphics. ■

Transparency in Views is implemented by the `isTransparent()` method, which by default returns true. If your custom view is not transparent, you should override the `isTransparent()` method to return false for better performance. When `isTransparent()` returns true, IFC draws the one or more views *behind* the transparent view before calling that view's `drawView()` method. Thus, drawing only a portion of the transparent view presents an illusion of transparency or irregularity.

Listing 2.3 is a simple example that shows custom drawing and transparency.

Listing 2.3 drawViewApp.java: *drawViewApp* Example

```
import netscape.application.*;

public class drawViewApp extends Application {

      public void init() {
            super.init();

            //.. add a bunch of circleView objects
            circleView cv;
            mainRootView().addSubview(cv = new circleView(0,0,100,100));
            mainRootView().addSubview(cv = new circleView(50,50,150,150));
            cv.color = Color.cyan;      //.. set its color
            mainRootView().addSubview(cv = new circleView(25,125,125,125));
            cv.color = Color.green; cv.border=true;     //.. set its color,
            ➥border
      }
```

continues

Listing 2.3 Continued

```
        /**
         *      standard GUI application main() routine
         */
        public static void main(String args[]) {

                drawViewApp app = new drawViewApp();
                ExternalWindow win = new ExternalWindow();
                app.setMainRootView(win.rootView());

                Size size = win.windowSizeForContentSize(200,300);
                win.sizeTo(size.width, size.height);
                win.setTitle("drawViewApp Example");
                win.show();

                app.run();
        }
}

/**
 * custom drawing view
 */
class circleView extends View {

        public Color color=Color.pink;
        public boolean border = false;

        public circleView(int x,int y,int w, int h) {
                super(x,y,w,h);
        }

        public void drawView(Graphics g) {
                if (border) {     //..draw border, if applicable
                        g.setColor(Color.black);
                        g.drawRect(0,0,width(),height());
                }
                g.setColor(color);      //..draw a circle with the current color
                g.fillOval(1,1,width()-2,height()-2);
        }
}
```

The code in Listing 2.3 here places three instances of the custom `circleView` object directly onto the main `RootView`, as shown in Figure 2.2.

Another popular method of supporting transparency in IFC is to use GIF89a image files, which support the transparent feature inside a `ContainerView` instance. Chapter 5, "Widgets," describes this method.

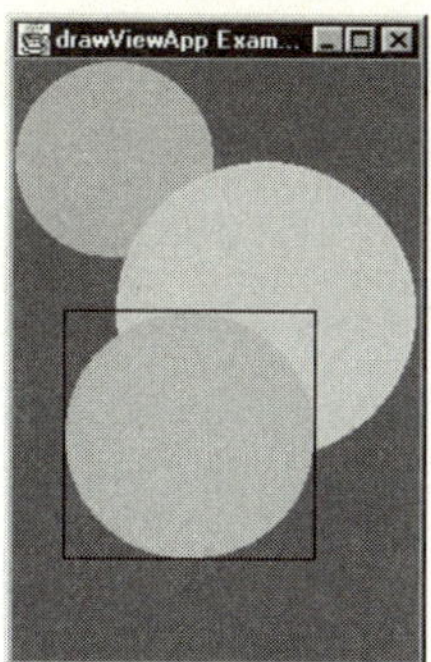

FIG. 2.2
drawViewApp example that shows custom drawing and transparency.

RootView

As first mentioned in Chapter 1, "Getting Started," the `RootView` object is the background on which IFC components are laid out. This section takes a closer look at this View subclass.

The *root view* is the top level of the view hierarchy in any IFC application; you might say, the ancestor of all other views. Each `ExternalWindow` object also has its own `RootView` instance along with its own view hierarchy. You will work with existing `RootViews` and will never instantiate a `RootView` directly.

`RootViews` also have the capability to display a Color and/or an Image (tiled, centered, or scaled). They also have a default set of `ColorChooser` and `FontChooser` utility widgets, which are covered in Chapter 10, "Utilities."

Listing 2.4 is the `RootView` class definition.

Listing 2.4 ***RootView* Class**

```
public class RootView extends View implements EventProcessor, ExtendedTarget {
      /* Constructors
      */
      public RootView();
      public RootView(Rect);
      public RootView(int, int, int, int);

      /* Methods
      */
      public boolean canBecomeSelectedView();
      public boolean canPerformCommand(String);
      public Color color();
      public ColorChooser colorChooser();
      public int cursor();
      public View defaultSelectedView();
```

continues

Listing 2.4 Continued

```
        public void draw(Graphics, Rect);
        public synchronized void drawDirtyViews();
        public void drawView(Graphics);
        public ExternalWindow externalWindow();
        public View focusedView();
        public FontChooser fontChooser();
        public Image image();
        public int imageDisplayStyle();
          public Vector internalWindows();
        public boolean isTransparent();
        public boolean isVisible();
        public InternalWindow mainWindow();
        public boolean mouseDown(MouseEvent);
        public Point mousePoint();
        public View mouseView();
          public FoundationPanel panel();
        public void performCommand(String, Object);
        public void processEvent(Event);
        public void redraw(Rect);
        public void removeOverrideCursor();
        public synchronized void resetDirtyViews();
        public RootView rootView();
        public void selectView(View, boolean);
        public void selectViewAfter(View);
        public void selectViewBefore(View);
        public void setColor(Color);
        public void setDefaultSelectedView(View);
        public void setFocusedView(View);
        public void setImage(Image);
        public void setImageDisplayStyle(int);
        public void setMouseView(View);
        public void setOverrideCursor(int);
        public void showColorChooser();
        public void showFontChooser();
        public void updateCursor();
        public void updateCursorLater();
        public View viewForMouse(int, int);
}
```

Besides providing methods to alter its appearance, such as `setColor()` and `setImage()`, the `RootView` class provides methods for mouse operations and keyboard interfacing. It also has methods for accessing the list of `InternalWindow` objects, as well as the `ExternalWindow` object, if any.

The most commonly used operations on the `RootView` include setting the color, which is dark gray by default, and setting an image as the background. You can tile, scale, or center this background image as you want. For example, to set a red background from anywhere, use the following code snippet:

```
Application.application().mainRootView().setColor(Color.red);
```

As shown in examples throughout the book, a standalone application must create an `ExternalWindow` object and designate that window's `RootView` as the application's root view. IFC manages this for Applets automatically.

View Layout

When you deal with multiple views, the position and size of the views become important. If your application uses fixed dimensions and places views at predefined locations, you don't need to worry about view layout issues. If your application locates views dynamically, however, or changes any superview's dimensions, then you might get results other than you hope to achieve. To address this issue, IFC furnishes layout managers.

Layout managers govern the layout behavior of a view within its superview. IFC implements its own View layout management scheme (called *relative layout* because views are laid out relative to their margins). By default, all IFC view components implement relative layout, which has no equivalent in AWT.

IFC also supports other layout managers via the `LayoutManager` interface and includes two—the `GridLayout` and `PackLayout` managers. You can also build your own layout manager by implementing the `LayoutManager` interface.

NOTE An important difference between relative layout and other layout managers is that relative layout applies to the View itself, whereas layout managers apply to that view's subviews.

It is possible to nest views that use different layout managers, providing greater flexibility in placement of views.

The `LayoutManager` interface definition is given in Listing 2.5.

Listing 2.5 *LayoutManager* Interface

```
public interface netscape.application.LayoutManager
{
      /* Methods
       */
      public abstract void addSubview(View);
      public abstract void layoutView(View, int, int);
      public abstract void removeSubview(View);
}
```

The `LayoutManager` definition has methods to add, remove, and lay out methods, and the `View.setLayoutManager()` method sets that view's layout manager.

Relative Layout

Views are anchored (by default) to their superview by their top-left corner (origin). The implication is that if you resize the view's superview, its origin and dimensions remain the same. There might be situations where you want more control over the placement of subviews when the superview is resized. For example, you might want to center a view such that even if the superview were resized, the view would remain centered.

The relative layout mechanism of the View class provides capabilities to effectively manage even complex layout scenarios, using the methods shown in Listing 2.6.

Listing 2.6 Relative Layout Methods and Constants in View Class

```
        public final static int LEFT_MARGIN_CAN_CHANGE;
        public final static int RIGHT_MARGIN_CAN_CHANGE;
        public final static int TOP_MARGIN_CAN_CHANGE;
        public final static int BOTTOM_MARGIN_CAN_CHANGE;
        public final static int WIDTH_CAN_CHANGE;
        public final static int HEIGHT_CAN_CHANGE;

        public void setHorizResizeInstruction(int);
        public void setVertResizeInstruction(int);
        public int horizResizeInstruction();
public int vertResizeInstruction();
```

As you can see, IFC's horizontal and vertical resize instructions control relative layout behavior. The default horizontal and vertical resize instructions are `RIGHT_MARGIN_CAN_CHANGE` and `BOTTOM_MARGIN_CAN_CHANGE`, respectively.

Figure 2.3 illustrates the behavior of the horizontal resize instruction. You can change any of the three parameters or, by default, leave them constant.

The horizontal resize instruction can specify any of the following values:

- **`LEFT_MARGIN_CAN_CHANGE`**. Specifies that the distance between the left edge of a view and the left edge of its superview can change.
- **`RIGHT_MARGIN_CAN_CHANGE`**. Specifies that the distance between the right edge of a view and the right edge of its superview can change.
- **`WIDTH_CAN_CHANGE`**. Specifies that the width of the view itself can change to maintain constant and distances on its sides.

FIG. 2.3
Horizontal resize instruction in relative layout.

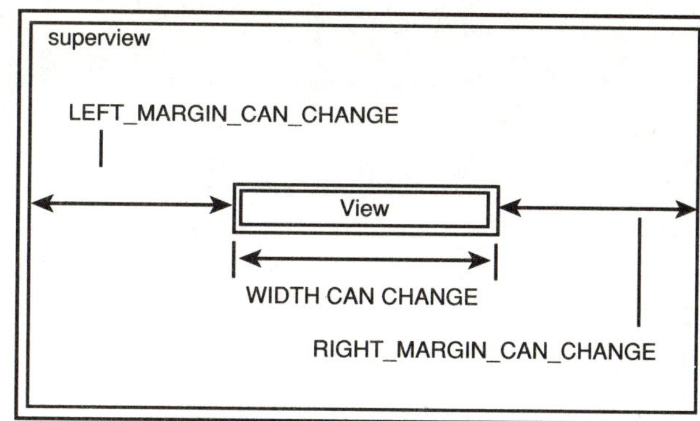

Similarly, the vertical resize instruction can specify any of the following values:

- **`TOP_MARGIN_CAN_CHANGE`**. Specifies that the distance between the top edge of a view and the top edge of its superview can change.
- **`BOTTOM_MARGIN_CAN_CHANGE`**. Specifies that the distance between the bottom edge of a view and the bottom edge of its superview can change.
- **`HEIGHT_CAN_CHANGE`**. Specifies that the height of the view itself can change.

GridLayout

A view with a `GridLayout` layout manager maintains its views in a two-dimensional matrix of equal-size cells. You may specify the exact dimensions of the matrix, or you may set the rows and/or columns to 0 to denote that the `GridLayout` can grow in that direction. If you set the number of columns to 0, for example (using a constructor or the `setColumnCount()` method), the layout manager uses as many rows as necessary to hold all of a view's subviews.

The position of the views in the `GridLayout` is determined by the order in which they are placed and begin in the top-left corner of the layout. The direction of placement, or *flow direction,* can be specified (the default is left-to-right). If you add a number of views exceeding the grid's capacity, IFC places them outside the view's clip region, and, therefore, outside of view.

NOTE When you use layout managers in IFC, you must explicitly call the `layoutView()` method after you add or remove subviews. This is required because the view doesn't know when the addition/removal is complete. It arranges all the subviews only when you call the `layoutView()`. Until then, newly added views are not visible.

When you use a grid layout to resize a view, the grid layout manager resizes each of the view's subviews to fit in a cell in the grid. It simply sizes the cells so that the grid fits into the view and ignores a view's minimum size.

Using the `GridLayout` layout manager is relatively simple, as Listing 2.7 demonstrates.

Listing 2.7 gridApp.java: *gridApp* Example

```
import netscape.application.*;

/**
 *      GridLayout example
 */
public class gridApp extends Application {

        public void init() {
                super.init();

                //.. create a internal window
                InternalWindow w = new InternalWindow(10,10,480,260);
                w.setResizable(true);
                w.setTitle("Resizable Window");

                //.. set the window's layout manager to a new GridLayout
                GridLayout g;
                w.contentView().setLayoutManager(g = new GridLayout(1,0));

                //.. set parameters for the GridLayout
                g.setFlowDirection(GridLayout.FLOW_ACROSS);
                g.setHorizGap(10); g.setVertGap(10);

                //.. add 4 containers to the window
                ContainerView c;
                c = new ContainerView();
                c.setTitle("Panel #1");
                w.addSubview(c);

                c = new ContainerView();
                c.setTitle("Panel #2");
                w.addSubview(c);

                c = new ContainerView();
                c.setTitle("Panel #3");
                w.addSubview(c);

                c = new ContainerView();
                c.setTitle("Panel #4");
                w.addSubview(c);

                //.. must explicitly lay out view (window)
                w.contentView().layoutView(0,0);

                w.show();     //.. explicitly show the window
```

```
        }

        /**
        *     standard GUI application main() routine
        */
        public static void main(String args[]) {

              gridApp app = new gridApp();
              ExternalWindow win = new ExternalWindow();
              app.setMainRootView(win.rootView());

              Size size = win.windowSizeForContentSize(640,480);
              win.sizeTo(size.width, size.height);
              win.setTitle("gridApp Example");
              win.show();

              app.run();
        }
}
```


The `gridApp` example brings up the screen shown in Figure 2.4.

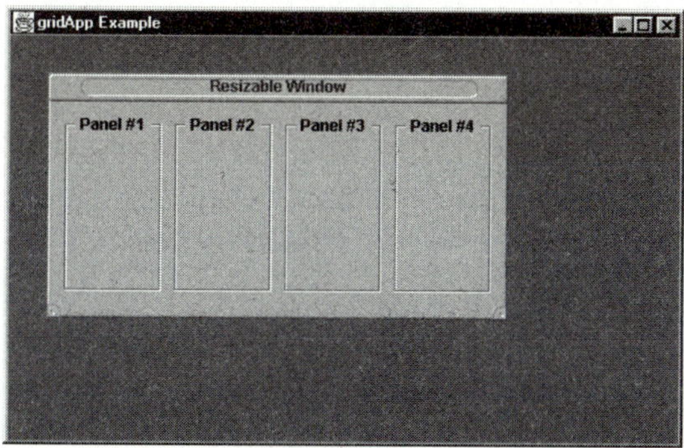

FIG. 2.4 `gridApp` example that shows usage of `GridLayout`.

Note that resizing the window causes the subviews to be resized automatically and that all subviews are of equal size.

PackLayout

The `PackLayout` manager provides asymmetric handling of view layout functionality by dealing with each view individually, as opposed to the `GridLayout` manager, which manages each view uniformly and maintains equal-sized subviews. Similar in concept and usage to the AWT `GridBagLayout` class, the `PackLayout` manager manages subviews based on a set of rules that is encapsulated by the `PackConstraints` class.

The IFC lays out subviews added to views managed by `PackLayout` managers according to their own constraints, and sometimes depends on other peer subviews, too.

The `PackConstraints` class specifies how a PackLayout manager should size and place a subview and includes the following parameters (which you can control):

- **Anchor.** Determines the location in which the view should be placed within its own area; used when the view is smaller than its allocated space (the default is `ANCHOR_CENTER`)
- **Side.** Sets the side of the view's allocated area to which the `PackLayout` manager should attach the view (the default is `SIDE_TOP`)
- **Expand.** Specifies whether the `PackLayout` manager should enlarge the view to fill any extra space within the view's allocated area (false by default)
- **Fill.** Specifies whether the `PackLayout` manager should enlarge the view to fill any extra space along the X- and Y-axes of the view's allocated area (false by default)
- **Padding.** Sets the padding that the `PackLayout` manager adds to the view's width and height (0 by default)

Listing 2.8 provides the definition of the `PackConstraints` class. It primarily contains methods for managing these five parameters.

Listing 2.8 ***PackConstraints* Class**

```
public class PackConstraints implements Codable, java.lang.Cloneable {
    /* Fields
    */
    public final static int ANCHOR_CENTER;
    public final static int ANCHOR_EAST;
    public final static int ANCHOR_NORTH;
    public final static int ANCHOR_NORTHEAST;
    public final static int ANCHOR_NORTHWEST;
    public final static int ANCHOR_SOUTH;
    public final static int ANCHOR_SOUTHEAST;
    public final static int ANCHOR_SOUTHWEST;
    public final static int ANCHOR_WEST;
    public final static int SIDE_BOTTOM;
    public final static int SIDE_LEFT;
    public final static int SIDE_RIGHT;
    public final static int SIDE_TOP;

    /* Constructors
    */
    public PackConstraints();
    public PackConstraints(int, boolean, boolean, boolean, int, int, int, int,
    ➥int);

    /* Methods
    */
    public int anchor();
    public Object clone();
```

```
        public void decode(Decoder);
        public void describeClassInfo(ClassInfo);
        public void encode(Encoder);
        public boolean expand();
        public boolean fillX();
        public boolean fillY();
        public void finishDecoding();
        public int internalPadX();
        public int internalPadY();
        public int padX();
        public int padY();
        public void setAnchor(int);
        public void setExpand(boolean);
        public void setFillX(boolean);
        public void setFillY(boolean);
        public void setInternalPadX(int);
        public void setInternalPadY(int);
        public void setPadX(int);
        public void setPadY(int);
        public void setSide(int);
        public int side();
}
```

The final result for a view managed by the `PackLayout` manager depends on the following factors:

- List of subviews as you add them
- Pack constraints associated with each subview
- Order in which you add the subviews (because the layout manager processes the subviews in the order in which you add them)

The following example, `packApp`, highlights various aspects of the `PackLayout` manager. The `packApp` example creates the layout shown in Figure 2.5.

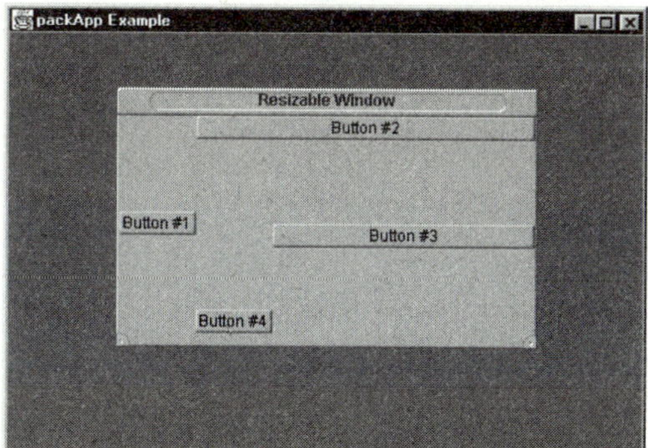

FIG. 2.5
`packApp` example that shows usage of `PackLayout`.

The packApp example lays out four buttons, using the PackLayout manager, and anchors each button to one of the four sides of the window, respectively. The Java code for this example (furnished in Listing 2.9) sets the fill parameter to true in the X direction, which causes the buttons to grow in the horizontal direction as shown in Figure 2.5. Note that the buttons have taken different widths depending on the sequence in which the code adds them and on the available space at the time.

Listing 2.9 packApp.java: *packApp* Example

```
import netscape.application.*;

/**
 *
 */
public class packApp extends Application {

     public void init() {
          super.init();

            //.. create an internal window
            InternalWindow w = new InternalWindow(10,10,320,200);
            w.setResizable(true);
          w.setTitle("Resizable Window");

          //.. set the window's view to have a new pack layout manager
          PackLayout p;
          PackConstraints pc = new PackConstraints();
          w.contentView().setLayoutManager(p = new PackLayout());
          //.. subviews should fill horizontally
          pc.setFillX(true);

          //.. add some buttons
          Button b;
          b = new Button(0,0,50,50);
          b.setTitle("Button #1");
          pc.setSide(PackConstraints.SIDE_LEFT);     //.. attach to left side
          p.setConstraints(b, pc);                 //.. associate the constraints
          w.addSubview(b);

          b = new Button(0,0,50,50);
          b.setTitle("Button #2");
          pc.setSide(PackConstraints.SIDE_TOP);          //.. attach to top side
          p.setConstraints(b, pc);
          w.addSubview(b);

          b = new Button(0,0,50,50);
          b.setTitle("Button #3");
          pc.setSide(PackConstraints.SIDE_RIGHT);     //.. attach to right side
          pc.setExpand(true);                      //.. should expand
          p.setConstraints(b, pc);
          w.addSubview(b);
```

```
            b = new Button(0,0,50,50);
            b.setTitle("Button #4");
            pc.setSide(PackConstraints.SIDE_BOTTOM);     //.. attach to bottom
            ➥side
            pc.setExpand(false);                         //.. should not expand
            p.setConstraints(b, pc);
            w.addSubview(b);

            //.. done adding views, so explicitly call layoutView()
            w.contentView().layoutView(0,0);

            w.show();      //..must show() window to make it visible
        }

        /**
           *     standard GUI application main() routine
        */
        public static void main(String args[]) {

              packApp app = new packApp();
              ExternalWindow win = new ExternalWindow();
               app.setMainRootView(win.rootView());

               Size size = win.windowSizeForContentSize(480,320);
               win.sizeTo(size.width, size.height);
               win.setTitle("packApp Example");
               win.show();

    app.run();
    }
    }
```

You can find a detailed explanation of the mechanics of the pack layout operation in the IFC cookbook examples (available at the IFC site) and related IFC documentation.

NOTE Existing AWT custom layout managers can be ported to IFC using IFC's LayoutManager interface.

Utility Classes

IFC provides some utility classes to manage measurement, data representation, and so on. Some of these utility classes are:

- **Point.** Represents an (x, y) coordinate in the IFC framework
- **Rect.** Represents a rectangular area with an origin and width, height values
- **Size.** Represents a width and height value (can be positive or negative)

- **Range.** Represents a set of contiguous indexed data with start and length parameters

IFC also provides classes to handle Fonts and Colors as discussed below.

Fonts

The IFC `Font` class represents a single font — its name, size, and style — and provides some additional convenience methods, such as the `fontNamed()` method, which is a static method. Ideally, you should use this method instead of creating your own fonts.

The `FontMetrics` class manages a font's dimensions and characteristics. (It presently contains only screen metric information.) It gives values such as the actual width and height of a character or string and is invaluable in laying out text precisely. Font characteristics that can be accessed by using the `FontMetrics` class are shown in Figure 2.6.

FIG. 2.6
Common font characteristics.

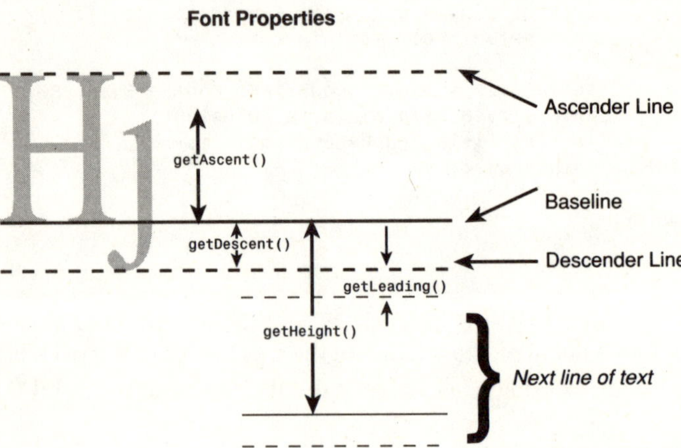

The font system also provides a font chooser standard dialog box for selecting fonts. Chapter 10, "Utilities," includes an examination of the `FontChooser` utility.

The `AWTCompatibility` class (presented in Listing 2.10) provides static methods for translating between IFC and AWT fonts.

Listing 2.10 *AWTCompatibility* Class Font-Related Methods

```
public static java.awt.Font awtFontForFont(Font);
public static java.awt.FontMetrics awtFontMetricsForFontMetrics(FontMetrics);
public static Font fontForAWTFont(java.awt.Font);
public static FontMetrics fontMetricsForAWTFontMetrics(java.awt.FontMetrics);
```

NOTE Like almost everything in IFC, the font class implements the codable interface, making it persistent.

Colors

The `Color` class manages colors, representing them by their red, green, and blue (RGB) values. The class also provides a standard set of ready-to-use colors, available as static values. It also provides convenient methods for translating RGB values to the Hue, Saturation, and Brightness (HSB) representation of color.

IFC also provides a color chooser utility, a standard dialog box in which you can select and create a custom color. Chapter 10, "Utilities," offers a look into the `ColorChooser` utility.

CHAPTER 3

Events

Target and _ExtendedTarget_ interfaces

We examine how IFC implements objects that accept commands.

Event classes and _EventLoop_

The abstract `Event` class and subclasses are studied, along with the queue data structure that manages the sequence of events.

EventProcessor, _EventFilter_ interfaces

Advanced event-handling operations like custom processing and filtering of events can be done.

Modern Graphical User Interface (GUI) systems use some form of event mechanism to handle the complex set of actions occurring within the system, most of which are generated when the user interacts with the system. These actions include user-initiated actions like keyboard operations and button clicks. Actions like timer events generated under program control are examples of events that occur without user interaction.

IFC provides a flexible event system, which allows complex event-driven programs to be designed. As events are generated in an IFC application, they are queued in each Application's `EventLoop` structure, where they are handled sequentially by the event handler. Programs have the power to process any of these events, to generate new ones, and to manipulate the event loop itself.

In this chapter we will look into the IFC event mechanism and build an example for command event processing.

Event Model

Because IFC is built on top of the default Java GUI system, called Another Windowing Toolkit (AWT), it must process AWT events along with its own. The entire AWT event mechanism is hidden from the IFC programmer and simplified into essentially the `Target` interface, which is examined in the next section.

Events are encapsulated in the `Event` class hierarchy, which is subclassed to handle various types of events. As events arrive from the AWT, along with some that are generated internally, IFC places them on the application's event queue, which is an `EventLoop` object. Each IFC application has a main thread that removes an event from the event queue and directs it to the object that should receive it.

In its main thread, the application removes an event from the queue, determines its destination, and then delivers the event, executing the event processing code in the receiving object. Once this code completes, the application's main thread removes the next event and repeats the cycle. This is illustrated in Figure 3.1.

FIG. 3.1
IFC Event Model.

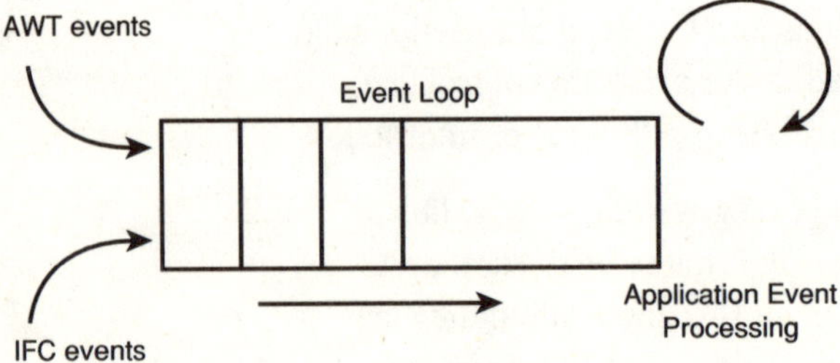

Unless your application creates additional threads, this design ensures that there is never more than one thread executing code in your application.

Target Interface

The `Target` interface is implemented by objects that want to receive and process commands and objects. It provides a generic mechanism to *classify* objects that process messages and is used widely by various parts of IFC. When objects need to send messages to other objects without knowing their type and structure, they can use the `Target` interface. It specifies a string command that describes the action that the target should perform, along with an arbitrary data parameter. Thus, without any prior knowledge of the destination, an object can send a command event to it.

For example, many widgets need to send their events to a destination, and this is done using their `setTarget()` method, which accepts a `Target` object. Thus, any object that implements the `Target` interface can accept that widget's events.

The interface definition consists of a single method that accepts the command name along with an argument of type Object. This is shown in Listing 3.1.

Listing 3.1 *Target* Interface

```
public interface Target {
        public abstract void performCommand(String command, Object data);
}
```

The `Target` object receives various commands via the command parameter and a generic argument via the data parameter.

targetApp Example

Let's work on a simple example that uses the Target interface. The `targetApp` example, shown in Listing 3.2, implements the `targetApp` class, which implements the `Target` interface. A `Button` component sends the programmed command event to this class.

Listing 3.2 *targetApp.java*: Using the *Target* Interface

```
import netscape.application.*;

/**
 *Application which implements the Target interface
 */
public class targetApp extends Application implements Target {

    public void init() {
        super.init();
            mainRootView().setColor(Color.lightGray);

            //.. put a button, which triggers all our events
            Button b = new Button(50,50,100,30);
            //.. set label on button
            b.setTitle("Click Me");
            //.. set Target for this button
            b.setTarget(this);
            //.. associate command for this button
            b.setCommand("cmdButton");
```

continues

Listing 3.2 Continued

```
            //.. add the button to the background
            mainRootView().addSubview(b);
    }

    public void performCommand(String command, Object arg) {
            //.. handle commands
            if (command.equals("cmdButton")) {
                    //.. display message box
                    Alert.runAlertInternally("Message","Button was
Pressed","OK",null,null);
            }
    }

    /**
     *      standard GUI application main() routine
     */
   public static void main(String args[]) {

        targetApp app = new targetApp();
        ExternalWindow win = new ExternalWindow();
        app.setMainRootView(win.rootView());

        Size size = win.windowSizeForContentSize(300,240);
        win.sizeTo(size.width, size.height);
            win.setTitle("targetApp Example");
        win.show();

        app.run();
   }
}
```

The example creates a Button and sets its command and target. When the user clicks the Button, the `cmdButton` command is sent to the Target, which in this case is the `targetApp` class itself. The `performCommand()` method receives this event and displays a dialog box with a message.

ExtendedTarget Interface

The `ExtendedTarget` interface extends the generic `Target` interface and allows the command processing framework to be extended. Objects implementing the `ExtendedTarget` interface can define custom commands by implementing the `canPerformCommand()` method. The IFC event processing framework will then query that object to see whether it can perform a particular command. For example, the `TextView` widget (explored in Chapter 5, "Widgets"), which implements the `ExtendedTarget` interface, returns `True` when asked if it can perform the `ExtendedTarget.SET_FONT` command. This is used to interface `TextView` with the `FontChooser` widget, which is explored in Chapter 10, "Utilities."

The `ExtendedTarget` interface consists of a single method, `canPerformCommand()`, which handles the interrogation as to whether the object can handle a specific command. It also has some class variables, as seen in Listing 3.3.

Listing 3.3 *ExtendedTarget* Interface

```
public interface ExtendedTarget implements Target {
        public final static String COPY;
        public final static String CUT;
        public final static String NEW_FONT_SELECTION;
        public final static String PASTE;
        public final static String SET_FONT;
        public final static String SHOW_COLOR_CHOOSER;
        public final static String SHOW_FONT_CHOOSER;

        public abstract boolean canPerformCommand(String);
}
```

Note that the interface also defines various constant values that have special meaning inside the IFC framework. For example, the `ExtendedTarget.NEW_FONT_SELECTION` tells the `FontChooser` widget to set the current font.

Event Class

The `Event` class is the abstract base class for all events in IFC. It encapsulates the common features and functions relating to events and is used to denote an entry in the application's event queue.

The `Event` class definition is shown in Listing 3.4.

Listing 3.4 *Event* Class

```
public class Event implements Cloneable {

        public Event();
        public Event(long);

        public Object clone();
        public EventProcessor processor();
        public void setProcessor(EventProcessor);
        public void setTimeStamp(long);
        public void setType(int);
        public long timeStamp();
        public int type();
}
```

In addition to setting and reading parameters like the time stamp and type, the class allows you to specify the `EventProcessor` associated with the `Event` object. This is covered in more detail in the section on the `EventProcessor` interface.

Under IFC, the `Event` class is subclassed into the following three subclasses to handle various events:

- `CommandEvent`

  Generic application command processing event subclass.

- `KeyEvent`

  Event subclass that handles events relating to keyboard actions and events.

- `MouseEvent`

  Subclass encapsulating events and values relating to mouse events in an IFC application.

NOTE In addition, IFC uses the `ApplicationEvent` class internally to handle events relating to the operation of the IFC Application. ■

`KeyEvent` and `MouseEvent` classes are examined in detail in Chapter 4, "Keyboard and Mouse."

If you have a requirement for specialized event handling, you may subclass any of the above classes or create a custom `Event` subclass.

CommandEvent Class

If your application needs to insert command events into the application event queue, you can use the `CommandEvent` class to achieve this. Another approach is to use the `performCommandAndWait()` and `performCommandLater()` methods in the `Application` class.

To use it, you must instantiate a `CommandEvent`, configure its `Target`, command and data, and add it to an `EventLoop`. Upon being processed, it sends the `performCommand()` message to its `Target`.

The class definition itself is given in Listing 3.5.

Listing 3.5 *CommandEvent* Class

```
public class CommandEvent extends Event implements EventProcessor {
      public CommandEvent();
      public CommandEvent(Target, String, Object);

      public String command();
```

```
        public Object data();
        public void processEvent(Event);
        public void setCommand(String);
        public void setData(Object);
        public void setTarget(Target);
        public Target target();
}
```

Notice that the `CommandEvent` class implements the `EventProcessor` interface, enabling it to send its command and argument to the specified `Target` object.

cmdEventApp Example

Let us construct an example that uses command event processing. The `cmdEventApp` example places a button that, when clicked, causes a chain of events to be generated and processed by the application. Details are given in Figure 3.2.

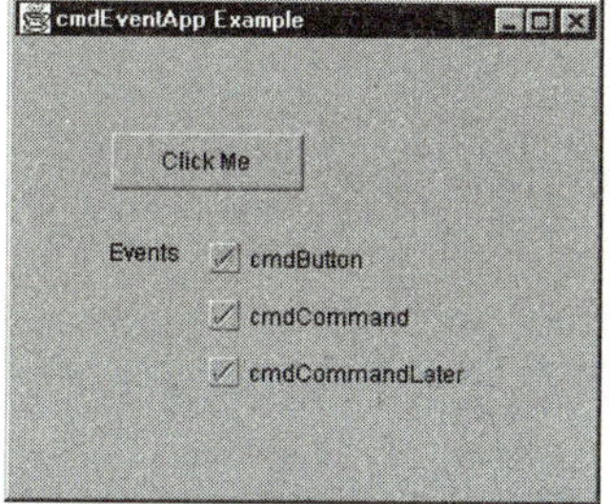

FIG. 3.2
`cmdEventApp` example.

The `cmdEventApp` example lays out a button along with three checkboxes for each of the three types of command events we are using. The button, when clicked, fires off a `cmdButton` command event. The `performCommand()` method, which receives all command events for a `Target` object, toggles the first check box and creates and inserts a new `cmdCommand` command event object into the main application event queue. When this is processed, again in the `performCommand()` method, it toggles the second check box and asks the application to perform the `cmdCommandLater` command using the `performCommandLater()` method. Finally, when the `cmdCommandLater` command is processed, the third check box is toggled. The program listing for the `cmdEventApp` example is shown in Listing 3.6.

Most IFC programs would use some form of command event processing, as these events constitute user-defined events. The IFC programmer ties together different components by handling the command events. Command processing using the `performCommand()` method is sufficient for most IFC programs. More advanced applications can use the `performCommandLater()` method to improve performance.

Listing 3.6 *cmdEventApp.java: cmdEventApp* Example

```
import netscape.application.*;

/**
 *     Application creates and uses command events
 */
public class cmdEventApp extends Application implements Target {

      Button btn1, btn2, btn3;

      public void init() {
            super.init();
            mainRootView().setColor(Color.lightGray);

//.. put a button, which triggers all our events
            Button b = new Button(50,50,100,30);
            b.setTitle("Click Me");
b.setTarget(this);
b.setCommand("cmdButton");
            mainRootView().addSubview(b);

            //.. add a label
            Label lab = new Label("Events",
Font.fontNamed("Arial",Font.PLAIN,12));
            lab.moveTo(50,105);
            mainRootView().addSubview(lab);

            //.. add the three display buttons
            mainRootView().addSubview(btn1 =
Button.createCheckButton(100,100,150,30));
            btn1.setTitle(" cmdButton");
            mainRootView().addSubview(btn2 =
Button.createCheckButton(100,130,150,30));
            btn2.setTitle(" cmdCommand");
            mainRootView().addSubview(btn3 =
Button.createCheckButton(100,160,150,30));
            btn3.setTitle(" cmdCommandLater");

      }

      public void performCommand(String command, Object arg) {

            if (command.equals("cmdButton")) {
                  //.. click the first button to reflect that we have received
this event
                  btn1.click();
                  //.. if the button was clicked, add a new CommandEvent object
to the
                  //   main application eventLoop
                  CommandEvent ev = new CommandEvent(this,"cmdCommand",null);
                  Application.application().eventLoop().addEvent(ev);
            }
            else if (command.equals("cmdCommand")) {
                  //.. click the second button to reflect that we have received
```

```
this event
                    btn2.click();
                    //.. we have received a user generated CommandEvent, add
another command
                    //   to the application event loop by using the
performCommand() method
         Application.application().performCommandLater(this,"cmdCommandLater",null);
             }
             else if (command.equals("cmdCommandLater")) {
                    //.. click the third button to reflect that we have received
this event
             btn3.click();
             }
      }

      /**
 *     standard GUI application main() routine
       */
      public static void main(String args[]) {

             cmdEventApp app = new cmdEventApp();
             ExternalWindow win = new ExternalWindow();
                      app.setMainRootView(win.rootView());

             Size size = win.windowSizeForContentSize(300,240);
             win.sizeTo(size.width, size.height);
             win.setTitle("cmdEventApp Example");
             win.show();

             app.run();
      }
}
```

EventProcessor Interface

Each `Event` object has an associated `EventProcessor` object that understands the action that should be taken based on the event and its data. Objects of this type implement the `EventProcessor` interface and process events as they are removed from an `EventLoop`.

For example, each `MouseEvent` specifies a `RootView` as its processor. As the `EventLoop` removes each `MouseEvent`, it calls the `RootView`'s `processEvent()` method, which forwards the `MouseEvent` to the appropriate `View`.

The `EventProcessor` interface consists of a single method, `processEvent()`, which handles the associated event. This can be seen in Listing 3.7.

Listing 3.7 *EventProcessor* Interface

```
public interface EventProcessor {
      public abstract void processEvent(Event);
}
```

EventLoop Class

The `EventLoop` manages the queue of events for an IFC application. There is a single instance of the `EventLoop` available to an IFC application that can be retrieved using the `eventLoop()` method in the `Application` class. Most IFC applications would not need to create an instance of the `EventLoop` class. The class definition is given in Listing 3.8.

Listing 3.8 *EventLoop* Class

```
public class EventLoop implements Runnable {
      public EventLoop();

      public void addEvent(Event);
      public void addEventAndWait(Event);
      public Object filterEvents(EventFilter);
      public Event getNextEvent();
      public synchronized boolean isRunning();
      public Event peekNextEvent();
      public void processEvent(Event);
      public void removeEvent(Event);
      public void run();
      public synchronized void stopRunning();
      public synchronized String toString();
}
```

The class provides methods to stop and start the loop, and also methods to add, remove, and peek at contents of the queue.

EventFilter Interface

IFC allows objects to filter events before they are processed from the `EventLoop`. These objects implement the `EventFilter` interface, which consists of a single method `filterEvents()`. This method is passed to the list of `Event` objects as a `Vector`, and suitable action may be taken here. Listing 3.9 shows the interface definition for `EventFilter`.

Listing 3.9 *EventFilter* Interface

```
public interface EventFilter {
      public abstract Object filterEvents(Vector);
}
```

The return value is the modified `Vector` of event objects. ●

CHAPTER 4

Keyboard and Mouse

The keyboard and mouse have traditionally been the main input devices for a computer. In this chapter, we will learn how to control the mouse and keyboard in the IFC environment. When the IFC application has multiple views, we will see how IFC determines the view to which keyboard and mouse events are sent.

We also see how IFC programs can be optimized by Event coalescing. Finally, we look into the autoscrolling feature found in modern Graphical User Interface (GUI) systems.

Managing the keyboard

Learn to control the keyboard in IFC applications by handling the `KeyEvent` class.

Keyboard focus

See how the keyboard focus affects IFC program behavior.

Managing the mouse

Explore the `MouseEvent` class and the various methods used to control mouse behavior.

Event coalescing

Learn to improve mouse response by handling event coalescing.

Autoscrolling

Look into how IFC handles autoscrolling behavior.

Keyboard

Software applications today use the keyboard to handle many data-entry tasks. In spite of new, innovative input devices, including speech input and pen-based systems, the traditional keyboard will continue to be one of the most important devices to support in most software applications.

IFC manages the keyboard by generating a `KeyEvent` object that's passed to the current view that is accepting input. It provides a number of methods that manage this and handles key input in a platform-independent manner.

KeyEvent Class

Keyboard events are encapsulated in the `KeyEvent` class given in Listing 4.1. Typically, this object is passed in as a parameter to keyboard-handling routines. Another important function is to define key constants such as `F1_KEY`, etc.

Listing 4.1 *KeyEvent* Class

```
public class KeyEvent extends Event {

     public final static int ALT_MASK;
     public final static int BACKSPACE_KEY;
     public final static int CONTROL_MASK;
     public final static int DELETE_KEY;
     public final static int DOWN_ARROW_KEY;
     public final static int END_KEY;
     public final static int ESCAPE_KEY;
     public final static int F10_KEY;
     public final static int F11_KEY;
     public final static int F12_KEY;
     public final static int F1_KEY;
     public final static int F2_KEY;
     public final static int F3_KEY;
     public final static int F4_KEY;
     public final static int F5_KEY;
     public final static int F6_KEY;
     public final static int F7_KEY;
     public final static int F8_KEY;
     public final static int F9_KEY;
     public final static int HOME_KEY;
     public final static int KEY_DOWN;
     public final static int KEY_UP;
     public final static int LEFT_ARROW_KEY;
     public final static int META_MASK;
     public final static int NO_MODIFIERS_MASK;
     public final static int PAGE_DOWN_KEY;
     public final static int PAGE_UP_KEY;
     public final static int RETURN_KEY;
```

```
    public final static int RIGHT_ARROW_KEY;
    public final static int SHIFT_MASK;
    public final static int TAB_KEY;
    public final static int UP_ARROW_KEY;

    public int key;
    public int modifiers;

    public KeyEvent();
    public KeyEvent(long, int, int, boolean);

    public boolean isAltKeyDown();
    public boolean isArrowKey();
    public boolean isBackTabKey();
    public boolean isBackspaceKey();
    public boolean isControlKeyDown();
    public boolean isDeleteKey();
    public boolean isDownArrowKey();
    public boolean isEndKey();
    public boolean isEscapeKey();
    public int isFunctionKey();
    public boolean isHomeKey();
    public boolean isLeftArrowKey();
    public boolean isMetaKeyDown();
    public boolean isPageDownKey();
    public boolean isPageUpKey();
    public boolean isPrintableKey();
    public boolean isReturnKey();
    public boolean isRightArrowKey();
    public boolean isShiftKeyDown();
    public boolean isTabKey();
    public boolean isUpArrowKey();
    public RootView rootView();
    public void setRootView(RootView);
    public String toString();
}
```

Most of the methods are query methods to test for certain keys. The modifiers variable contains the modifier keys that the user held down when the `KeyEvent` was generated. Example modifier keys include the Control and Alt keys.

Keyboard Focus

Many applications requiring keyboard input have more than one view that accept keystrokes. In such a situation, directing keyboard input to a particular view requires some processing. For some of its widgets such as `TextField` and `TextView`, IFC manages this implicitly by handling appropriate events. For example, a `TextField` may lose focus if the user presses the Tab key, or if the user clicks another view that accepts keyboard input.

To manage the keyboard focus for applications and their views, IFC uses the methods in the View class shown in Listing 4.2.

Listing 4.2 Keyboard Focus Methods in View Class

```
public void setFocusedView();

public void startFocus();
public void stopFocus();
public void resumeFocus();
public void pauseFocus();
```

The `setFocusedView()` method explicitly gives keyboard focus to the view. The `startFocus()` and `stopFocus()` methods get called when the view is gaining and losing keyboard focus, respectively. The `resumeFocus()` and `pauseFocus()` are also provided to tell the view that it is *temporarily* gaining and losing focus. The most common occurrence of this is when the user starts working with another application.

In addition, the `ApplicationObserver` class has the `applicationFocusDidChange()` abstract method, which is called when the keyboard focus of one of views changes. The `ExternalWindow.applicationFocusDidChange()` is similar.

The `RootView.focusedView()` and `InternalWindow.focusedView()` can be used to find the current view that has the keyboard focus in the `RootView` and `InternalWindow` objects, respectively.

keyEventApp Example

This example places three view subclasses that accept keystrokes when in focus. They buffer only printable keystrokes and paint their screen with the stored buffer on a white background when in focus, as seen in Figure 4.1. If the view is out of focus, the buffer is painted on a gray background. The user may change focus to either of the views by clicking them.

The `keyEventApp` example program is shown in Listing 4.3.

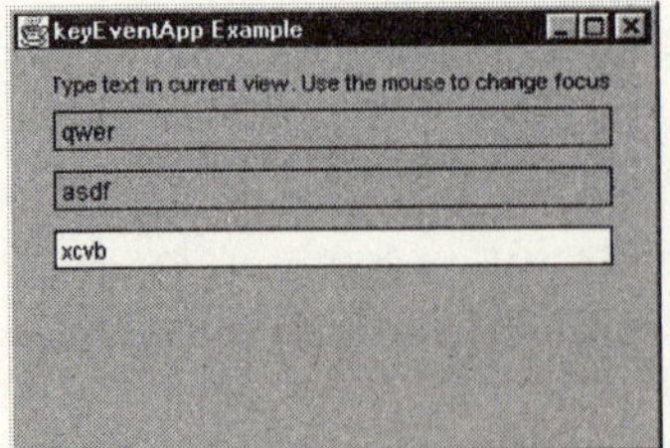

FIG. 4.1 `keyEventApp` example that handles `keyEvent`.

Listing 4.3 keyEventApp.java: *keyEventApp* Example

```
import netscape.application.*;

/**
 *     Application that demonstrates key events, focus
 */
public class keyEventApp extends Application {

      public void init() {
            super.init();
            //.. set background to light gray
            mainRootView().setColor(Color.lightGray);

            //.. create a label
            Label lab = new Label("Type text in current view. Use the mouse to
change focus",
                                    Font.fontNamed("Arial",Font.PLAIN,11));
            lab.moveTo(20,10);
            mainRootView().addSubview(lab);

            //.. attach the keyEventView
            mainRootView().addSubview(new keyEventView(20,90,280,20));
            mainRootView().addSubview(new keyEventView(20,60,280,20));
            keyEventView view;
            mainRootView().addSubview(view = new keyEventView(20,30,280,20));
            view.setFocusedView();
      }

      /**
      *     standard GUI application main() routine
      */
      public static void main(String args[]) {

            keyEventApp app = new keyEventApp();
            ExternalWindow win = new ExternalWindow();
            app.setMainRootView(win.rootView());

            Size size = win.windowSizeForContentSize(320,200);
            win.sizeTo(size.width, size.height);
            win.setTitle("keyEventApp Example");
            win.show();

            app.run();
      }
}

/**
 *     View that handles key events and input focus
 */
class keyEventView extends View {

      protected StringBuffer buf;
      protected boolean focussed = false;
```

continues

Listing 4.3 Continued

```
    public keyEventView(int x, int y, int w, int h) {
            super(x,y,w,h);
            buf = new StringBuffer();
            setBuffered(true);
    }

    //.. print only printable characters, ignore rest
    public void keyDown(KeyEvent ev) {
if (ev.key > ' ' && ev.key < 'z') {          //.. is printable char ?
                    buf.append((char)ev.key);
                    setDirty(true);
            }
    }

    public void keyUp(KeyEvent ev) { }

    public boolean mouseDown(MouseEvent event) { setFocusedView(); return
false; }

    public void drawView(Graphics g) {

            //.. draw appropriate background color
            g.setColor((focussed) ? Color.white : Color.lightGray);
            g.fillRect(1,1,width()-2,height()-2);

            //.. draw a black 1 pixel boundary
            g.setColor(Color.black);
            g.drawRect(0,0,width(),height());

            //.. draw text
            g.setFont(Font.defaultFont());
            g.drawString(buf.toString(),4,height()/2 +
            Font.defaultFont().fontMetrics().height()/2-2);
    }

    //.. manage input focus
public void startFocus() { focussed = true; setDirty(true);     }

public void stopFocus() { focussed = false; setDirty(true);     }
}
```

The example places three `keyEventView` objects, which are our subclassed views, along with a label. The topmost view is explicitly given focus by calling its `setFocusedView()` method.

The `keyEventView` subclass handles the `keyDown()` method by storing printable characters in a buffer, which is painted in the `drawView()` method. The `setDirty()` method is called immediately after storing to cause an immediate update on the screen. A similar action occurs in the `stopFocus()` and `startFocus()` methods, which also save the focus state. This state is used to paint the background color in the `drawView()` method.

Notice that we have enabled buffered drawing in our view, which helps reduce screen flicker.

Mouse

The mouse is an extremely important input device for today's Graphical User Interface (GUI) applications. Many users manage their entire software sessions using only the mouse, which emphasizes the importance of managing the mouse in an optimal manner.

IFC manages the mouse via the `MouseEvent` object and some methods in the View class. Subclasses usually override one or more of these methods to customize behavior. Some of these methods are as shown in Listing 4.4.

Listing 4.4 Mouse-Related Methods in the View Class

```
public boolean mouseDown(MouseEvent);
public void mouseDragged(MouseEvent);
public void mouseEntered(MouseEvent);
public void mouseExited(MouseEvent);
public void mouseMoved(MouseEvent);
public void mouseUp(MouseEvent);

public View viewForMouse(int, int);
public boolean wantsAutoscrollEvents();
public boolean wantsMouseEventCoalescing();
```


The `mouseDown()` and related methods are called at various stages of mouse handling. Note that the return value from the `mouseDown()` determines whether subsequent `mouseDragged()` and `mouseUp()` events are generated. Returning false prevents these `mouseDragged()` and `mouseUp()` events from being processed by the view.

MouseEvent Class

The `MouseEvent` class handles data relating to mouse events and is typically used as a parameter to many mouse event methods. (See Listing 4.5.)

Listing 4.5 *MouseEvent* Class

```
public class MouseEvent extends Event {

      public final static int MOUSE_DOWN;
      public final static int MOUSE_DRAGGED;
      public final static int MOUSE_ENTERED;
      public final static int MOUSE_EXITED;
```

continues

Listing 4.5 Continued

```
        public final static int MOUSE_MOVED;
        public final static int MOUSE_UP;

        public int x;
        public int y;

        public MouseEvent();
        public MouseEvent(long, int, int, int, int);

        public int clickCount();
        public boolean isAltKeyDown();
        public boolean isControlKeyDown();
        public boolean isMetaKeyDown();
        public boolean isShiftKeyDown();
        public int modifiers();
        public RootView rootView();
        public void setClickCount(int);
        public void setModifiers(int);
        public void setRootView(RootView);
        public String toString();
}
```

Besides defining some constants, it provides some query methods to check for modifiers and number of mouse clicks via the `clickCount()` method. The mouse coordinates are passed in the x and y variables.

mouseApp Example

Here is a simple example that prints out mouse events received, using the `System.out` stream. The check box on the right controls the return value of the view's `mouseDown()` method as shown in Figure 4.2. Notice that when the checkbox is off, i.e. the `mouseDown()` method is returning false, no mouse drag and mouse up events are generated for this view.

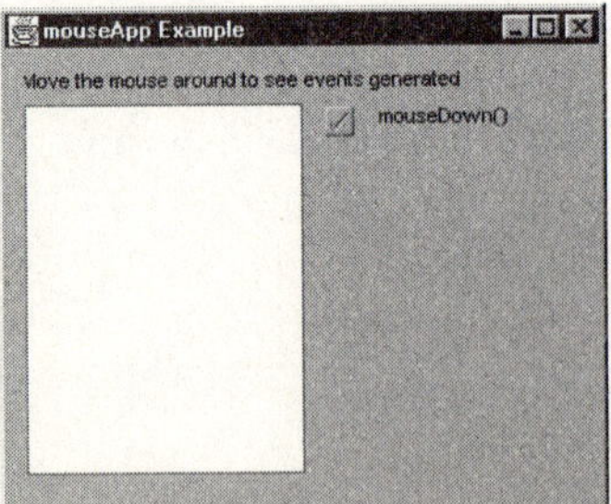

FIG. 4.2 `mouseApp` example that handles `mouseEvent`.

The mouseApp example is shown in Listing 4.6.

Listing 4.6 mouseApp.java: *mouseApp* Example

```
import netscape.application.*;

/**
 *     Application that prints mouse events
 */
public class mouseApp extends Application implements Target {

      public static String COMMAND = "cmdMouseDown";
      protected mouseView view;

      public void init() {
super.init();

            //.. set background to light gray
            mainRootView().setColor(Color.lightGray);

            //.. create a label
            Label lab = new Label("Move the mouse around to see events
            ➥generated",
            Font.fontNamed("Arial",Font.PLAIN,11));
            lab.moveTo(10,10);
            mainRootView().addSubview(lab);

            //.. check button that controls event coalesense
            Button b;
            mainRootView().addSubview(b =
Button.createCheckButton(170,30,20,20));
            b.setCommand(COMMAND); b.setTarget(this);

            //.. add label for check button
            lab = new Label("
mouseDown()",Font.fontNamed("Arial",Font.PLAIN,11));
            lab.moveTo(200,30);
            mainRootView().addSubview(lab);

            //.. attach the mouseView
            mainRootView().addSubview(view = new mouseView(10,30,150,200));
      }

      public void performCommand(String command, Object arg) {
            //.. handle the checkButton event
//      set the coaleseView's flag from the checkButton's state
            if (command.equals(COMMAND))
                  view.setMouseDn(((Button)arg).state());

      }
```

continues

Part I Ch 4

Listing 4.6 Continued

```
        /**
        *     standard GUI application main() routine
        */
        public static void main(String args[]) {

              mouseApp app = new mouseApp();
              ExternalWindow win = new ExternalWindow();
              app.setMainRootView(win.rootView());

              Size size = win.windowSizeForContentSize(320,250);
              win.sizeTo(size.width, size.height);
              win.setTitle("mouseApp Example");
              win.show();

              app.run();
        }
}

/**
 *     View that prints our various mouse events
 */
class mouseView extends View {

        protected boolean mouseDn = false;

        public mouseView(int x, int y, int w, int h) { super(x,y,w,h); }

        public boolean mouseDn() { return mouseDn; }
        public void setMouseDn(boolean value) { mouseDn = value; }

        public boolean mouseDown(MouseEvent ev) {
              System.out.println("mouseDown:"+ev);
              return mouseDn;
        }

        public void mouseDragged(MouseEvent ev) {
        System.out.println("mouseDragged:"+ev);
        }

        public void mouseEntered(MouseEvent ev) {
              System.out.println("mouseEntered:"+ev);
        }

        public void mouseExited(MouseEvent ev) {
              Syste
m.out.println("mouseExited:"+ev);
        }

        public void mouseMoved(MouseEvent ev) {
              System.out.println("mouseMoved:"+ev);
        }

        public void mouseUp(MouseEvent ev) {
```

```
            System.out.println("mouseUp:"+ev);
      }

      //.. draw a gray 1-pixel boundary around a white background
      public void drawView(Graphics g) {
            g.setColor(Color.white);
            g.fillRect(0,0,width()-1,height()-1);
            g.setColor(Color.gray);
            g.drawRect(0,0,width(),height());
      }
}
```

Listing 4.6 places our subclassed view, called `mouseView`, along with the checkbox and two labels. The `mouseView` itself prints out the `mouseEvent` object passed in as a parameter from each of the mouse methods. Sample output generated is shown in Listing 4.7.

Listing 4.7 Sample Output from *mouseApp*

```
mouseDown:MouseEvent: Down at: (153,177) modifiers: 0 clicks: 1
mouseDragged:MouseEvent: Dragged at: (154,177) modifiers: 0 clicks: 1
mouseDragged:MouseEvent: Dragged at: (155,178) modifiers: 0 clicks: 1
mouseExited:MouseEvent: Exited at: (155,178) modifiers: 0 clicks: 0
mouseUp:MouseEvent: Up at: (155,178) modifiers: 0 clicks: 1
```


Event Coalescing

High-frequency events, like mouse move and mouse drag events, are queued in the event queue for processing by the application. If the application can't keep up with the rate of new events generated, this could slow down performance drastically. Because such mouse events usually aren't critical for an application, most applications can afford to handle only the latest event of a particular type. This is the concept of *event coalescence.*

Event coalescing is disabled by default and may be enabled by returning true from the `wantsMouseEventCoalescing()` method of a View subclass.

coalesceApp Example

To demonstrate this feature, we will implement the `coalesceApp` example. This example draws an icon that follows the mouse being dragged after a 100-millisecond delay, as shown in Figure 4.3. Due to the delay in processing, the mouse dragged events get queued up in the application. With the Coalesce events checkbox unchecked, you will notice a delay before the application redraws the icon, which will continue even after the mouse has been released. If you check the Coalesce events checkbox, you will see improved performance in the icon-drawing operations. This is because only the latest mouse dragged event is processed by the application.

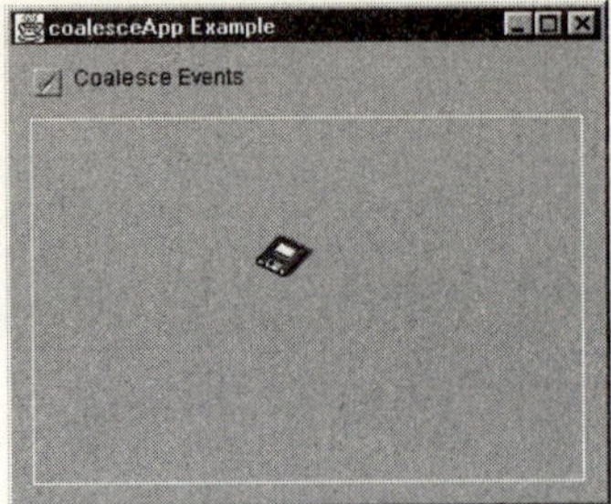

FIG. 4.3
`coalesceApp` example shows mouse event coalescence.

The `coalesceApp` example is shown in Listing 4.8.

Listing 4.8 coalesceApp.java: *coalesceApp* Example

```
import netscape.application.*;

/**
 * Application that demonstrates event coalesence
 */
public class coalesceApp extends Application implements Target {

      public static String CMD_COALESCE = "cmdCoalesce";
      protected coalesceView view;

      public void init() {
            super.init();
            //.. set background to light gray
            mainRootView().setColor(Color.lightGray);

            //.. check button that controls event coalesense
            Button b;
            mainRootView().addSubview(b =
Button.createCheckButton(10,10,20,20));
            b.setCommand(CMD_COALESCE); b.setTarget(this);

            //.. create a label
            Label lab = new Label("Coalesce Mouse Events ",
Font.fontNamed("Arial",Font.PLAIN,12));
            lab.moveTo(35,10);
            mainRootView().addSubview(lab);

            //.. attach the coalesce view
            mainRootView().addSubview(view = new coalesceView(10,40,300,200));
      }

      public void performCommand(String command, Object arg) {
            //.. handle the checkButton event
            //   set the coalesceView's flag from the checkButton's state
            if (command.equals(CMD_COALESCE))
                  view.setCoalesce(((Button)arg).state());
```

```
        }

        /**
        *     standard GUI application main() routine
        */
        public static void main(String args[]) {

              coalesceApp app = new coalesceApp();
              ExternalWindow win = new ExternalWindow();
              app.setMainRootView(win.rootView());

              Size size = win.windowSizeForContentSize(320,250);
              win.sizeTo(size.width, size.height);
              win.setTitle("coalesceApp Example");
              win.show();

              app.run();
        }
}

/**
 *     View that exhibits AutoScrolling
 */
class coalesceView extends View {

     public static Bitmap ICON = Bitmap.bitmapNamed("floppy.gif");

     private Point prev = new Point(0,0);          //.. stores previous image
     ➥position
     protected boolean coalesce=false;          //.. determines if this view
     ➥coalesces

     public coalesceView(int x, int y, int w, int h) { super(x,y,w,h); }

     //.. get/set coalesce flag
     public void setCoalesce(boolean value) { coalesce = value; }
     public boolean coalesce() { return coalesce; }

     //.. overriden for event coalescing
     public boolean wantsMouseEventCoalescing()     { return coalesce; }

     //.. mouseDown always returns true
public boolean mouseDown(MouseEvent ev)     { return true; }

     //.. mouseDown always returns true
public void mouseDragged(MouseEvent ev) {

          //.. force a 100 millisecond delay in processing this event
          try { Thread.currentThread().sleep(100); }
          catch (InterruptedException e) { }

          Graphics g = createGraphics();

          //.. erase previously drawn icon
```

continues

Listing 4.8 Continued

```
        g.setXORMode(Color.lightGray);
        g.drawBitmapAt(ICON,prev.x-ICON.width(),prev.y-ICON.height());

        //.. draw icon at new mouse location
        g.drawBitmapAt(ICON,ev.x-ICON.width(),ev.y-ICON.height());

        //.. save position for next draw operation
        prev.x=ev.x; prev.y=ev.y;
    }

    //.. draw a white 1-pixel boundary around the view
    public void drawView(Graphics g) {
        g.setColor(Color.white);
        g.drawRect(0,0,width(),height());
    }
}
```

The example starts by laying out a label and `coalesceView`, along with the check button that controls whether the `coalesceView` will coalesce events onto the background view. The `coalesceView` is our subclassed view that sends commands to a target upon receiving mouse dragged operations. It dynamically enables and disables the coalesce feature by returning the appropriate value from the `wantsMouseEventCoalescing()` method.

Autoscrolling

There are situations in which a view in your application will want to receive mouse drag events if the user drags the mouse outside your view's bounds—provided, of course, that the drag operation started inside the view. This is the concept of *autoscrolling*, which can be found in applications that scroll data, such as word processors and paint programs.

For a view to receive autoscroll events, it must be subclassed and made to return true from the `wantsAutoscrollEvents()` method. Henceforth that view will receive autoscroll events, which are essentially mouse drag events with the `MouseEvent` parameter containing coordinates that are outside the bounds of the view.

Following is an example that shows autoscrolling behavior.

autoScrollApp Example

This example shows how autoscrolling works in an IFC application. You may click and drag the mouse around, which sends mouse dragged events to the application, as shown in Figure 4.4. Each event toggles the LED, which flashes as a result. When you drag the mouse outside the view's bounds, notice that the view will continue getting mouse dragged events. This behavior is called autoscrolling.

FIG. 4.4
`autoScrollApp` example that shows autoscrolling.

The `autoScrollApp` example is shown in Listing 4.9.

Listing 4.9 autoScrollApp.java: *autoScrollApp* Example

```
import netscape.application.*;

/**
 *     AutoScrolling example
 */
public class autoScrollApp extends Application implements Target {

       protected static Color RED = new Color(255,0,0);
       protected ContainerView led;

       public void init() {
             super.init();
             //.. set background to light gray
             mainRootView().setColor(Color.lightGray);

             //.. put a label
             Label lab = new Label("Receiving Events:",
             Font.fontNamed("Arial",Font.PLAIN,12));
             lab.moveTo(10,10);
             mainRootView().addSubview(lab);

             //.. add a blinking LED
             led = new ContainerView(120,13,15,10);
             led.setBackgroundColor(Color.lightGray);
             led.setBorder(LineBorder.grayLine());
             mainRootView().addSubview(led);

             //.. add out autoScrollView object
             autoScrollView v = new autoScrollView(10,30,150,200);
             mainRootView().addSubview(v);
             v.setTarget(this);
       }

       public void performCommand(String command, Object arg) {
             //.. handle commands from autoScrollView
//      that flash(toggle) the LED's color
```

continues

Listing 4.9 Continued

```
        if (command.equals(autoScrollView.COMMAND)) {
                    if (led.backgroundColor()==Color.lightGray)
                          led.setBackgroundColor(RED);
                    else
                          led.setBackgroundColor(Color.lightGray);
              }
        }

        /**
   *     standard GUI application main() routine
         */
        public static void main(String args[]) {

              autoScrollApp app = new autoScrollApp();
              ExternalWindow win = new ExternalWindow();
              app.setMainRootView(win.rootView());

              Size size = win.windowSizeForContentSize(320,250);
              win.sizeTo(size.width, size.height);
              win.setTitle("autoScrollApp Example");
              win.show();

              app.run();
        }
  }

  /**
   *     View that exhibits AutoScrolling
   */
  class autoScrollView extends View {

        public static String COMMAND = "cmdAutoScroll";
        protected Target target;

        public autoScrollView(int x, int y, int w, int h) { super(x,y,w,h); }

        //.. get/set target
        public Target target() { return target; }
        public void setTarget(Target tgt) { target = tgt; }

        //.. overriden to accept AutoScrollEvents
  public boolean wantsAutoscrollEvents()          { return true; }

        //.. mouse methods
  public boolean mouseDown(MouseEvent ev)          { return true; }

        //.. send command to target, if any
        public void mouseDragged(MouseEvent ev) {
              if (target!=null) target.performCommand(COMMAND,this);
        }

        //.. paint a white background
```

```
        public void drawView(Graphics g) {
              g.setColor(Color.white);
              g.fillRect(0,0,width(),height());
        }
}
```

The example places a label and a `ContainerView` object, which simulates an LED (light-emitting diode). Then our subclassed `autoScrollView` object is added and its target is set to the application. This ensures that the application will receive events with the command value of `autoScrollView.COMMAND`. The `performCommand()` method flashes the LED color.

The `autoScrollView` view overrides the `autoScrollView()` method of the View class by returning True. This causes IFC to send autoscroll events to this view. The `mouseDown()` returns True such that subsequent mouse drag events are received. The `mouseDragged()` method sends its command to the target.

The `drawView()` method is overridden to draw a white background. ●

PART II

Visual Frameworks

CHAPTER 5

Widgets

- *Borders*
- *Buttons*
- *ColorWell*
- *ContainerView*
- *Lists*
- *Popups*
- *Scrolling*
- *Slider*
- *Textfield*
- *TextView*

IFC provides a rich and powerful set of widgets. GUI-based applications are the order of the day, and using the IFC widgets helps you write advanced applications in a short time. These ready-to-use widgets provide an extensible design that can be suitably modified and enhanced to suit your needs.

These IFC components cover most common operations and features found in modern GUI applications. Additional widgets are available from leading vendors. And you can always write your own widgets from scratch by subclassing the View base class.

Most widgets have the following `setXXX()` to set an attribute and `XXX()` to query attributes.

In general, the widgets have attributes that are set with a `setXXX()` method and queried with an `XXX()` method, e.g., `setFont()` and `font()`.

Borders

Borders are low-level objects that are used in conjunction with other widgets. Many IFC widgets need to display a border, and IFC has provided a separate Border class hierarchy providing a set of border types.

To give the programmer maximum flexibility, each Border object may be subclassed further to implement custom behavior. Views normally use the `setBorder()` method to add and remove a border, with the `setBorder(null)` method removing the border.

The Border class hierarchy consists of the following classes:

- Border

  The abstract base class for borders that encapsulates generic border behavior
- BezelBorder

  Different varieties of 3-D borders. These include most of the commonly used borders, such as Button border
- EmptyBorder

  Dummy border used as a placeholder internally inside components such as TextField
- LineBorder

  A thin, 1-pixel-wide border, commonly used with TextFields

Border

This implements the base functionality for borders and is used by subclasses to provide different kinds of borders. It also provides many border-related convenience methods.

The Border class definition is shown in Listing 5.1.

Listing 5.1 Border Class

```
public abstract class Border implements Codable {
public Border();

public Rect interiorRect(int, int, int, int);          //.. dimensions
public Rect interiorRect(Rect);
public void computeInteriorRect(int, int, int, int, Rect);
public void computeInteriorRect(Rect, Rect);

public void drawInRect(Graphics, Rect);               //.. drawing
public abstract void drawInRect(Graphics, int, int, int, int);

public void decode(Decoder);                          //.. persistence
```

```
public void describeClassInfo(ClassInfo);
public void encode(Encoder);
public void finishDecoding();

public int heightMargin();                              //.. margin
public int widthMargin();
public abstract int bottomMargin();
public abstract int leftMargin();
public abstract int rightMargin();
public abstract int topMargin();
}
```

Looking at the Border classes, we see that derived classes would need to implement the `xxxMargin()` and `drawInRect()` abstract methods at a minimum.

NOTE Most visual components have a public constructor with no arguments. This is a requirement of the IFC persistence framework, which we will cover in Chapter 9, "Persistence."

BezelBorder

This is a 2-pixel-wide border and is the most common type of border used in applications. It provides a 3-D look and feel to the Widget it adorns.

The following styles are available: raised, lowered, grooved, raised button, and lowered button. These are shown in Figure 5.1.

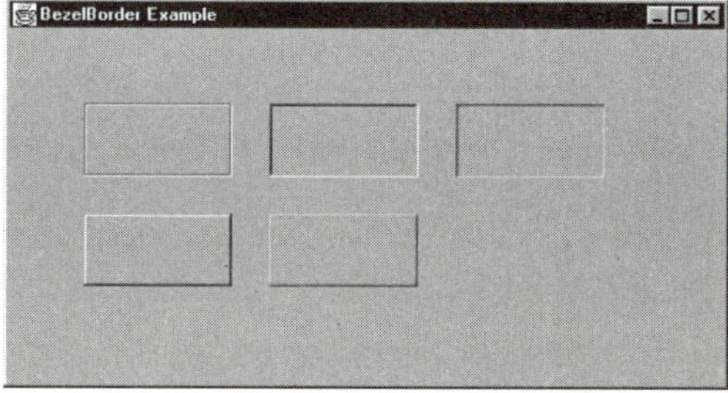

FIG. 5.1 Different BezelBorder types.

A complete example that displays what's seen in Figure 5.1 is available on the CD-ROM as the `borderApp` example application.

The BezelBorder class is defined in Listing 5.2.

Listing 5.2 BezelBorder Class

```
public class BezelBorder extends Border {

public final static int GROOVED;
public final static int LOWERED;
public final static int LOWERED_BUTTON;
public final static int RAISED;
public final static int RAISED_BUTTON;

public BezelBorder();
public BezelBorder(int);
public BezelBorder(int, Color);
public BezelBorder(int, Color, Color, Color);

public static void drawBezel(Graphics, int, int, int, int, Color, Color, Color,
Color, boolean);
public static void drawGroovedBezel(Graphics, int, int, int, int, Color, Color);
public static void drawLoweredButtonBezel(Graphics, int, int, int, int);
public static void drawRaisedButtonBezel(Graphics, int, int, int, int);
public static Border groovedBezel();
public static Border loweredBezel();
public static Border loweredButtonBezel();
public static Border raisedBezel();
public static Border raisedButtonBezel();

public int bottomMargin();
public void decode(Decoder);
public void describeClassInfo(ClassInfo);
      public void drawInRect(Graphics, int, int, int, int);
public void encode(Encoder);
public void finishDecoding();
public int leftMargin();
public int rightMargin();
      public int topMargin();
public int type();
}
```

Notice that the class provides a number of static methods that provide all the Border styles in a convenient manner. Most applications will use these static functions directly, as shown in Listing 5.3.

Listing 5.3 BezelBorder Example

```
ContainerView panel = new ContainerView(0,0,100,100);
panel.setBorder(BezelBorder. RaisedBezel());
```

EmptyBorder

The EmptyBorder class is a subclass of Border with a zero margin border that draws nothing. EmptyBorders act as placeholders for classes that take Borders but do not want to check for null everywhere. This class is rarely used by IFC programs directly. One example of its usage is in components such as Slider, which use it as a placeholder when their borders are set to null using the `setBorder()` method. (See Listing 5.4.)

Listing 5.4 EmptyBorder Class

```
public class EmptyBorder extends Border {
public EmptyBorder();

public static Border emptyBorder();
public int bottomMargin();
public void decode(Decoder);
public void drawInRect(Graphics, int, int, int, int);
public int leftMargin();
public int rightMargin();
public int topMargin();
}
```

Notice that this class also provides a static `emptyBorder()` method, which is sufficient for most applications. For example, a program can assign an EmptyBorder instance by calling the static method as follows:

```
newBorder = EmptyBorder.emptyBorder();
```


LineBorder

For visual components requiring a simple 1-pixel-wide frame around them, IFC provides the LineBorder class. (See Listing 5.5.) The color can be specified in the constructor or set later.

Listing 5.5 LineBorder Class

```
public class LineBorder extends Border {

public LineBorder();
public LineBorder(Color);

public static Border blackLine();
public static Border grayLine();

public int bottomMargin();
public Color color();
public void decode(Decoder);
public void describeClassInfo(ClassInfo);
```

continues

Listing 5.5 Continued

```
public void drawInRect(Graphics, int, int, int, int);
public void encode(Encoder);
public void finishDecoding();
public int leftMargin();
public int rightMargin();
public void setColor(Color);
public int topMargin();
}
```

As with the other border classes, LineBorder also provides static members that are sufficient for most applications. For example, a program can assign a black LineBorder instance by calling the static method, as follows:

```
newBorder = LineBorder.blackLine();
```

Buttons

Buttons represent a visual component that responds to a user's click with an action. In the IFC context, this action is the sending of the button's command to its target. Buttons are in either their *normal* state or their *depressed* state, and they trigger events when they change states.

The IFC Button class provides a rich set of functions that allow you to control many parameters of a button, such as type, image, border, etc.

The Button class definition is shown in Listing 5.6.

Listing 5.6 Button Class

```
public class Button extends View Target, DrawingSequenceOwner {
public final static java.lang.String CLICK;                     //.. constants
public final static int CONTINUOUS_TYPE;
public final static int IMAGE_ABOVE;
public final static int IMAGE_BELOW;
public final static int IMAGE_BENEATH;
public final static int IMAGE_ON_LEFT;
public final static int IMAGE_ON_RIGHT;
public final static int PUSH_TYPE;
       public final static int RADIO_TYPE;
public final static java.lang.String SEND_COMMAND;
public final static int TOGGLE_TYPE;

public Button();                                          //.. constructors
public Button(Rect);
public Button(int, int, int, int);
```

```
public String command();                              //.. events
public void sendCommand();
public void setCommand(String);
public Target target();
public void setTarget(Target);
public void performCommand(String, Object);

public boolean isEnabled();                             //.. enable
public void setEnabled(boolean);

public void setState(boolean);                        //.. state
public boolean state();

public void setType(int);                             //.. type
public int type();
public int repeatDelay();          //.. for CONTINOUS_TYPE
public void setRepeatDelay(int);

public static Button createCheckButton(int, int, int, int);          //.. static
public static Button createPushButton(int, int, int, int);
public static Button createRadioButton(int, int, int, int);

public String title();
public void setTitle(String);
public String altTitle();                             //..title
public void setAltTitle(String);
public Color disabledTitleColor();
public void setDisabledTitleColor(Color);
public Color titleColor();
public void setTitleColor(Color);
public Font font();
public void setFont(Font);

public Image image();                                  //.. image
public void setImage(Image);
public Image altImage();
public void setAltImage(Image);
public int imagePosition();
public void setImagePosition(int);
public Size imageAreaSize();

public void click();                                  //.. clicks
public int clickCount();

public boolean isTransparent();                        //.. transparent
public void setTransparent(boolean);

public Color loweredColor();                             //.. color
public Color raisedColor();
public void setRaisedColor(Color);
public void setLoweredColor(Color);

public boolean isBordered();                             //.. border
public void setBordered(boolean);
```

continues

Listing 5.6 Continued

```
public void setRaisedBorder(Border);
public void setLoweredBorder(Border);
public Border loweredBorder();
public Border raisedBorder();

public boolean mouseDown(MouseEvent);                               //.. mouse
public void mouseDragged(MouseEvent);
public void mouseUp(MouseEvent);
public Sound mouseDownSound();                               //.. mouse sound
public Sound mouseUpSound();
public void setMouseDownSound(Sound);
public void setMouseUpSound(Sound);

public void drawView(Graphics);                               //.. drawing
public void drawViewBackground(Graphics, Rect, boolean);
public void drawViewInterior(Graphics, String, Image, Rect);
public void drawViewTitleInRect(Graphics, String, Font, Rect, int);
public void drawingSequenceCompleted(DrawingSequence);
public void drawingSequenceFrameChanged(DrawingSequence);
public Size minSize();

protected void ancestorWasAddedToViewHierarchy(View);

public void decode(Decoder);                               //.. persistent
public void describeClassInfo(ClassInfo);
public void encode(Encoder);
}
```

The Button class is a View subclass, which implements the Target and DrawingSequence interfaces. The Target interface is discussed in Chapter 3, "Events," and the DrawingSequence interface is discussed in Chapter 10, "Utilities."

The Button class provides a set of constant values that include values to define the Button type (CONTINUOUS_TYPE, PUSH_TYPE, RADIO_TYPE, TOGGLE_TYPE), location of the image (IMAGE_ABOVE, IMAGE_BELOW, IMAGE_BENEATH, IMAGE_ON_LEFT, IMAGE_ON_RIGHT) in an image button, and other values mainly used internally (CLICK, SEND_COMMAND).

A button works by sending a command, set by the `setCommand()` method, to a target, set by the `setTarget()` method. You may also force the button to send its command by calling the button's `sendCommand()` method. The `performCommand()` method implements the Target interface and is not directly called. It may be overridden by subclasses for custom behavior.

Using the `setEnabled()` method allows you to enable and disable the button. In the disabled state, the button will not respond to user actions and consequently will not send any events.

The state of the button may be queried by the `state()` methods, and the button may be forced to change its state by the `setState()` method.

There are four types of buttons possible in IFC that are set using the `setType()` method and one of the constant values for the type defined. As the constant names suggest, they are:

- Continuous buttons

  When depressed, these send out a periodic stream of events. The time period is controlled by the `setRepeatDelay()` method. A continuous button can be used to implement the button found with scroll bars on most platform windows. When the user presses and holds the button, the scrollbar "thumb" can move continuously as it receives events. Using this button involves setting its type to `Button.CONTINUOUS_TYPE`.

- Push buttons

  The most common type of buttons, which can be pushed and *spring* back when released.

- Radio buttons

  May be used in a group that exhibits a mutually exclusive behavior; for example, only one button may be depressed at any time, and it resets all other buttons in the group.

- Toggle buttons

  Buttons that have a *sticky* behavior and toggle between the normal and depressed states.

The class defines three static convenience methods to quickly instantiate the most common buttons: `createPushButton()`, `createRadioButton()`, `createToggleButton()`.

Buttons may have one or more optional titles and images associated with them. These are set using the `setTitle()` and `setImage()` methods, respectively. Buttons can have different titles and images for the *depressed* state, which are set using the `setAltTitle()` and `setAltImage()` methods. In addition, the title's font may be set using the `setFont()` method, and its color controlled by the `setTitleColor()` and `setDisabledTitleColor()`. The image can be positioned on the button using the `setImagePosition()` method, which takes one of the five constant values discussed earlier.

The `click()` method causes the button to simulate a user click, and the `clickCount()` returns the number of user clicks for a depressed button.

The transparency of the button is controlled by the `setTransparent()` method, and the color of the button can be controlled by the `setRaisedColor()` and `setLoweredColor()`

methods. Similarly, the border around the button is enabled with the `setBordered()` method and is set with the `setRaisedBorder()` and `setLoweredBorder()` methods.

The `mouseDown()`, `mouseDragged()`, and `mouseUp()` methods are usually used by subclasses for custom behavior.

You may set a sound to play at mouse clicks by using the `setMouseDownSound()` and `setMouseUpSound()`.

NOTE Note that Applications must use external classes to implement sound. The `sun.audio.*` is one such set of classes. Applets, on the other hand, have built-in audio support.

The `draw()` methods are used by subclasses to implement custom drawing behavior, which we will illustrate in our example, and the `ancestorWasAddedToViewHierarchy()` method is used internally for radio buttons.

Finally, the classes implement the Codable interface, making this class persistent.

Button Example

Now let's work on an example that illustrates some attributes of the Button class. The `buttonApp` application displays various kinds of buttons on a panel, as shown in Figure 5.2. Among the buttons displayed are custom buttons that we will implement as the checkBox class.

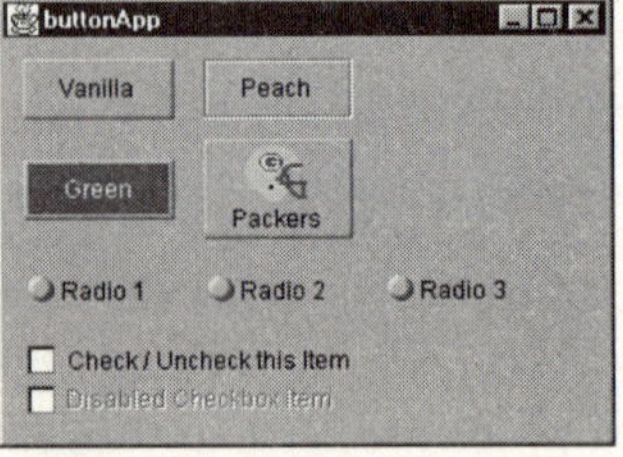

FIG. 5.2 Some example buttons.

We first add a push button, setting its title to "Vanilla." Its command is set to "btnVanilla" and the target to itself (see Listing 5.7). This and all buttons are added directly to the root view.

NOTE A good practice is to name commands with a sensible prefix like "btn" or "cmd". This helps in the command processing routines to *group* commands based on their type and/or context by using the `String.startsWith()` method.

Next, we add a similar "Peach" button but with a different border. A button with a green face is implemented, followed by one with an image. Next, a group of three radio buttons is implemented. Lastly, we create two instances of our custom checkBox buttons and disable the second one.

The `performCommand()` routine displays the command and the state of the button.

Listing 5.7 buttonApp.java: *buttonApp* Example

```
import netscape.application.*;

/**
 *     Application which illustrates usage of Buttons
 */
public class buttonApp extends Application implements Target {

public void init() {

     mainRootView().setColor(Color.lightGray);
     Button b;
     //.. create a push Button (default)
     b = new Button(10,10,75,30);

     //.. set title, command, target
     b.setTitle("Vanilla");
     b.setCommand("btnVanilla");
     b.setTarget(this);

     //.. add to container
     mainRootView().addSubview(b);

     //.. create another push Button
     b = new Button(100,10,75,30);
     b.setTitle("Peach");
     b.setCommand("btnPeach");
     b.setTarget(this);

     //.. set a different border
     b.setRaisedBorder(BezelBorder.groovedBezel());
     mainRootView().addSubview(b);

     //.. create another push Button
     b = new Button(10,60,75,30);
     b.setTitle("Green");
     b.setCommand("btnGreen");
     b.setTarget(this);

     //.. set its background color and title color
     b.setRaisedColor(new Color(0,128,0));
     b.setTitleColor(Color.white);
     b.setLoweredColor(new Color(0,128,0));
     mainRootView().addSubview(b);
```

continues

Listing 5.7 Continued

```
        //.. create another push Button
        b = new Button(100,50,75,50);
        //.. set its image to be above the title
        b.setImage(Bitmap.bitmapNamed("Packers.gif"));
        b.setImagePosition(Button.IMAGE_ABOVE);
        b.setTitle("Packers");
        b.setCommand("btnPackers");
        b.setTarget(this);
        mainRootView().addSubview(b);

        //.. create 3 radio buttons
        mainRootView().addSubview(b=Button.createRadioButton(10,110,75,30));
        b.setTitle("Radio 1");
        b.setCommand("btnRadio1");
        b.setTarget(this);

        mainRootView().addSubview(b=Button.createRadioButton(100,110,75,30));
        b.setTitle("Radio 2");
        b.setCommand("btnRadio2");
        b.setTarget(this);

        mainRootView().addSubview(b=Button.createRadioButton(190,110,75,30));
        b.setTitle("Radio 3");
        b.setCommand("btnRadio3");
        b.setTarget(this);

        //.. create 2 custom checkBox buttons
        checkBox cb;
        cb = new checkBox("Check / Uncheck this Item",10,150,200,20);
        mainRootView().addSubview(cb);
        cb.setCommand("btnCheckBox1");
        cb.setTarget(this);

        cb = new checkBox("Disabled Checkbox item",10,170,200,20);
        cb.setEnabled(false);
        cb.setCommand("btnCheckBox2");
        cb.setTarget(this);
        mainRootView().addSubview(cb);
}

        //.. command processing routine
        public void performCommand(String command, Object arg) {

             if (arg instanceof Button) {
                  //.. display commands sent by Button objects only
                  boolean state = ((Button)arg).state();
                  String which = command.substring(3);
                  System.out.println("Button = "+which+", state="+state);
             }
        }

        /**
         *     standard GUI application main() routine
```

```
      */
public static void main(String args[]) {

buttonApp app = new buttonApp();
ExternalWindow win = new ExternalWindow();
          win.setTitle("buttonApp");
app.setMainRootView(win.rootView());

Size size = win.windowSizeForContentSize(300, 200);
win.sizeTo(size.width, size.height);
win.show();

app.run();
System.exit(0);
}
}
```

checkBox class

The checkBox class, a subclass of the Button class, is implemented by setting certain characteristics of the button, such as the border, image, and type (see Listing 5.8). The `drawViewTitleInRect()` method is overridden to draw the title with a grayed-out style if the button is disabled.

Listing 5.8 checkBox.java: checkBox Class

```
import netscape.application.*;

/**
 *     Button subclass which implements checkBox behaviour
 */
public class checkBox extends Button {

     public checkBox(String title, int x, int y, int w, int h) {
          super(x,y,w,h); setTitle(" "+title);

          //.. hardcode certain attributes
          setBordered(false); setBuffered(true);
          setImage(Bitmap.bitmapNamed("cbox1.gif"));
          setAltImage(Bitmap.bitmapNamed("cbox2.gif"));
          setType(TOGGLE_TYPE);
     }

     public void drawViewTitleInRect(Graphics g, String title,
                    Font titleFont, Rect textBounds, int justification)
     {
          //.. nothing to draw
    if (title == null || title.length() == 0) return;
```

continues

Listing 5.8 Continued

```
        //.. set color, font
        if (isEnabled())
            g.setColor(titleColor());
        else
            g.setColor(Color.white);
    g.setFont(titleFont);

        //.. only handle single-line titles
        if (title.indexOf('\n') == -1) {
g.drawStringInRect(title, textBounds, justification);

        if (!isEnabled()) {
                //.. if disabled draw dark gray text over white text
                g.setColor(Color.gray);
                textBounds.x-=1;
                textBounds.y-=1;
                g.drawStringInRect(title, textBounds, justification);
        }
return;
    }
        else    //.. multiline titles are handled by default routine
super.drawViewTitleInRect(g,title,titleFont,textBounds,justification);
    }
}
```

ColorWell

The ColorWell class provides a convenient View subclass with built-in support for the dragging and dropping of color objects. When you drop a color object onto it, a ColorWell object changes its own color to that of the dropped object. It's usually used in conjunction with the `ColorChooser()` class, which is discussed in Chapter 10, "Utilities."

By default, a double-click on a ColorWell object brings up the `ColorChooser()` window associated with the main application root view. A sophisticated graphics program, such as a paint application, will use a ColorWell subclass in places that it wants the user to change color by simply dragging and dropping a Color.

NOTE A good example is the simpledraw example by Jason Beaver and Tyler Gingrich, which is available on the CD-ROM.

The `ColorChooser()` class definition is shown in Listing 5.9.

Listing 5.9 ColorWell Class

```
public class ColorWell extends DragWell implements DragDestination {

public ColorWell();
public ColorWell(Rect);
public ColorWell(int, int, int, int);


public String command();
public void sendCommand();
public void setCommand(String);
public void setTarget(Target);
public Target target();

public void decode(Decoder);                     //.. persistence
public void describeClassInfo(ClassInfo);
public void encode(Encoder);

public boolean dragDropped(DragSession);           //.. drag and drop support
public boolean dragEntered(DragSession);
public void dragExited(DragSession);
public boolean dragMoved(DragSession);
public DragDestination acceptsDrag(DragSession, int, int);
public void setData(Object);
public void setDataType(String);
public String dataType();

public void drawView(Graphics);                  //.. drawing

public Color color();
public void setColor(Color);

public boolean mouseDown(MouseEvent);              //.. mouse
public void mouseDragged(MouseEvent);
public void mouseUp(MouseEvent);

public Image image();
public void setImage(Image);
}
```

Also note that by default, a ColorWell Object has a border of type `BezelBorder.LOWERED`.

colorWellApp example

Let's use the ColorWell class in an example, which generates the screen shown in Figure 5.3.

The colorWellApp example, whose listing is given in Listing 5.10, starts by placing a yellow ColorWell object directly onto the main application root view. The command and target are set for the ColorWell object.

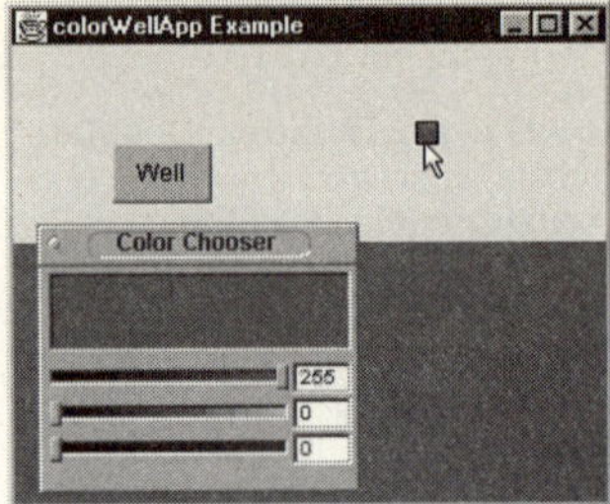

FIG. 5.3 Screen from colorWelAPP Example.

A button is added to the ColorWell object. When the user clicks the button, it queries the ColorWell's color and prints it.

The `performCommand()` method displays the ColorWell's color value in the case of both events being generated here:

- When a Color object is dropped onto it.
- When the user clicks the button.

Listing 5.10 colorWellApp.java: ColorWell Application

```
import netscape.application.*;

/**
 *     Application illustrating the ColorWell class
 */
public class colorWellApp extends Application implements Target {

     protected ColorWell well;

public void init() {

          //.. create a yellow ColorWell with no border
          well = new ColorWell(0,0,300,200);
          well.setColor(Color.yellow);
          well.setBorder(null);
          //.. set its command and target
          well.setCommand("cmdWell");
          well.setTarget(this);

          Button b;
          //.. add a Button to the ColorWell
          well.addSubview(b = new Button(50,50,50,30));
          b.setTitle("Well");
          b.setCommand("btnWell");
          b.setTarget(this);

          mainRootView().addSubview(well);
     }
```

```
//.. command processing routine
public void performCommand(String command, Object arg) {

     if (command.equals("btnWell")) {
          //.. if the button was pressed, print the ColorWell's value
          System.out.println("ColorWell Color="+well.color());
     }
     else if (command.equals("cmdWell")) {
          //.. if the ColorWell sends its command, print its value
System.out.println("ColorWell Color="+((ColorWell)arg).color());
     }
}

/**
 *     standard GUI application main() routine
 */
public static void main(String args[]) {

colorWellApp app = new colorWellApp();
ExternalWindow win = new ExternalWindow();
app.setMainRootView(win.rootView());

Size size = win.windowSizeForContentSize(320, 480);
win.sizeTo(size.width, size.height);
win.show();

app.run();
}
}
```

ContainerView

The ContainerView is the basic GUI container class used to hold other Views and Images. A ContainerView has a border with a title and space to contain other objects. The space within the ContainerView can be made transparent to achieve some special effects. Custom behavior can be implemented by subclassing it and overriding appropriate methods.

NOTE The ContainerView class is the equivalent to the `java.awt.Panel` class.

The class definition is shown in Listing 5.11.

Listing 5.11 ContainerView Class

```
public class ContainerView extends View {
public ContainerView();                      //.. constructors
public ContainerView(Rect);
public ContainerView(int, int, int, int);
```

continues

Listing 5.11 Continued

```
public Border border();                          //.. appearance
public void setBorder(Border);
public boolean isTransparent();
public void setTransparent(boolean);
public Color backgroundColor();
public void setBackgroundColor(Color);
public Rect interiorRect();
public Size minSize();

public void decode(Decoder);                           //.. persistence
public void describeClassInfo(ClassInfo);
public void encode(Encoder);
public void finishDecoding();

public void drawSubviews(Graphics);                      //.. custom drawing
public void drawView(Graphics);
public void drawViewBackground(Graphics);
public void drawViewBorder(Graphics);

public Image image();                                //.. image
public int imageDisplayStyle();
public void setImage(Image);
public void setImageDisplayStyle(int);

public void setTitle(String);                          //.. title
public void setTitleColor(Color);
public void setTitleFont(Font);
public String title();
public Color titleColor();
public Font titleFont();
}
```

The API for ContainerView may be broadly classified into:

- Appearance

  Parameters that may be controlled include border, transparency, and background color
- Persistence

  Methods to support persistent behavior
- Custom drawing

  Subclasses override these methods to implement custom drawing
- Image

  Methods to manipulate the contained image
- Title

  Attributes for the title, which shows up in the center of the top border

Listing 5.12 shows its usage.

Listing 5.12 ContainerView Example

```
ContainerView panel = new ContainerView(0,0,300,200);
panel.setTransparent(false);
panel.setBackgroundColor(Color.white);
panel.setBorder(BezelBorder.raisedBezel());
panel.setTitle("This is a title");
mainRootView().addSubview(panel);
```

One of the more common uses for this is to hold an image, since an image is not a view and needs one to *hold* it. A code fragment showing this usage is shown in Listing 5.13.

Listing 5.13 ContainerView with Image

```
ContainerView panel = new ContainerView(0,0,300,200);
mainRootView().setColor(Color.lightGray);
panel.setImage(Bitmap.bitmapNamed("Packers.gif"));
     panel.setImageDisplayStyle(Image.TILED);
     mainRootView().addSubview(panel);
```

Lists

Lists present the user with a sequence of items, from which one or more may be selected. Each item may consist of a text string and/or an icon, and represents one row in the list. Events may be generated when the user selects one or more items, and also when the user double-clicks an item.

IFC has broken up management of lists into the following classes:

- ListItem

  Represents a single item of a ListView

- ListView

  The GUI container that holds ListItem objects

ListItem

To make lists as extensible and modular as possible, IFC has encapsulated the functionality of the list entry into the ListItem class. This class handles most functions that a list member should have, such as the title to display, icon, and color. There is also a provision to store user data in a ListItem.

Drawing is handled by the parent ListView class based on information provided by each ListItem object.

The API is shown in Listing 5.14.

Listing 5.14 ListItem Class

```
public class ListItem implements Cloneable, Codable {

public ListItem();

public Object clone();

public String command();
public void setCommand(String);
public Object data();
public void setData(Object);

public Font font();
public void setFont(Font);
public void setTitle(String);
public String title();
public Image image();
public void setImage(Image);
public Image selectedImage();
public void setSelectedImage(Image);
public Color selectedColor();
public void setSelectedColor(Color);

public boolean isEnabled();
public void setEnabled(boolean);
public boolean isSelected();
public void setSelected(boolean);
public ListView listView();

protected void drawBackground(Graphics, Rect);          //.. drawing
public void drawInRect(Graphics, Rect);
protected void drawStringInRect(Graphics, String, Font, Rect, int);
public boolean isTransparent();

public int minHeight();
public int minWidth();

public void decode(Decoder);                            //.. persistent
public void describeClassInfo(ClassInfo);
public void encode(Encoder);
public void finishDecoding();
}
```

Using the ListItem involves creating it and setting its attributes, as shown in the following code snippet:

```
ListItem item = new ListItem();
item.setImage(Bitmap.bitmapNamed("blusq.gif"));
item.setSelectedImage(Bitmap.bitmapNamed("yelsq.gif"));
```

The `clone()` method implements the Clonable interface. The `setCommand()` method sets the command for the ListItem. If set, it will be used by the parent ListView for events relating to this object. The `setData()` provides a mechanism to store a user-defined object inside a ListItem.

The `setFont()`, `setImage()`, `setTitle()`, `setSelectedImage()`, and `setSelectedColor()` methods control the appearance. Note that the selected item's image must be set separately. The selected color refers to the highlight bar that reflects the currently selected item.

The `setEnabled()` method is used to enable and disable this item. A disabled item is grayed out and cannot be selected, and hence will not generate any events. The `setSelected()` method forces this item to be selected, and `listView()` returns the ListView container that holds this ListItem, if set.

The `draw()` and `isTransparent()` methods are used by subclasses to implement custom drawing behavior. If a subclass returns True for the `isTransparent()` method, the parent ListView will draw this item transparently.

Finally, the Codable interface implements persistence.

ListView

The ListView class implements the actual list that is displayed to the user and manages all resources to achieve the same. By definition, a ListView shows a vertical list of ListItem objects, which may be selected individually or in multiples. Events may be generated when the user single- or double-clicks an item.

When the number of items exceeds the physical bounds of the ListView, scrolling may be implemented. In the reverse case of fewer items, the `View.sizeToMinSize()` method may be used to shrink the ListView to an optimum size.

The ListView class is normally used with the *prototype* item. This is similar to a standard *template* that the ListView uses to construct the list. After a certain ListItem is designated as the prototype for the list, the ListView uses it to construct its other items.

Let's examine the ListView class definition, as presented in Listing 5.15.

Listing 5.15 ListView Class

```
public class ListView extends View {

public ListView();
public ListView(Rect);
public ListView(int, int, int, int);

public int count();

public ListItem prototypeItem();                        //.. prototype
public void setPrototypeItem(ListItem);

public ListItem addItem();                              //.. item
public ListItem addItem(ListItem);
public ListItem insertItemAt(ListItem, int);
public ListItem insertItemAt(int);
public void removeItem(ListItem);
public void removeItemAt(int);
public void removeAllItems();

public int indexOfItem(ListItem);
public ListItem itemAt(int);
public ListItem itemForPoint(int, int);

public void selectItem(ListItem);
public void selectItemAt(int);
public void selectOnly(ListItem);
public void deselectItem(ListItem);

public int selectedIndex();
public ListItem selectedItem();
public Vector selectedItems();

public void scrollItemAtToVisible(int);
public void scrollItemToVisible(ListItem);
public int rowHeight();
public void setRowHeight(int);
public int minItemHeight();
public int minItemWidth();
public Size minSize();

public boolean allowsEmptySelection();                  //.. selection
public void setAllowsEmptySelection(boolean);
public boolean allowsMultipleSelection();
public void setAllowsMultipleSelection(boolean);
public boolean multipleItemsSelected();

public boolean isEnabled();
public void setEnabled(boolean);
public boolean isTransparent();
public void setTransparent(boolean);
public Color backgroundColor();
public void setBackgroundColor(Color);
```

```
public String command();                              //.. events
public void sendCommand();
public void setCommand(String);
public Target target();
public void setTarget(Target);
public String doubleCommand();
public void sendDoubleCommand();
public void setDoubleCommand(String);

public void drawItemAt(int);                             //.. drawing
public void drawView(Graphics);
public void drawViewBackground(Graphics, int, int, int, int);
public Rect rectForItem(ListItem);
public Rect rectForItemAt(int);

public boolean mouseDown(MouseEvent);                        //.. mouse
public void mouseDragged(MouseEvent);
public void mouseUp(MouseEvent);
public void setTracksMouseOutsideBounds(boolean);
public boolean tracksMouseOutsideBounds();
public boolean wantsAutoscrollEvents();

public void decode(Decoder);                             //.. persistence
public void describeClassInfo(ClassInfo);
public void encode(Encoder);
}
```

Using the ListView involves creating it and setting its default prototype item, as shown in the following code snippet:

```
ListView list = new ListView(0,0,100,100);
list.setPrototypeItem(item);
```

The `count()` returns the number of ListItems contained within it. The `setPrototypeItem()` sets the prototype item to be used with this object. The `addItem()` adds a ListItem based on the prototype item, whereas the `addItem(ListItem)` adds a new ListItem. The `insertItemAt()` methods insert ListItems in a similar manner at a particular position in the ListView. The `remove` methods remove ListItem(s) from the ListView.

The `indexOfItem()` returns the position of the item, which `itemAt()` returns the item at the position. The `itemForPoint()` returns the item at the specified coordinates.

To select and deselect items under program control, use the `selectItem()`, `selectItemAt()`, and `deselectItem()` methods. Note that selection of an item causes an event to be sent to the target. This can be avoided by using the `selectOnly()` method.

The `selectedIndex()` and `selectedItem()` methods return the currently selected item, while multiple selections are returned via the `selectedItems()` method, which returns a Vector of ListItem objects.

The scroll methods scroll the view to make the requested item visible, while the `setRowHeight()` method forces each item to the specified size. The `setAllowsEmptySelection()` and `setAllowsMultipleSelection()` methods control empty and multiple selection options, respectively. The `multipleItemsSelected()` method determines if there are multiple items selected at that time.

The `setEnabled()`, `setTransparent()`, `setBackgroundColor()`, `setCommand()`, and `setTarget()` methods do functions that were described earlier. The `setDoubleCommand()` method sets the command to be sent when the user double-clicks an entry. The `sendCommand()` and `sendDoubleCommand()` force the ListView to send its command and double command to the target.

The `draw` and `mouse` methods are overridden by subclasses for custom behavior, and the Codable interface implementation makes this object persistent.

listApp Example

The listApp example, as shown in Figure 5.4, uses the ListView and ListItem components. We build a list of birds, associating a bitmap with each item and allowing multiple selections. The list is directly attached to the main application root view. The example starts by constructing a ListItem object that has images associated with it and designating it to the prototype item for a newly constructed ListView.

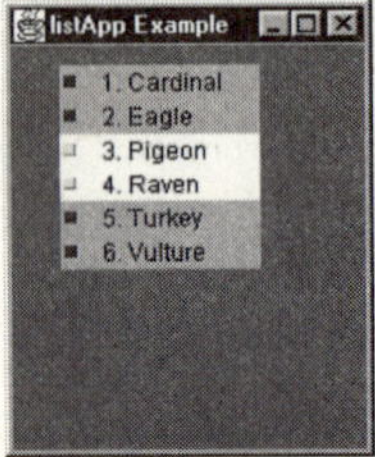

FIG. 5.4
Screen from listApp Example.

Next, the bird strings are added to the list. Note that we have to first add the item, retrieve it back, and set its title. This is more efficient than the alternate approach of constructing a new ListItem each time, setting its images, etc.

We then enable multiple selections and shrink its size to exactly fit the list of items. Lastly, we set its command and target and add it directly to the main application root view. The program listing is given in Listing 5.16.

The `performCommand()` handles commands sent by the ListView, retrieves its selections, and prints them out.

Listing 5.16 listApp.java: listApp Application

```
public class listApp extends Application implements Target {

public void init() {
super.init();

          String[] birds = {
               "Cardinal", "Eagle", "Pigeon", "Raven", "Turkey", "Vulture"
          };

          ListItem item = new ListItem();
          item.setImage(Bitmap.bitmapNamed("blusq.gif"));
          item.setSelectedImage(Bitmap.bitmapNamed("yelsq.gif"));

          ListView list = new ListView(0,0,100,100);
          list.setPrototypeItem(item);
          for (int i=0;i<birds.length;i++) {
               list.addItem();
               item = list.itemAt(i);
item.setTitle(" "+(i+1)+". "+birds[i]);
          }
          list.setAllowsMultipleSelection(true);
          list.sizeToMinSize();
          list.setCommand("cmdListView");
          list.setTarget(this);
          mainRootView().addSubview(list);

     }

     public void performCommand(String command, Object arg) {
          if (command.equals("cmdListView")) {
               ListView list = (ListView)arg;
               if (list.multipleItemsSelected()) {
                    Vector v = list.selectedItems();
                    for (int i=0;i<v.size();i++)
                         System.out.println(((ListItem)v.elementAt(i)).title());
               }
               else
                    System.out.println(list.selectedItem().title());
          }
     }

public static void main(String args[]) {

listApp app = new listApp();
ExternalWindow win = new ExternalWindow();
app.setMainRootView(win.rootView());

Size size = win.windowSizeForContentSize(640, 480);
win.sizeTo(size.width, size.height);
win.show();

app.run();
}
}
```

Popup Lists

Popup Lists, when activated, display a list of items (just like ListView), and when an item is selected, hide the list and set their value to the selected item. Most native platforms implement similar behavior in the form of popup menus, drop-down list/combo boxes, etc.

Similar to the list-management system discussed earlier, the popup system is also divided into the following classes:

- PopupItem

  Represents a single entry in the Popup view
- Popup

  The GUI container that holds PopupItem(s)

PopupItem

The PopupItem is a subclass of the ListItem and inherits its functionality from it. The only extra functionality it implements relates to the parent Popup object that holds it, which may be changed by the `setPopup()` method. (See Listing 5.17.)

Listing 5.17 PopupItem Class

```
public class PopupItem extends ListItem {
public PopupItem();

public Popup popup();                          //.. owner
public void setPopup(Popup);

public void drawInRect(Graphics, Rect);          //.. draw

public void decode(Decoder);                     //.. persistence
public void describeClassInfo(ClassInfo);
public void encode(Encoder);
}
```

Popup

The Popup class is similar in some respects to the ListView class discussed earlier. Since it behaves differently, it was decided not to subclass ListView, but instead to implement the Popup from the base View class.

Normally, a Popup object will contain PopupItems, but ListItems may be used instead. Also note that a ListView may be constructed and passed on to the Popup to operate upon.

The API is shown in Listing 5.18.

Listing 5.18 Popup Class

```
public class Popup extends View implements Target {

public Popup();
public Popup(Rect);
public Popup(int, int, int, int);

public int count();

public ListItem prototypeItem();                    //.. prototype
public void setPrototypeItem(ListItem);

public ListItem addItem(String, String);            //.. items
public void removeAllItems();
public void removeItem(String);
public ListItem itemAt(int);
public void selectItem(ListItem);
public void selectItemAt(int);
public int selectedIndex();
public ListItem selectedItem();

public String command();                            //.. event
public void sendCommand();
public void setCommand(String);
public void setTarget(Target);
public Target target();
public void performCommand(String, Object);

public boolean isTransparent();                     //.. appearance
public Border border();
public void setBorder(Border);
public Image popupImage();
public void setPopupImage(Image);

public ListView popupList();
public void setPopupList(ListView);
public Window popupWindow();
public void setPopupWindow(Window);

public void drawView(Graphics);                     //.. draw
protected void layoutPopupWindow();
protected void showPopupWindow(MouseEvent);

public boolean mouseDown(MouseEvent);               //.. mouse

public void decode(Decoder);                        //.. persistence
public void describeClassInfo(ClassInfo);
public void encode(Encoder);


}
```

We will not discuss methods that are common with the ListView class because they perform very similar functions. Instead, we will focus on the extra functionality of the Popup class.

NOTE Note that the items in a Popup may be PopupItem or ListItem objects.

The `setPopupImage()` sets the image that is displayed by the selected item. The `setPopupList()` designates a ListView for the Popup to operate upon.

Another extra feature available with the Popup class is the ability to associate a Window object to it by using the `setPopupWindow()` method. One use of this feature is to implement a popup menu.

Popup Example

Let's build an example that uses Popups. The example is similar to the one used in the ListView discussion in that it uses the same data. When you run the example, you get the screen shown in Figure 5.5. On activation, it will show the entire list.

The example program is very similar to the ListView example, with minor changes. Notice that the Popup object is decorated with a BezelBorder and the popup image is assigned with the `setPopupImage()` method. (See Listing 5.19.)

FIG. 5.5 Screen from popupApp Example.

Listing 5.19 popupApp.java: popupApp Class

```
import netscape.application.*;

public class popupApp extends Application implements Target {


public void init() {
        //.. sample data
        String[] birds = {
             "Cardinal", "Eagle", "Pigeon", "Raven", "Turkey", "Vulture"
        };
```

```
        //.. create new list item and set its images
        ListItem item = new ListItem();
        item.setImage(Bitmap.bitmapNamed("blusq.gif"));
        item.setSelectedImage(Bitmap.bitmapNamed("yelsq.gif"));

        //.. create new popup
        Popup list = new Popup(10,10,100,20);
        //.. set its default prototype item and border
        list.setPrototypeItem(item);
        list.setBorder(BezelBorder.raisedBezel());
        //.. add data to the popup
        for (int i=0;i<birds.length;i++)
             list.addItem(" "+birds[i],null);

        //.. set its command, target and popup image
        list.setCommand("cmdPopup");
        list.setTarget(this);
        list.setPopupImage(Bitmap.bitmapNamed("blusq.gif"));

        mainRootView().addSubview(list);
    }

    //.. command processing routine
    public void performCommand(String command, Object arg) {
         if (command.equals("cmdPopup")) {
           //.. get the pop object, which is passed as the argument
              Popup popup = (Popup)arg;
           //.. get the selected item and display its value
              ListItem item = popup.selectedItem();
              System.out.println("Selected:"+item.title());
         }
    }

     /**
      *       standard GUI application main() routine
      */
       public static void main(String args[]) {

               popupApp app = new popupApp();
               ExternalWindow win = new ExternalWindow();
               app.setMainRootView(win.rootView());

               Size size = win.windowSizeForContentSize(640, 480);
               win.sizeTo(size.width, size.height);
               win.show();

               app.run();
       }
}
```

Scrolling

Larger views are managed in smaller areas with Scrolling mechanisms. IFC implements an extensible framework of classes and interfaces to support scrolling operations. Applications may use high-level classes like ScrollGroup that handle most operations, or may subclass various component classes to implement custom scrolling behavior.

There are two approaches to implementing scrolling in IFC:

- ScrollGroup

  A high-level component that manages the scrolling view with minimal programming
- ScrollView

  A discrete approach, offering more control

ScrollGroup

The preferred way to implement scrolling is by using the ScrollGroup class. It consists of ScrollView and ScrollBars objects that are linked up internally.

Using the ScrollGroup involves setting the content view to the view that needs to be managed by using the `setContentView()` method.

scrollGroupApp Example

The scrollGroupApp example uses the ScrollGroup component to demonstrate a scrolling image panel. The example output is displayed in Figure 5.6.

FIG. 5.6 Scrolling example output.

The program listing is given in Listing 5.20.

Listing 5.20 scrollGroupApp.java: ScrollGroup Example

```
import netscape.application.*;

/**
 *     ScrollGroup Application
```

```
 */
public class scrollGroupApp extends Application {

public void init() {

        //.. image panel
        ContainerView panel = new ContainerView(0,0,350,400);
        panel.setImage(Bitmap.bitmapNamed("watch.gif"));

        //.. create ScrollGroup with buffered drawing, scrollbars
        ScrollGroup scroll = new ScrollGroup(0,0,300,200);
        scroll.setBuffered(true);
          scroll.setHasVertScrollBar(true); scroll.setHasHorizScrollBar(true);

          //.. make image scrolling manageable by the ScrollGroup
          scroll.setContentView(panel);

          //.. add the ScrollGroup object to the Application root view
          mainRootView().addSubview(scroll);
    }

    /**
     *      standard GUI application main() routine
     */
  public static void main(String args[]) {

      scrollGroupApp app = new scrollGroupApp();
      ExternalWindow win = new ExternalWindow();
      app.setMainRootView(win.rootView());

      Size size = win.windowSizeForContentSize(300, 200);
      win.sizeTo(size.width, size.height);
          win.setTitle("scrollGroupApp Example");
      win.show();

      app.run();
  }
}
          scroll.setHasVertScrollBar(true); scroll.setHasHorizScrollBar(true);

          //.. make image scrolling manageable by the ScrollGroup
          scroll.setContentView(panel);

          //.. add the ScrollGroup object to the Application root view
          mainRootView().addSubview(scroll);
    }

    /**
     *     standard GUI application main() routine
     */
public static void main(String args[]) {

scrollGroupApp app = new scrollGroupApp();
ExternalWindow win = new ExternalWindow();
app.setMainRootView(win.rootView());
```

continues

Listing 5.20 Continued

```
Size size = win.windowSizeForContentSize(640, 480);
win.sizeTo(size.width, size.height);
win.show();

app.run();
}
}
```

The example attaches a ScrollGroup object to a ContainerView object that contains an image.

NOTE While scrolling a view, you might notice *flashing* or *flickering*. This may be avoided by using the double buffering offered by the View class via its `setBuffered()` method. This is at the cost of extra memory resources being used.

ScrollView

There are situations in which you might need more control over scrolling operations, or there might be certain components like the ListView that would not support the use of ScrollGroup. In these situations, you might use the ScrollView directly.

When using the ScrollView, you have to create and manage the ScrollBar components. This involves allocating and placing the ScrollBar objects and linking them with the ScrollView.

Listing 5.21 shows an example that uses ScrollView.

Listing 5.21 scrollViewApp.java: ScrollView Example

```
import netscape.application.*;

/**
 *      ScrollView Application
 */
public class scrollViewApp extends Application {


public void init() {
super.init();

//.. image panel
        ContainerView panel = new ContainerView(0,0,350,400);
        panel.setImage(Bitmap.bitmapNamed("watch.gif"));

        //.. new ScrollView with buffered drawing
```

```
            ScrollView scroll = new ScrollView(0,0,300,200);
            scroll.setBuffered(true);

            //.. make image manageable by the ScrollView
            scroll.setContentView(panel);

            //.. add horizontal, vertical scrollbars and link them
            ScrollBar hbar,vbar;
            scroll.addScrollBar(hbar=new
ScrollBar(0,200,300,20,Scrollable.HORIZONTAL));
            scroll.addScrollBar(vbar=new
ScrollBar(300,0,20,200,Scrollable.VERTICAL));
            hbar.setScrollableObject(scroll);
            vbar.setScrollableObject(scroll);

            //.. add the ScrollView, ScrollBar items to the Application RootView
            mainRootView().addSubview(scroll);
            mainRootView().addSubview(hbar);
            mainRootView().addSubview(vbar);
            vbar.scrollLineForward();
}

/**
 * standard GUI application main() routine
 */
public static void main(String args[]) {

scrollViewApp app = new scrollViewApp();
ExternalWindow win = new ExternalWindow();
app.setMainRootView(win.rootView());

Size size = win.windowSizeForContentSize(640, 480);
win.sizeTo(size.width, size.height);
win.show();

app.run();
}
}
```

In addition to the preceding, there are other Scrolling-related classes and interfaces:

- ScrollBar

  Class that implements a ScrollBar
- Scrollable

  Interface implemented by objects controlled by the ScrollBar class. The ScrollView class implements this interface
- ScrollBarOwner

  Interface implemented by objects interested in ScrollBar-related actions. The setScrollBarOwner( ) method of the ScrollBar class accepts this interface

Slider

The Slider widget emulates the familiar sliding controls found on consumer electronic equipment. It is used in software applications to control values in a linear fashion and presents the user with a familiar interface, as shown in Figure 5.7.

The user controls values by dragging the ***knob***, causing it to send events to a predesignated `Target`.

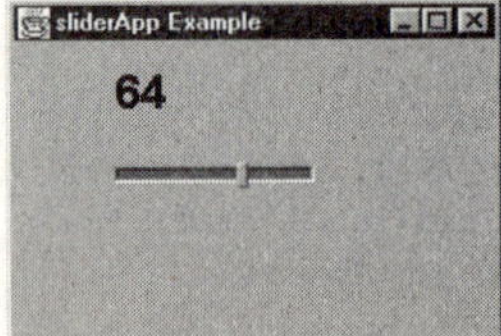

FIG. 5.7
Slider example.

The Slider class definition is given in Listing 5.22.

Listing 5.22 Slider Class

```
public class Slider extends View {

public Slider();                          //.. constructors
public Slider(Rect);
public Slider(int, int, int, int);

public String command();                   //.. event
public void setCommand(String);
public void sendCommand();
public Target target();
public void setTarget(Target);

public void drawView(Graphics);             //.. drawing
public void drawViewGroove(Graphics);
public void drawViewKnob(Graphics);
public Size minSize();
public void didSizeBy(int, int);

public int grooveHeight();                  //.. appearance
public void setGrooveHeight(int);
public Image image();
public void setImage(Image);
public int imageDisplayStyle();
public void setImageDisplayStyle(int);
public void setBackgroundColor(Color);
public Color backgroundColor();
public Border border();
public void setBorder(Border);
```

```
public boolean isEnabled();                    //.. enabled
public void setEnabled(boolean);

public int knobHeight();                    //.. knob
public Image knobImage();
public Rect knobRect();
public int knobWidth();
public void setKnobHeight(int);
public void setKnobImage(Image);

public int maxValue();                         //.. value
public int minValue();
public int value();
public void setValue(int);
public void setLimits(int, int);

public boolean mouseDown(MouseEvent);              //.. mouse
public void mouseDragged(MouseEvent);

}
```

The API has methods in the following broad categories:

- Event handling

  These methods handle the command and target
- Custom drawing

  Subclasses override these methods to do custom drawing
- Appearance

  Control various parameters that affect the appearance of this widget. Image overrides background color
- Enable and disable

  Activate and deactivate this control
- Knob control

  Controls various parameters for the knob
- Value-related methods

  Direct manipulation of the value, which defaults to the range (0,255)
- Mouse

  Subclasses override these methods for better control of the mouse

The sliderApp example program presented in Listing 5.23 uses some of these Slider methods to implement a simple example that causes a slider value to be displayed as its knob is moved, as shown in Figure 5.7.

Listing 5.23 sliderApp.java: Slider Example

```
import netscape.application.*;

public class sliderApp extends Application implements Target {

    protected TextField value;

   public void init() {

           //.. set background color
           mainRootView().setColor(Color.lightGray);

           //.. create a slider component
           Slider sldr = new Slider(50,50,100,32);

           //.. set its command and target
           sldr.setCommand("SLIDER");
           sldr.setTarget(this);
           //.. set limits for the slider
           sldr.setLimits(0,100);

           //.. add it to the background
           mainRootView().addSubview(sldr);

           //.. add a label which will reflect the slider's value
           value = TextField.createLabel("100",
Font.fontNamed("Arial",Font.BOLD,24));
           value.setStringValue("0");
           value.moveTo(50,10);
           mainRootView().addSubview(value);
    }

    //.. command processing routine
    public void performCommand(String command, Object arg) {
          //.. if the slider has sent its command
          if (command.equals("SLIDER")) {
                //.. reflect it in the label
                value.setStringValue(((Slider)arg).value()+"");
             }
    }

    /**
     *      standard GUI application main() routine
     */
   public static void main(String args[]) {

       sliderApp app = new sliderApp();
       ExternalWindow win = new ExternalWindow();
       app.setMainRootView(win.rootView());

       Size size = win.windowSizeForContentSize(240, 150);
       win.sizeTo(size.width, size.height);
           win.setTitle("sliderApp Example");
```

```
        win.show();

        app.run();
    }
}
```

The preceding fragment creates a Slider, sets its command and target, sets its limit to the range (0,100), and adds it to the main background view of the application.

When the user drags the knob, it sends out its command to itself, which is shown in Figure 5.7.

TextField

The TextField class performs many useful functions on text strings, including display and user edits. The string is characterized by a single font and may contain control characters that are handled appropriately.

Another salient feature of the TextField class is the ability to notify a TextFieldOwner object of certain changes occurring within it. This way another object can keep track of events in a TextField object. Filtering of user input is provided via the TextFilter interface. Labels are provided by the `createLabel()` static methods.

The class definition is shown in Listing 5.24.

Listing 5.24 TextField Class

```
public class TextField extends View implements Target {

public final static java.lang.String SELECT_TEXT;

public TextField();
public TextField(Rect);
public TextField(int, int, int, int);

public static TextField createLabel(String, Font);
public static TextField createLabel(String);

public boolean isEmpty();                           //.. value
public int intValue();
public void setIntValue(int);
public String stringValue();
public void setStringValue(String);
public void replaceRangeWithString(Range, String);
public String stringForRange(Range);
public void cancelEditing();
```

continues

Listing 5.24 Continued

```
public void completeEditing();
public int baseline();
public boolean isBeingEdited();

public boolean hasInsertionPoint();
public void setInsertionPoint(int);
public int leftIndent();
public int rightIndent();
public Size minSize();

public boolean hasSelection();
public boolean isSelectable();
public void setSelectable(boolean);
public void selectRange(Range);
public void selectText();
public Range selectedRange();
public String selectedStringValue();
public int charCount();
public int charNumberForPoint(int);
public int cursorForPoint(int, int);
public int xPositionOfCharacter(int);

public TextField backtabField();                          //.. tabbing
public void setBacktabField(TextField);
public TextField tabField();
public void setTabField(TextField);

public String command();                                  //.. event
public void setCommand(String);
public Target target();
public void setTarget(Target);
public void performCommand(String, Object);
public String contentsChangedCommand();
public Target contentsChangedTarget();
public void setContentsChangedCommandAndTarget(String, Target);

public Color backgroundColor();                           //.. appearance
public void setBackgroundColor(Color);
public Border border();
public void setBorder(Border);
public Color caretColor();
public void setCaretColor(Color);
public boolean drawsDropShadow();
public void setDrawsDropShadow(boolean);
public boolean isEditable();
public void setEditable(boolean);
public Font font();
public void setFont(Font);
public Color selectionColor();
public void setSelectionColor(Color);
public boolean isTransparent();
public void setTransparent(boolean);
public Color textColor();
public void setTextColor(Color);
```

```
public int justification();
public void setJustification(int);
public boolean wrapsContents();
public void setWrapsContents(boolean);

public TextFieldOwner owner();                    //.. support
public void setOwner(TextFieldOwner);
public TextFilter filter();
public void setFilter(TextFilter);

public void startFocus();                         //.. keyboard
public void stopFocus();
public void pauseFocus();
public void resumeFocus();
public void setFocusedView();
public void keyDown(KeyEvent);

public void drawInterior();                        //.. drawing
public void drawView(Graphics);
public void drawViewBorder(Graphics);
public void drawViewInterior(Graphics, Rect);
public void drawViewStringAt(Graphics, String, int, int);

public boolean mouseDown(MouseEvent);                  //.. mouse
public void mouseDragged(MouseEvent);
public void mouseUp(MouseEvent);
public boolean wantsAutoscrollEvents();

public void decode(Decoder);                        //.. persistence
public void describeClassInfo(ClassInfo);
public void encode(Encoder);
public void finishDecoding();
}
```


As we see, the API may be broadly classified into certain categories of methods. Details can be found in the IFC reference documentation. Using the TextField class involves creating it and setting its attributes as shown:

```
        //.. label
        tf = TextField.createLabel("Email Account",
Font.fontNamed("Arial",Font.BOLD,20)));
        tf.moveTo(70,10);
        //.. add fields for data entry
        name = new TextField(120,50,150,20);
        name.setJustification(Graphics.CENTERED);
```

TextFieldOwner Interface

The TextFieldOwner interface provides a mechanism to monitor TextFields. Upon setting the owner for a TextField, via its `setOwner()` method, the TextField notifies its owner of important events, like the end of editing, via the TextFieldOwner interface methods. Four such methods are available, as can be seen from the interface definition in Listing 5.25.

Listing 5.25 TextFieldOwner Interface

```
public interface TextFieldOwner {
     public final static int BACKTAB_KEY;
     public final static int LOST_FOCUS;
     public final static int RESIGNED_FOCUS;
     public final static int RETURN_KEY;
     public final static int TAB_KEY;

     public abstract void textEditingDidBegin(TextField);
     public abstract void textEditingDidEnd(TextField, int, boolean);
     public abstract boolean textEditingWillEnd(TextField, int, boolean);
     public abstract void textWasModified(TextField);
}
```

The TextFieldOwner interface is used with the `TextField.setOwner()` method, as shown:

```
name = new TextField(120,50,150,20);
name.setOwner((TextFieldOwner)owner);
```

TextFilter Interface

The TextFilter interface is implemented by objects that are interested in *intercepting* keystrokes before they are passed to the text-processing objects, like the TextField and TextView classes. This is useful for data validation and tasks such as keystroke translation. (See Listing 5.26.)

The API is as follows.

Listing 5.26 TextFilter Interface

```
public interface TextFilter {
     public abstract boolean acceptsEvent(Object, KeyEvent, Vector);
}
```

The TextFilter interface is used with the `TextField.setFilter()` method as shown:

```
name = new TextField(120,50,150,20);
name.setFilter((TextFilter)filter);
```

TextField Example

Let's use some of the preceding concepts in an example that implements an authentication window with TextFields.

The TextField example uses the PasswordField class provided with the IFC samples kit and implements tab movement between the two TextField objects, as shown in Figure 5.8.

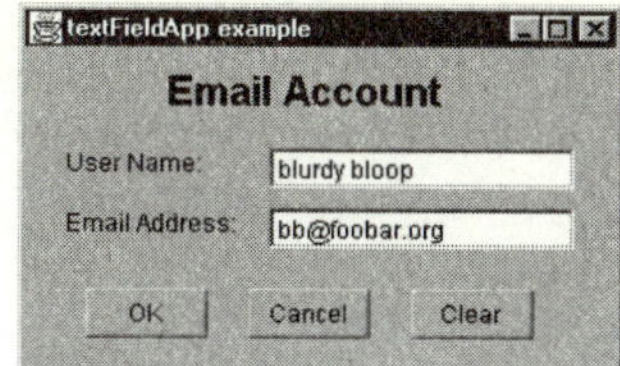

FIG. 5.8
TextFieldApp example.

Listing 5.27 textFieldApp.java: TextField Example

```
import netscape.application.*;

/**
 *     TextField Application
 */
public class textFieldApp extends Application implements Target, TextFieldOwner
{
     protected TextField name;
     protected TextField email;

public void init() {
         super.init();
//.. set background color
     mainRootView().setColor(Color.lightGray);

          TextField tf;

     //.. place labels
          mainRootView().addSubview(tf = TextField.createLabel("Email Account",
                              Font.fontNamed("Arial",Font.BOLD,20)));
     tf.moveTo(70,10);
     mainRootView().addSubview(tf = TextField.createLabel("User Name:"));
          tf.moveTo(20,50);
     mainRootView().addSubview(tf = TextField.createLabel("Email Address:"));
          tf.moveTo(20,80);

     //.. add fields for data entry
          mainRootView().addSubview(name = new TextField(120,50,150,20));
     mainRootView().addSubview(email = new TextField(120,80,150,20));
          //..set the TextFieldOwner's for these TextFields
          name.setOwner(this);          email.setOwner(this);

     //.. set Tab/Backtab links
          name.setTabField(email);     name.setBacktabField(email);
     email.setTabField(name);     email.setBacktabField(name);

          //.. add buttons which cause action
     Button b;
          mainRootView().addSubview(b = Button.createPushButton(30,120,60,25));
     b.setTitle("OK");
b.setCommand("btnOk");
b.setTarget(this);
```

continues

Listing 5.27 Continued

```
        mainRootView().addSubview(b = Button.createPushButton(110,120,60,25));
    b.setTitle("Cancel");
b.setCommand("btnCancel");
b.setTarget(this);

        mainRootView().addSubview(b = Button.createPushButton(190,120,60,25));
    b.setTitle("Clear");
b.setCommand("btnClear");
b.setTarget(this);
}

//.. command processing routine
public void performCommand(String command, Object arg) {
        if (command.equals("btnOk")) {
            System.out.println("name="+name.stringValue()+
                ", email="+email.stringValue());
        //.. stop application/applet
if (isApplet()) stopRunning(); else System.exit(0);
    }
        else if (command.equals("btnCancel")) {
            System.out.println("operation was cancelled");
if (isApplet()) stopRunning(); else System.exit(0);
    }
        else if (command.equals("btnClear")) {
            name.setStringValue("");     //.. clear both fields
        email.setStringValue("");
        }
}

/**
 *     TextFieldOwner interface
 */
public void textEditingDidBegin(TextField text) { }

//.. called when editing is about to end
public void textEditingDidEnd(TextField text, int cond, boolean edit) {
//.. figure out which text field caused this event
        String fieldName = (text==name) ? "userName" : "emailAddress";
        String event=null;
//.. find the condition for which this routine was called
        if (cond==TAB_KEY)                event="Tab Key";
        else if (cond==BACKTAB_KEY)          event="BackTab Key";
        else if (cond==RETURN_KEY)          event="Return Key";
        else if (cond==LOST_FOCUS)          event="Lost Focus";
        else if (cond==RESIGNED_FOCUS)     event="Resign Focus";

        System.out.println(fieldName+" got the following event - "+event);
    }

public boolean textEditingWillEnd(TextField text, int cond, boolean edit) {
        return true;
    }
```

```
public void textWasModified(TextField text) { }

     /**
      *     standard GUI application main() routine
      */
public static void main(String args[]) {

textFieldApp app = new textFieldApp();
ExternalWindow win = new ExternalWindow();
    app.setMainRootView(win.rootView());

         Size size = win.windowSizeForContentSize(290, 160);
    win.sizeTo(size.width, size.height);
          win.setTitle("textFieldApp example");
         win.show();

    app.run();
}
}
```

TextView

One of the most powerful features of IFC is its ability to handle multifont text. The TextView object handles this operation in an elegant and extendible manner. The TextView class is also the foundation for handling HTML-based hyperlinked documents. We will look into this aspect in Chapter 11, "Advanced Topics."

The TextView holds collections of text strings, with each collection having a common set of attributes. This collection is called a *run* of text. Each set of attributes is held in a Hashtable object. Thus, each run has a Hashtable associated with it, with the TextView itself having a default attributes Hashtable. Attributes include such properties as text font, color, and caret color.

A paragraph of text is a collection of runs terminating with a carriage return. Each paragraph can have its own set of attributes, as defined by the TextParagraphFormat class. These can include such properties as tab spacing, justification, etc.

Using the preceding features of the TextView class, it's possible to build sophisticated text-processing programs.

Note that you cannot set a maximum height of the TextView because it's always sized according to what you add. You can clip the TextView by placing it inside another view of desired size. Most commonly, the ScrollGroup is used to hold a TextView.

When one or more characters are inserted into the TextView by typing or by using the insertion methods, the following rules determine how attributes apply to the new ranges:

- If there's a run *after* the inserted range, the inserted characters' attributes will be: `defaultAttributes() UNION` the following run's attributes.
- If a run appears *before* the inserted range, the inserted characters' attributes will be: `defaultAttributes() UNION` the previous run's attributes.
- If the previous two conditions don't apply, the inserted characters' attributes will be `defaultAttributes()`.

The TextView API is shown in Listing 5.28.

Listing 5.28 TextView Class

```
public class TextView extends View implements ExtendedTarget, EventFilter,
DragDestination {

    //.. constants
public final static java.lang.String CARET_COLOR_KEY;
public final static java.lang.String FONT_KEY;
public final static java.lang.String LINK_COLOR_KEY;
public final static java.lang.String LINK_DESTINATION_KEY;
public final static java.lang.String LINK_KEY;
public final static java.lang.String PARAGRAPH_FORMAT_KEY;
public final static java.lang.String PRESSED_LINK_COLOR_KEY;
public final static java.lang.String TEXT_ATTACHMENT_BASELINE_OFFSET_KEY;
public final static java.lang.String TEXT_ATTACHMENT_KEY;
public final static java.lang.String TEXT_ATTACHMENT_STRING;
public final static java.lang.String TEXT_COLOR_KEY;

    public TextView();                                  //.. constructors
public TextView(Rect);
public TextView(int, int, int, int);

public static String stringWithoutCarriageReturns(String);     //.. static
functions

     public void addAttributeForRange(String, Object, Range);     //..
➥attributes
public void addAttributesForRange(Hashtable, Range);
public void addDefaultAttribute(String, Object);
public Hashtable attributesAtIndex(int);
public Hashtable defaultAttributes();
public void setAttributesForRange(Hashtable, Range);
public void setDefaultAttributes(Hashtable);

public boolean canPerformCommand(String);              //.. ExtendedTarget

     public void decode(Decoder);                          //.. persistence
public void describeClassInfo(ClassInfo);
public void encode(Encoder);
public void finishDecoding();

public boolean dragDropped(DragSession);              //.. drag & drop
```

```
public boolean dragEntered(DragSession);
public void dragExited(DragSession);
public boolean dragMoved(DragSession);
public DragDestination acceptsDrag(DragSession, int, int);

public TextFilter filter();                        //.. filter
public void setFilter(TextFilter);
public Object filterEvents(Vector);

public void importHTMLFromURLString(String);             //.. HTML
public void importHTMLInRange(InputStream, Range, URL);

public boolean isEditable();                       //.. properties
public void setEditable(boolean);
public void disableResizing();
public boolean isResizingEnabled();
public void enableResizing();
public boolean isSelectable();
public void setSelectable(boolean);
public boolean isTransparent();
public void setTransparent(boolean);
public Font font();
public void setFont(Font);
public Color backgroundColor();
public void setBackgroundColor(Color);
public Color caretColor();
public void setCaretColor(Color);
public void setUseSingleFont(boolean);
public boolean usesSingleFont();
public Color selectionColor();
public void setSelectionColor(Color);
public Color textColor();
public void setTextColor(Color);

public void keyDown(KeyEvent);                     //.. keyboard
public void pauseFocus();
public void resumeFocus();
public void startFocus();
public void stopFocus();

public boolean mouseDown(MouseEvent);                   //.. mouse
public void mouseDragged(MouseEvent);
public void mouseUp(MouseEvent);
public boolean wantsAutoscrollEvents();

public TextViewOwner owner();                        //.. owner
public void setOwner(TextViewOwner);

public Range paragraphForIndex(int);                   //.. paragraph
public Range paragraphForPoint(int, int);
public Vector paragraphsForRange(Range);
public Vector rectsForRange(Range);
public void removeAttributeForRange(String, Range);
public void replaceRangeWithString(Range, String);
```

continues

Listing 5.28 Continued

```
public Range runForIndex(int);                          //.. runs
public Range runForPoint(int, int);
public Range runWithLinkDestinationNamed(String);
public Vector runsForRange(Range);

public void selectRange(Range);                          //.. select
public Range selectedRange();

public Range appendString(String);                          //.. get/set
public void setString(String);
public String string();
public String stringForRange(Range);

public void replaceRangeWithTextAttachment(Range, TextAttachment);

public boolean hasSelection();
public int indexForPoint(int, int);
public int cursorForPoint(int, int);

public void didMoveBy(int, int);
public void didSizeBy(int, int);
public void sizeBy(int, int);
public void sizeToMinSize();

public void drawView(Graphics);

public void performCommand(String, Object);

public void scrollRangeToVisible(Range);

public int length();

public String toString();
}
```

TextViewOwner Interface

The TextViewOwner provides a mechanism to monitor TextView objects. Similar to the TextFieldOwner discussed earlier, the TextViewOwner interface is used to communicate important events back to the owner of a TextView.

Listing 5.29 shows the TextViewOwner interface.

Listing 5.29 TextViewOwner Interface

```
public interface TextViewOwner {
public abstract void attributesDidChange(TextView, Range);
public abstract void attributesWillChange(TextView, Range);
public abstract void linkWasSelected(TextView, Range, String);
```

```
public abstract void selectionDidChange(TextView);
public abstract void textDidChange(TextView, Range);
public abstract void textEditingDidBegin(TextView);
public abstract void textEditingDidEnd(TextView);
public abstract void textWillChange(TextView, Range);
}
```

TextParagraphFormat

The TextParagraphFormat class represents a single paragraph in a TextView object. The recommended way to use it is to get the default paragraph format from the TextView's default attributes, clone it, and modify the clone. This is easier than creating a new TextParagraphFormat, because doing so entails setting a number of values.

Some of the properties that can be controlled by the TextParagraphFormat class are:

- Tab positions
- Justification
- Margins and Indents
- Line spacing

The TextParagraphFormat class definition is shown in Listing 5.30.

Listing 5.30 TextParagraphFormat

```
public class TextParagraphFormat implements Cloneable, Codable {

public TextParagraphFormat();

public void addTabPosition(int);
public void clearAllTabPositions();
public Object clone();
public void decode(Decoder);
public void describeClassInfo(ClassInfo);
public void encode(Encoder);
public void finishDecoding();
public int justification();
public int leftIndent();
public int leftMargin();
public int lineSpacing();
public int positionForTab(int);
public int rightMargin();
public void setJustification(int);
public void setLeftIndent(int);
       public void setLeftMargin(int);
public void setLineSpacing(int);
public void setRightMargin(int);
public void setTabPositions(int[]);
public int[] tabPositions();
}
```

To apply a TextParagraphFormat, use TextView's `addAttributeForRange()` method as follows:

```
        para = new TextParagraphFormat();
        para.setJustification(Graphics.RIGHT_JUSTIFIED);
        tv = new TextView(120,50,150,20);
        tv.addAttributeForRange(TextView.PARAGRAPH_FORMAT_KEY, para,
    Range.rangeFromIndices(0,1));
```

TextView Example

Let's look at an example that uses some the features of the TextView widget. This example places a TextView inside a ScrollGroup and places three buttons that toggle attributes for a selected range of text, as shown in Figure 5.9. When you select a range of text and press a button, the appropriate attribute is toggled.

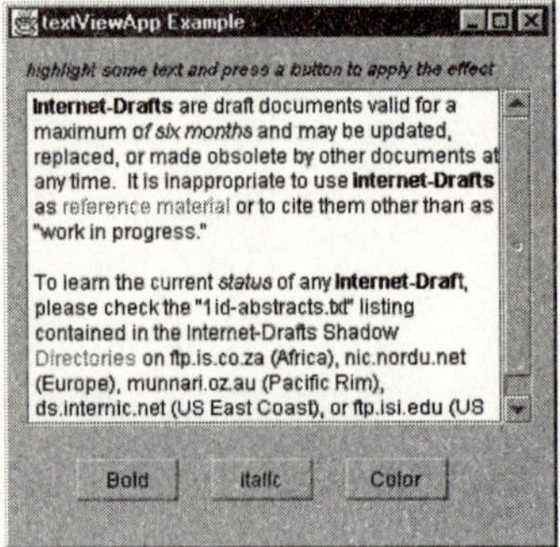

FIG. 5.9
textViewApp example.

The code is shown in Listing 5.31.

Listing 5.31 textViewApp.java: TextView Example

```
import netscape.application.*;
import netscape.util.*;

/**
 *      TextView sample Application
 */
public class textViewApp extends Application implements Target {

protected TextView text;

public void init() {

super.init();
mainRootView().setColor(Color.lightGray);

//.. instructions label
```

```
TextField label;
mainRootView().addSubview(label = TextField.createLabel("highlight some "+
                            "text and press a button to apply the effect"));
label.moveTo(10,10);
label.setFont(Font.fontNamed("Dialog", Font.ITALIC, 11));

//.. ScrollGroup to hold the TextView
ScrollGroup scroll = new ScrollGroup(10,30,300,200);
scroll.setBorder(BezelBorder.groovedBezel());
scroll.setBackgroundColor(Color.white);

//.. TextView
text = new TextView(0,0,300-scroll.vertScrollBar().width(),400);
text.setTransparent(true);

//.. set the default attributes for the TextView
Hashtable h = new Hashtable();
h.put(TextView.TEXT_COLOR_KEY,Color.black);
h.put(TextView.FONT_KEY,Font.fontNamed("Arial", Font.PLAIN, 12));
text.setDefaultAttributes(h);

//.. attach TextView to the ScrollGroup
scroll.setContentView(text);
scroll.setHasVertScrollBar(true);
mainRootView().addSubview(scroll);

//.. Buttons which cause action
Button b;
mainRootView().addSubview(b = Button.createPushButton(40,250,60,25));
b.setTitle("Bold");
b.setCommand("btnBold");
b.setTarget(this);
mainRootView().addSubview(b = Button.createPushButton(120,250,60,25));
b.setTitle("Italic");
b.setCommand("btnItalic");
b.setTarget(this);
mainRootView().addSubview(b = Button.createPushButton(200,250,60,25));
b.setTitle("Color");
b.setCommand("btnColor");
b.setTarget(this);
}

/**
 *
 */
public void performCommand(String command, Object arg) {

if (command.startsWith("btn")) {

//.. get selected range, if any
if (!text.hasSelection()) return;
Range r = text.selectedRange();

//.. get the attributes of the run at the
Hashtable h = text.attributesAtIndex(r.index());
```

Part II Ch 5

continues

Listing 5.31 Continued

```
if (command.equals("btnBold") ¦¦ command.equals("btnItalic")) {
//.. extract the font and its style
Font f = (Font)h.get(TextView.FONT_KEY);
int style = f.style();

//.. toggle the bold/italic attributes
if (command.equals("btnBold"))
style = (f.isBold()) ? style & ~Font.BOLD : style ¦ Font.BOLD;
else if (command.equals("btnItalic"))
style = (f.isItalic()) ? style & ~Font.ITALIC :
style ¦ Font.ITALIC;
//.. set back the font attributes
text.addAttributeForRange(TextView.FONT_KEY,
Font.fontNamed("Arial", style, 12),r);
}
else
if (command.equals("btnColor")) {
//.. extract the font color
Color c = (Color)h.get(TextView.TEXT_COLOR_KEY);
c = (c == Color.red) ? Color.black : Color.red;
//.. set back the font color
text.addAttributeForRange(TextView.TEXT_COLOR_KEY,c,r);
}
}
}

/**
 *      standard GUI application main() routine
 */
public static void main(String args[]) {

textViewApp app = new textViewApp();
ExternalWindow win = new ExternalWindow();
app.setMainRootView(win.rootView());
win.setTitle("TextView Application");

Size size = win.windowSizeForContentSize(320, 300);
win.sizeTo(size.width, size.height);
win.setTitle("textViewApp Example");
win.show();

app.run();
}
}
```

CHAPTER 6

Windows

Windowing represents an extremely important aspect of Graphical User Interfaces (GUI), as can be seen from most current-generation platforms. Windows allow the user to process more data than will physically fit on the screen display and are not limited to graphical programs. In fact, in the Unix world, a lot of tasks are still performed in text mode, albeit they are done inside one or more text windows.

IFC provides a powerful windowing system that enables you to build applications in a convenient fashion. Capabilities such as resizeable and movable subwindows, with features such as transparency support and custom drawing, allow powerful applications to be rapidly developed.

IFC Windows come in two flavors—`InternalWindow` and `ExternalWindow`. Internal windows exist inside the application space and provide the familiar windowing environment found in popular platforms inside a Java application space. External windows map to the standard platform windows.

Study the basics of IFC Windows

Study Window characteristics and behavior that are common to all IFC Window objects.

Create and manage *InternalWindows*

`InternalWindows` are subwindows that exist inside an `ExternalWindow` and present information in an intuitive manner.

Work with *ExternalWindows*

These are frame windows that map directly to a native window and may contain menus.

Learn how to implement menus

The IFC pull-down and cascade menus provide the same functionality found on popular platforms such as Windows 95.

Window

The `Window` interface represents the abstraction of window functionality in the IFC context. Most of the common characteristics and behavior of the different IFC window types are defined in this interface. Both the `InternalWindow` and `ExternalWindow` objects implement this interface.

The interface definition is shown in Listing 6.1.

Listing 6.1 *Window* Interface

```
public interface Window implements Target {

public final static int BLANK_TYPE;                          //.. constants
public final static java.lang.String HIDE;
public final static java.lang.String SHOW;
public final static int TITLE_TYPE;

public abstract void addSubview(View);                      //.. add

public abstract void moveBy(int, int);                      //.. move
public abstract void moveTo(int, int);

public abstract WindowOwner owner();                          //.. owner
public abstract void setOwner(WindowOwner);

public abstract boolean isResizable();                      //.. attributes
public abstract void setResizable(boolean);
public abstract String title();
public abstract void setTitle(String);

public abstract void center();                            //.. display
public abstract void hide();
public abstract boolean isVisible();
public abstract void show();
public abstract void showModally();

public abstract Size contentSize();                          //.. size
public abstract Rect bounds();
public abstract void setBounds(int, int, int, int);
public abstract void setBounds(Rect);
public abstract void setMinSize(int, int);
public abstract Size minSize();
public abstract void sizeBy(int, int);
public abstract void sizeTo(int, int);
public abstract Size windowSizeForContentSize(int, int);

public abstract View viewForMouse(int, int);                   //.. mouse
}
```

The API covers aspects to add, move, display views, and so on. Detailed descriptions of individual methods can be found in the IFC reference documentation.

The superMail screen, shown in Figure 6.1, demonstrates the power of the IFC windowing system.

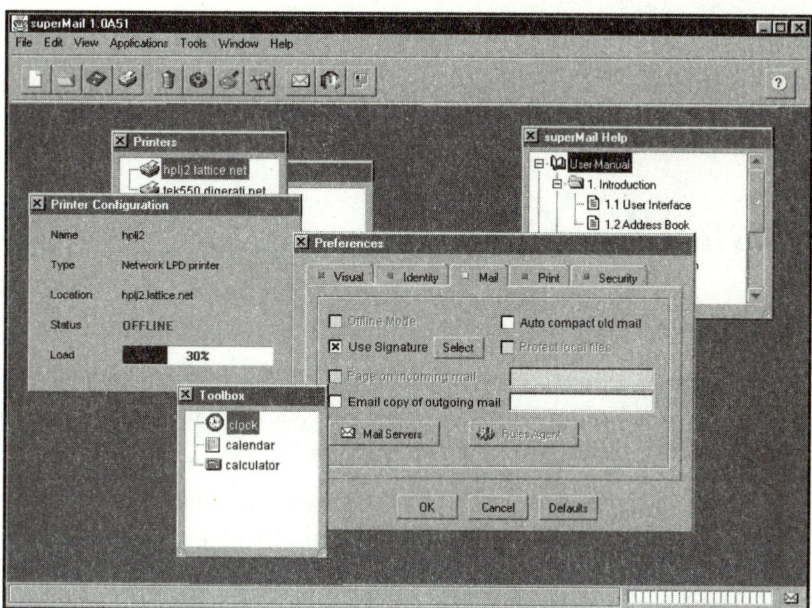

FIG. 6.1
superMail! screen.

WindowOwner

The WindowOwner interface is provided by IFC for managing window behavior by using external entities. The interested object implements this interface and sets itself as the owner via the setOwner() method of the Window object. Henceforth, the owner is notified by the window of important events such as window resizing, closing, and so on.

The owner can also determine the outcome of some of these events by the return of appropriate results. For example, if windowWillHide() returns false, the window will cancel its hide operation.

The WindowOwner interface definition is given in Listing 6.2.

Listing 6.2 *WindowOwner* Interface

```
public interface WindowOwner {
public abstract void windowDidBecomeMain(Window);
public abstract void windowDidHide(Window);
```

continues

Part II Ch 6

Listing 6.2 Continued

```
public abstract void windowDidResignMain(Window);
public abstract void windowDidShow(Window);
public abstract boolean windowWillHide(Window);
public abstract boolean windowWillShow(Window);
public abstract void windowWillSizeBy(Window, Size);
}
```

Notice that each method is also passed the `Window` object that is generating the event. This allows a single `WindowOwner` to manage multiple Window objects.

InternalWindow

`InternalWindow` objects are `View` subclasses that simulate window behavior with operations like move, resize, and close, and may have a title bar.

`InternalWindow` objects have a base view, which is the ancestor of all Views added to it. Calling `InternalWindow`'s `addSubview()` adds the View to the `InternalWindow`'s `contentView` rather than directly to the `InternalWindow`.

`InternalWindows` are rectangular regions, but can be made to appear irregular by using the transparency property. Using the `setTransparent()` method along with either of the following techniques achieves the effect of irregularly shaped windows:

- Use an image that supports transparency, such as GIF89A format images, as the background
- Override the `drawView()` method to draw to an irregular region

Some sample `InternalWindow` objects are shown in Figure 6.2, as generated by the `intWinApp` example.

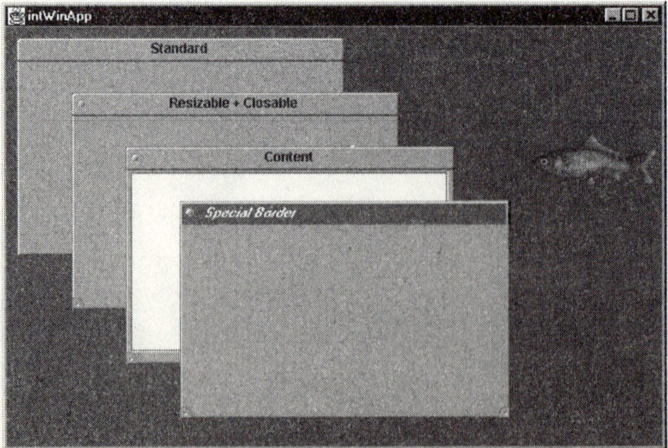

FIG. 6.2
`intWinApp` example.

The `InternalWindow` API is presented in Listing 6.3.

Listing 6.3 *InternalWindow* Class

```
public class InternalWindow extends View implements Window {

public final static int DEFAULT_LAYER;          //.. constants
public final static int DRAG_LAYER;
public final static int MODAL_LAYER;
public final static int PALETTE_LAYER;
public final static int POPUP_LAYER;

public InternalWindow();                     //.. constructors
public InternalWindow(Rect);
public InternalWindow(int, int, int, int);
public InternalWindow(int, int, int, int, int);

public void addSubview(View);                   //.. add,remove
public void addSubviewToWindow(View);

public WindowContentView contentView();
protected Button createCloseButton();

public void decode(Decoder);                    //.. persistence
public void describeClassInfo(ClassInfo);
public void encode(Encoder);

public void didBecomeMain();                    //.. inform
public void didResignMain();

public void draw(Graphics, Rect);               //.. drawing
public void drawBottomBorder();
public void drawTitleBar();
public void drawView(Graphics);
public void layoutParts();
public void setRootView(RootView);

public Size contentSize();                    //.. size
public Size minSize();
public void setBounds(int, int, int, int);
public void subviewDidResize();
public Size windowSizeForContentSize(int, int);

public boolean mouseDown(MouseEvent);               //.. mouse
public void mouseDragged(MouseEvent);
public void mouseUp(MouseEvent);
public View viewForMouse(int, int);

public void performCommand(String, Object);

public Border border();                     //.. attributes
public void setBorder(Border);
```

continues

Listing 6.3 Continued

```
public boolean canBecomeMain();
public boolean isMain();
public void setCanBecomeMain(boolean);
public boolean isCloseable();
public void setCloseable(boolean);
public View focusedView();
public void setFocusedView(View);
public int layer();
public void setLayer(int);
public boolean isResizable();
public void setResizable(boolean);
public String title();
public void setTitle(String);
public boolean isTransparent();
public void setTransparent(boolean);
public void setType(int);
public int type();

public WindowOwner owner();                              //.. owner
public void setOwner(WindowOwner);

public void center();                                    //.. display
public void hide();
public boolean isVisible();
public void show();
public void showBehind(InternalWindow);
public void showInFrontOf(InternalWindow);
public void showModally();

public boolean isPointInBorder(int, int);
public InternalWindow window();
public String toString();
}
```

The API has methods to support various features and attributes, such as controlling the layer on which the window is displayed, the kind of border the window will have, whether the window is resizeable, and so on. As you can see, the API is quite exhaustive and details are available in the IFC reference documentation.

InternalWindowBorder

The `InternalWindowBorder` class is available to enhance the look of the default `InternalWindow`. It provides control over the way the titlebar and borders are drawn.

Using this class entails overriding the appropriate methods and setting them to the desired `InternalWindow`. Thus, when the `InternalWindow` needs to be painted, the corresponding methods of `InternalWindowBorder` class will be called.

The class definition is shown in Listing 6.4.

Listing 6.4 *InternalWindowBorder* Class

```
public class InternalWindowBorder extends Border {

public InternalWindowBorder();                    //.. constructors
public InternalWindowBorder(InternalWindow);

public void decode(Decoder);                        //.. persistence
public void describeClassInfo(ClassInfo);
public void encode(Encoder);

public void drawBottomBorder(Graphics, int, int, int, int);          //..
➥drawing
public void drawInRect(Graphics, int, int, int, int);
public void drawLeftBorder(Graphics, int, int, int, int);
public void drawRightBorder(Graphics, int, int, int, int);
public void drawTitleBar(Graphics, int, int, int, int);

public int bottomMargin();                        //.. margins
public int leftMargin();
public int rightMargin();
public int topMargin();
public int resizePartWidth();

public void setWindow(InternalWindow);              //.. owner
public InternalWindow window();
}
```

As you can see, the class provides default methods to handle drawing methods and size.

An example class that implements custom drawing behavior is presented in Listing 6.5.

Listing 6.5 *intWinApp.java: intWinBorder* Class

```
class intWinBorder extends InternalWindowBorder {

     public static Color COLOR = new Color(128,128,216);
      //.. standard color

      //.. constructor
      public intWinBorder(InternalWindow win) {
            super(win);
}

      //.. method to draw the title bar
      public void drawTitleBar(Graphics g, int x, int y, int width, int height)
{
            g.setColor(Color.lightGray);
            g.fillRect(x,y,width,height);      //.. fill entire title bar region
with light gray
```

continues

Part II Ch 6

Listing 6.5 Continued

```
            g.setColor(Color.black);       //.. draw black lines on bottom,right
border
             g.drawLine(x,height-1,width,height-1);
             g.drawLine(width-1,y,width-1,height-1);

             g.setColor(Color.white);      //.. draw white lines on top, left
border
             g.drawLine(x+1,y+1,width-2,y+1);
             g.drawLine(x+1,y+1,x+1,height-2);

             g.setColor(Color.gray);       //.. draw dark gray lines above black
border
             g.drawLine(x+1,height-2,width-2,height-2);
             g.drawLine(width-2,y+1,width-2,height-2);

             g.setColor(COLOR);            //.. fill center of titlebar with
standard color
             g.fillRect(x+2,y+3,width-6,height-8);

             //.. draw the title string, only if required
                   if (window().title()!=null) {
                   g.setFont(Font.fontNamed("Dialog", Font.BOLD ¦ Font.ITALIC,
12));
                   g.setColor(Color.white);
           g.drawString(window().title(),(window().isCloseable())?x+20:x+10,y+15);
             }
      }
}
```

This class is used in the `intWinApp` example whose results were shown previously in Figure 6.2.

WindowContentView

The `WindowContentView` class is a `View` subclass used by the `InternalWindow` to hold to its content. Normally, you will have little need to use this class directly. One common use for this class is to collectively manipulate all the views inside the `InternalWindow`. This is possible since they are all subviews of that window's `WindowContentView`.

The class definition for `WindowContentView` is shown in Listing 6.6.

Listing 6.6 *WindowContentView* Class

```
public class WindowContentView extends View {
public WindowContentView();
```

```
public WindowContentView(Rect);
public WindowContentView(int, int, int, int);

public void decode(Decoder);
public void describeClassInfo(ClassInfo);
public void encode(Encoder);

public void drawView(Graphics);
public boolean isTransparent();
public void setColor(Color);
public void setTransparent(boolean);
}
```

The class contains methods to manage its background color and transparency features.

intWinApp Example

A complete example that illustrates some common features of `InternalWindow` is presented. The example builds different kinds of `InternalWindow` objects, including one that employs the `intWinBorder` class described earlier.

The complete `intWinApp` example is given in Listing 6.7.

Listing 6.7 *intWinApp.java: intWinApp* Example

```
import netscape.application.*;
import netscape.util.*;

/**
 *     Application which creates different kinds of InternalWindows
 */
public class intWinApp extends Application {

protected Button btn;

public void init() {
super.init();

InternalWindow win;
//.. create a 'standard' type window
win = new InternalWindow(10,10,300,200);
win.setTitle("Standard");
win.show();

//.. make it resizable and closable
win = new InternalWindow(60,60,300,200);
win.setTitle("Resizable + Closable");
win.setCloseable(true); win.setResizable(true);
win.show();
```

continues

Listing 6.7 Continued

```
//.. create another similar windowwin = new InternalWindow(110,110,300,200);
win.setTitle("Content");
win.setCloseable(true); win.setResizable(true);
//.. add a containerview to it
ContainerView c;
c = new ContainerView(2,2,win.contentSize().width-6,win.contentSize().height-2);
c.setBackgroundColor(Color.white);
win.addSubview(c);
win.show();

//.. create yet another similar window
win = new InternalWindow(160,160,300,200);
win.setTitle("Special Border");
win.setCloseable(true); win.setResizable(true);
//.. this window has a special border
win.setBorder(new intWinBorder(win));
win.show();

//.. create a blank window (without titlebar and borders)
Image img = Bitmap.bitmapNamed("fish.gif");
win = new InternalWindow(Window.BLANK_TYPE,480,100,img.width(),img.height());
//.. set its layer and tranparency
win.setLayer(InternalWindow.PALETTE_LAYER);
win.setTransparent(true);
//.. add a containerview which holds a transparent image
c = new ContainerView(0,0,img.width(),img.height());
c.setTransparent(true); c.setBorder(null);
c.setImage(img);
win.addSubview(c);
win.show();
}

//.. standard GUI application main() routine
public static void main(String args[]) {

intWinApp app = new intWinApp();
ExternalWindow win = new ExternalWindow();
app.setMainRootView(win.rootView());

Size size = win.windowSizeForContentSize(640, 480);
win.sizeTo(size.width, size.height);
win.setTitle("intWinApp");
win.show();

app.run();
}
}
```

Notice that the borderless window that displays a fish image exhibits an *always-on-top* behavior and is not movable, since you specified a default BLANK_TYPE window. To make it movable, you would have to subclass the `InternalWindow` and handle the appropriate mouse events.

ExternalWindow

The `ExternalWindow` class is the top-level window class that creates a platform-dependent native window. The `ExternalWindow` can optionally have an associated menu system, and it implements the `Window` interface. It also implements the `ApplicationObserver` interface, as it is commonly used as the top-level window in IFC applications.

A simple `ExternalWindow` with an enclosed Alert subwindow is shown in Figure 6.3, as generated by the `extWinApp` example discussed later in this section.

FIG. 6.3
`extWinApp` example.

The class definition for the `ExternalWindow` class is shown in Listing 6.8.

Listing 6.8 *ExternalWindow* Class

```
public class ExternalWindow implements Window,  ApplicationObserver {

public ExternalWindow();                          //.. constructors
public ExternalWindow(int);

public void applicationDidPause(Application);      //.. application
public void applicationDidResume(Application);
public void applicationDidStart(Application);
public void applicationDidStop(Application);

protected FoundationDialog createDialog();          //.. foundation
protected FoundationFrame createFrame();
protected FoundationPanel createPanel();
public FoundationPanel panel();
```

continues

Listing 6.8 Continued

```
public WindowOwner owner();                           //.. owner
public void setOwner(WindowOwner);

public void addSubview(View);                         //.. add

public Rect bounds();                                 //.. size
public void setBounds(int, int, int, int);
public void setBounds(Rect);
public Size contentSize();
public Size minSize();
public void setMinSize(int, int);
public void sizeBy(int, int);
public void sizeTo(int, int);
public Size windowSizeForContentSize(int, int);

public void center();                                 //.. display
public void hide();
public boolean isVisible();
public void show();
public void showModally();
public boolean hidesWhenPaused();
public void setHidesWhenPaused(boolean);
public void moveBy(int, int);
public void moveTo(int, int);

public boolean isResizable();                         //.. attributes
public void setResizable(boolean);
public Menu menu();
public void setMenu(Menu);
public void setTitle(String);
public String title();

public View viewForMouse(int, int);                   //.. mouse

public RootView rootView();
public void dispose();
public void performCommand(String, Object);
}
```

The API is quite comprehensive and includes methods to interact with certain AWT components via the foundation methods.

extWinApp Example

The `extWinApp` example illustrates some common techniques used with `ExternalWindow`. Listing 6.9 also illustrates using the `WindowOwner` interface to intercept the window-closing event.

Listing 6.9 *extWinApp.java: extWinApp* Example

```
import netscape.application.*;
import netscape.util.*;

/**
 *     ExternalWindow example application
 */
public class extWinApp extends Application implements Target, WindowOwner {

protected Button demo;

public void init() {
super.init();

//.. if an applet, display a button which sends the cmdDemo command to us
if (isApplet()) {
demo=new Button(0,0,50,30); demo.setTitle("DEMO");
demo.setFont(Font.fontNamed("Dialog", Font.PLAIN, 12));
demo.setCommand("cmdDemo"); demo.setTarget(this);
mainRootView().addSubview(demo);
}
else
create();
}

public void create() {
            //.. get the main external window and set its owner
            ExternalWindow win = mainRootView().externalWindow();
            win.setOwner(this);

            mainRootView().setColor(Color.lightGray);
            //.. add a label description
            TextField label = TextField.createLabel("Example of a
ExternalWindow\n"+
                        "Try closing this window");
            label.moveTo(50,50); label.sizeTo(200,40);
            label.setWrapsContents(true);
            mainRootView().addSubview(label);
}

public void performCommand(String command, Object arg) {

if (command.equals("cmdDemo")) {
//.. the demo button was pressed, change button's label
demo.setTitle("Wait..");
mainRootView().setColor(Color.lightGray);      //.. set the applet backgound
➥color

//.. create an ExternalWindow of size 320x320
ExternalWindow win = new ExternalWindow();
Size size = win.windowSizeForContentSize(320,320);
win.sizeTo(size.width, size.height);
```

continues

Listing 6.9 Continued

```
win.show();
setMainRootView(win.rootView());

create();
demo.setTitle("DEMO");            //.. set the button's label
}
else if (command.equals("cmdFileExit")) {
//.. application is ending
if (isApplet()) stopRunning(); else System.exit(0);
}
else
System.out.println("command = "+command);
}

/**
 *     WindowOwner interface
 */
public void windowDidBecomeMain(Window w)     { }
public void windowDidHide(Window w)          { }
public void windowDidResignMain(Window w)     { }
public void windowDidShow(Window w)          { }

public boolean windowWillHide(Window w) {
//. Window is closing, ask permission to close via message box
return (Alert.DEFAULT_OPTION ==
Alert.runAlertInternally(Alert.warningImage(),
"Unsaved Data", "Are you sure that \nyou want to close \nthe Window ?",
"Yes", "No", null));
}

public boolean windowWillShow(Window w)          { return true; }
public void windowWillSizeBy(Window w, Size sz)      { }

/**
 *     standard GUI application main() routine
 */
public static void main(String args[]) {

extWinApp app = new extWinApp();
ExternalWindow win = new ExternalWindow();
app.setMainRootView(win.rootView());

Size size = win.windowSizeForContentSize(320,320);
win.sizeTo(size.width, size.height);
win.setTitle("extWinApp Example");
win.show();

app.run();
}
}
```

The `Alert` class used in the `windowWillHide()` method is a standard message dialog box and will be covered in Chapter 10, "Utilities."

Menus

Menus represent a container of `MenuItems` objects. They are attached to the top margin of `ExternalWindow` objects and send command events to a `Target` instance. On most platforms, they map directly onto the native menu system.

NOTE Netscape has indicated that it will provide an independent menu system, similar to the one found in Constructor. This should work inside any `View` subclass, including `InternalWindow`.

A menu system attached to an `ExternalWindow`, shown in Figure 6.4, is generated by your `menuApp` example.

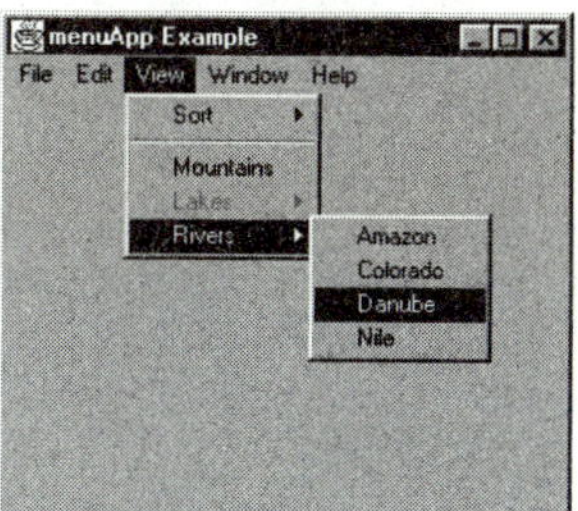

FIG. 6.4 `menuApp` example.

The `Menu` class definition is as shown in Listing 6.10.

Listing 6.10 *Menu* Class

```
public class Menu {

public Menu();                                        //.. constructors
public Menu(boolean);

public MenuItem addItem(String, String, Target);          //.. add
public MenuItem addItem(String, char, String, Target);
public void addItemAt(MenuItem, int);
public MenuItem addItemWithSubmenu(String);

public void removeItem(MenuItem);                       //.. remove
public void removeItemAt(int);
```

continues

Listing 6.10 Continued

```
public int indexOfItem(MenuItem);                        //.. position
public MenuItem itemAt(int);

public MenuItem prototypeItem();                         //.. prototype
public void setPrototypeItem(MenuItem);

public Menu createMenuAsSubmenu();
public boolean handleCommandKeyEvent(KeyEvent);
public int itemCount();
}
```

NOTE When using menus on Windows 95/NT platforms and JDK 1.02, `MenuItems` cannot change their titles once they have been created, due to a bug in the AWT.

The method `addItemAt()` in `Menu` ignores the specified index and adds the `MenuItem` at the end of its list of MenuItems. This is because the API in the AWT Menus does not allow for adding at arbitrary indices. To avoid this, always add MenuItems to a Menu in the order you want them to appear.

MenuItem

The `MenuItem` class represents a single item in a Menu and may or may not contain submenus. It may also have a hot key, or menu *accelerator,* associated with it. This is a single character that is activated along with the meta key.

NOTE Note that hot keys do not work on submenus, and may be fixed in future IFC releases.

When a `MenuItem` is selected from a menu, the associated command is sent to the designated `Target`.

Normally you would not create a MenuItem directly, but instead use `MenuItem` objects returned by the Menu objects `addItem()` and `addItemWithSubmenu()` methods.

The class definition is shown in Listing 6.11.

Listing 6.11 *MenuItem* Class

```
public class MenuItem implements Cloneable, EventProcessor {

public MenuItem();                               //.. constructors
public MenuItem(String, String, Target);
public MenuItem(String, char, String, Target);
```

```
public Object clone();

public void processEvent(Event);
public String command();                    //.. command
public char commandKey();
public void sendCommand();
public void setCommand(String);
public void setCommandKey(char);
public void setTarget(Target);
public Target target();

public boolean isEnabled();                   //.. attributes
public void setEnabled(boolean);
public Font font();
public void setFont(Font);
public void setTitle(String);
public String title();

public boolean hasSubmenu();                   //.. parent/child
public void setSubmenu(Menu);
public Menu submenu();
public void setSupermenu(Menu);
public Menu supermenu();
}
```

menuApp example

We now build a complete example that uses pull-down and cascade menus. The output was shown in Figure 6.4 and the code is given in Listing 6.12.

Listing 6.12 ***menuApp.java: menuApp*** **Example**

```
import netscape.application.*;
import netscape.util.*;

/**
 *     Menu Example Application
 */
public class menuApp extends Application implements Target {

protected Button demo;

public void init() {

super.init();

          //..      if an applet, show only a button,
//     which when activated, will call create()
if (isApplet()) {
demo=new Button(0,0,50,30); demo.setTitle("Menu");
demo.setFont(Font.fontNamed("Dialog", Font.PLAIN, 12));
```

continues

Part II Ch 6

Listing 6.12 Continued

```
demo.setCommand("cmdDemo"); demo.setTarget(this);
mainRootView().addSubview(demo);
}
else     //.. if an application, directly call create()
create();
}

public void create() {

ExternalWindow win = mainRootView().externalWindow();

mainRootView().setColor(Color.lightGray);     //.. set the background color

Menu menu; MenuItem menuItem, menuItem2, menuItem3;
java.awt.Menu awtMenu;

menu = new Menu(true);          //.. create a top level menu

menuItem = menu.addItemWithSubmenu("File");
awtMenu = AWTCompatibility.awtMenuForMenu(menuItem.submenu());

          //.. add various menu items along with accelarators
menuItem.submenu().addItem("New", 'N', "cmdFileNew",  this);
menuItem.submenu().addItem("Open",'O', "cmdFileOpen", this);
menuItem.submenu().addItem("Save",'S', "cmdFileSave", this);
menuItem.submenu().addItem("Save As", "cmdFileSaveAs",this);

//.. add a menu separator
awtMenu.addSeparator();
menuItem.submenu().addItem("Print...", 'P', "cmdFilePrint", this);

//.. disable this menu item
menuItem.submenu().itemAt(menuItem.submenu().itemCount()-1).setEnabled(false);
menuItem.submenu().addItem("Print Setup", "cmdFilePrintSetup", this);
awtMenu.addSeparator();
menuItem.submenu().addItem("Exit", 'X', "cmdFileExit", this);

menuItem = menu.addItemWithSubmenu("Edit");
awtMenu = AWTCompatibility.awtMenuForMenu(menuItem.submenu());
menuItem.submenu().addItem("Undo", 'Z', "cmdEditUndo", this);
awtMenu.addSeparator();
menuItem.submenu().addItem("Cut",  "cmdEditCut", this);
menuItem.submenu().addItem("Copy", "cmdEditCopy", this);
menuItem.submenu().addItem("Paste", "cmdEditPaste", this);
menuItem.submenu().itemAt(menuItem.submenu().itemCount()-1).setEnabled(false);
menuItem.submenu().addItem("Delete", 'D', "cmdEditDelete", this);
menuItem.submenu().addItem("Clear", "cmdEditClear", this);
awtMenu.addSeparator();
menuItem.submenu().addItem("Find", 'F', "cmdEditFind", this);
menuItem.submenu().addItem("Replace", 'R', "cmdEditReplace", this);
awtMenu.addSeparator();
menuItem.submenu().addItem("Properties", "cmdEditProperties", this);
```

```
menuItem = menu.addItemWithSubmenu("View");
awtMenu = AWTCompatibility.awtMenuForMenu(menuItem.submenu());

//.. add a sub menu
menuItem2 = menuItem.submenu().addItemWithSubmenu("Sort");
menuItem2.submenu().addItem("Ascending", "cmdViewSortAsc",  this);
menuItem2.submenu().addItem("Descending", "cmdViewSortDesc",  this);
menuItem2.submenu().itemAt(menuItem2.submenu().itemCount()-1).setEnabled(false);
awtMenu.addSeparator();
menuItem.submenu().addItem("Mountains", "cmdViewMountains",  this);
menuItem2 = menuItem.submenu().addItemWithSubmenu("Lakes");

//.. disable the submenu itself
menuItem2.setEnabled(false);
menuItem2 = menuItem.submenu().addItemWithSubmenu("Rivers");
menuItem2.submenu().addItem("Amazon", "cmdViewRiverAmazon",  this);
menuItem2.submenu().addItem("Colorado", "cmdViewRiverColorado", this);
menuItem2.submenu().addItem("Danube", "cmdViewRiverDanube",  this);
menuItem2.submenu().addItem("Nile", "cmdViewRiverNile",  this);

menuItem = menu.addItemWithSubmenu("Window");
awtMenu = AWTCompatibility.awtMenuForMenu(menuItem.submenu());
menuItem.submenu().addItem("Cascade", "cmdWindowCascade", this);
menuItem.submenu().addItem("Tile Horizontal", "cmdWindowTileHoriz", this);
menuItem.submenu().addItem("Tile Vertical", "cmdWindowTileVert", this);
menuItem.submenu().addItem("Close", "cmdWindowClose", this);
awtMenu.addSeparator();
menuItem.submenu().addItem("All Windows ...", 'W', "cmdWindowAll", this);

menuItem = menu.addItemWithSubmenu("Help");
awtMenu = AWTCompatibility.awtMenuForMenu(menuItem.submenu());
menuItem.submenu().addItem("Search for help on...", "cmdHelpSearch", this);
menuItem.submenu().addItem("Contents", 'B', "cmdHelpContents", this);
awtMenu.addSeparator();
menuItem.submenu().addItem("About...", "cmdHelpAbout", this);

win.setMenu(menu);
}

public void performCommand(String command, Object arg) {

if (command.equals("cmdDemo")) {

demo.setTitle("Wait..");
mainRootView().setColor(Color.lightGray);

ExternalWindow win = new ExternalWindow();
Size size = win.windowSizeForContentSize(320,320);
win.sizeTo(size.width, size.height);
win.show();
setMainRootView(win.rootView());

create();
demo.setTitle("DEMO");
```

continues

Listing 6.12 Continued

```
}
else if (command.equals("cmdFileExit")) {
if (isApplet()) stopRunning(); else System.exit(0);
}
else
System.out.println("command = "+command);
}

/**
 *     standard GUI application main() routine
 */
public static void main(String args[]) {

menuApp app = new menuApp();
ExternalWindow win = new ExternalWindow();
app.setMainRootView(win.rootView());

Size size = win.windowSizeForContentSize(320,320);
win.sizeTo(size.width, size.height);
win.setTitle("menuApp Example");
win.show();

app.run();
}
}
```

Notice the interaction between IFC menus and the underlying AWT menu classes. Also note the techniques used to add menu separator items. ●

CHAPTER 7

Graphics and Sound

This chapter covers graphics and sound support under IFC. Graphics operations include drawing and filling geometric shapes, creating text, and handling images. IFC provides a variety of classes to support these operations and enhances many methods and techniques found in the Java AWT package. ■

Discover IFC techniques to handle images and bitmaps

The Image and Bitmap classes provide powerful capabilities for managing images in IFC applications.

Explore the Graphics class

We will look into the `Graphics` class, along with its DebugGraphics subclass used for advanced debug operations.

Look into custom painting operations

Using methods from the `Graphics` class, we will create some examples that do custom painting operations.

Learn to use sound in IFC applications

Audio support under IFC is encapsulated in the `Sound` class, which provides methods suitable for most purposes.

Images and Bitmaps

Images are collections of pixels (or "pels" for picture elements) arranged in a matrix to represent visual information. Such an arrangement of discrete pels constitutes *raster* images as compared to *vector* images, which consist of *vectors,* such lines and arcs. Thus, vector images can be thought of as collections of discrete shapes and patterns. Examples of raster images include most of the images you see on the World Wide Web, such as GIF and JPEG images, and examples of vector images include graphics produced by traditional Computer Aided Design (CAD) packages and drawing packages such as CorelDraw.

IFC provides the `Image` virtual class, which encapsulates all image properties — both raster and vector images. The `Bitmap` class is a subclass designed to handle raster images. The `DrawingSequence` class, covered in Chapter 10, is another derived class of the `Image` class and handles animation-like effects.

Image Class

The `Image` class virtualizes all the characteristics of images in general to provide a common set of methods. Listing 7.1 presents the code that defines the `Image` class.

Listing 7.1 *Image* Class

```
public abstract class Image implements Codable {

     public final static int CENTERED;               //.. constants
     public final static java.lang.String IMAGE_TYPE;
     public final static int SCALED;
     public final static int TILED;

     public Image();

     public void decode(Decoder);                         //.. persistence
     public void describeClassInfo(ClassInfo);
     public void encode(Encoder);
     public void finishDecoding();

     public abstract void drawAt(Graphics, int, int);          //.. drawing
     public void drawCentered(Graphics, int, int, int, int);
     public void drawCentered(Graphics, Rect);
     public void drawScaled(Graphics, int, int, int, int);
     public void drawScaled(Graphics, Rect);
     public void drawTiled(Graphics, int, int, int, int);
     public void drawTiled(Graphics, Rect);
     public void drawWithStyle(Graphics, int, int, int, int, int);
     public void drawWithStyle(Graphics, Rect, int);
```

```
        public String name();
        public boolean isTransparent();
        public abstract int height();
        public abstract int width();
}
```

Notice that the `Image` class handles a minimal set of image-related methods and specifies many abstract methods for subclasses to implement.

Bitmap Class

The `Bitmap` class constitutes a subclass of the `Image` class, and it handles bitmapped, or *raster,* images. In addition to implementing the abstract methods of the `Image` class, it includes some static convenience methods for directly loading an image from a URL or disk.

The `Bitmap` class supports off-line loading of images by allowing an event to be generated and sent while it is loading. This is achieved by first setting the mode via the `setLoadsIncrementally()` method. Then the `setUpdateCommand()` and `setUpdateTarget()` specify the command and target, which are sent after the image is loaded incrementally. From then on, the image fires off events and draws as data is made available, and it does not wait for all of the data to be available.

Another powerful feature provided in the Bitmap class is support for transparency. Transparent images are supported via the `setTransparent()` method.

NOTE To use the transparency feature, the image format you use must support the transparency option. For example, GIF89a images have the transparency option.

The `Bitmap` class definition is given in Listing 7.2.

Listing 7.2 *Bitmap* Class

```
public class Bitmap extends Image {

        public Bitmap();
        public Bitmap(int, int);
        public Bitmap(int[], int, int);
        public Bitmap(int[], int, int, int, int);

        public static Bitmap bitmapFromURL(URL);                    //.. static
        public static synchronized Bitmap bitmapNamed(String, boolean);
        public static Bitmap bitmapNamed(String);

        public Graphics createGraphics();
```

continues

Listing 7.2 Continued

```
    public void drawAt(Graphics, int, int);                        //.. drawing
    public void drawScaled(Graphics, int, int, int, int);

    public void decode(Decoder);                                   //.. persistence
    public void describeClassInfo(ClassInfo);
    public void encode(Encoder);

    public boolean grabPixels(int[]);                              //.. capture
    public boolean grabPixels(int[], int, int, int, int, int, int);

    public boolean isTransparent();                                //.. transparent
    public void setTransparent(boolean);

    public boolean isValid();                                      //.. loading
    public void loadData();
    public boolean hasLoadedData();
    public boolean loadsIncrementally();
    public void setLoadsIncrementally(boolean);
    public synchronized void setUpdateCommand(String);
    public synchronized void setUpdateTarget(Target);
    public synchronized String updateCommand();
    public synchronized Rect updateRect();
    public synchronized Target updateTarget();

    public String name();
    public void flush();
    public int height();
    public int width();
    public String toString();
}
```

The static `bitmapNamed()` API would load the image file from the `<codebase>/images/` subdirectory, where `<codebase>` represents the current directory or location of the IFC program. Note that the IFC application maintains a cache of named bitmaps that it checks before loading any new images.

An image may also be accessed using the static `bitmapFromURL()` method, as follows:

```
Image.imageFromURL(new URL("http://foolbar.com/images/foo.gif"));
```

The `grabPixels()` methods allow applications to *capture* parts of the image (and it is so used in the following `imageApp` example).

imageApp Example

The `imageApp` example implements a simple image processor (see Figure 7.1) to illustrate some techniques used in handling images.

FIG. 7.1
imageApp example that shows simple image processing.

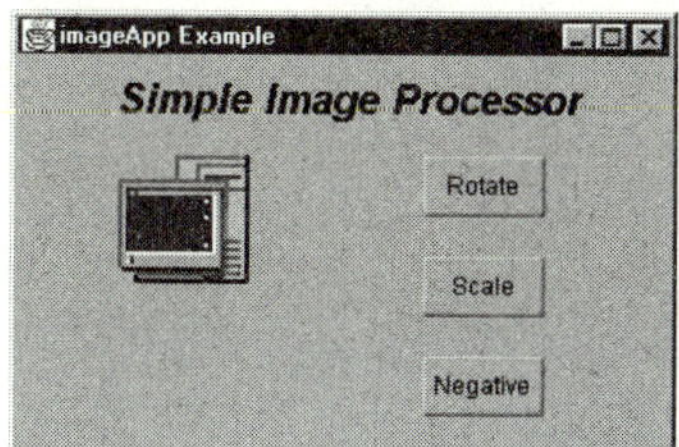

The example implements simple rotate, scaling, and binary complement (negative) operations on images. These operations are reversible and mutually exclusive, and you may apply them to the image independently. The scale button toggles between the normal-sized image and a scaled image. Listing 7.3 presents the code that generates the screen output shown in Figure 7.1.

Listing 7.3 imageApp.java: *imageApp* Example

```
import netscape.application.*;

/**
 *     Application
 */
public class imageApp extends Application implements Target {

     protected ContainerView img;
     protected Size sz;

     /**
      *
      */
     public void init() {

          super.init();

          mainRootView().setColor(Color.lightGray);

          TextField label = TextField.createLabel("Simple Image Processor",
                    Font.fontNamed("Arial",Font.BOLD¦Font.ITALIC,20));
          label.moveTo(50,10);
          mainRootView().addSubview(label);

          Bitmap bmp = Bitmap.bitmapNamed("computer.gif");
          sz = new Size(bmp.width(),bmp.height());
          img = new ContainerView(50,50,bmp.width(),bmp.height());
          img.setBorder(null); img.setImageDisplayStyle(Image.SCALED);
          img.setImage(bmp); img.setTransparent(false);
          mainRootView().addSubview(img);
```

continues

Listing 7.3 Continued

```
        Button b;
        b = new Button(200,50,60,30);
        b.setTitle("Rotate");
        b.setTarget(this); b.setCommand("cmdRotate");
        mainRootView().addSubview(b);

        b = new Button(200,100,60,30);
        b.setTitle("Scale");
        b.setTarget(this); b.setCommand("cmdScale");
        mainRootView().addSubview(b);

        b = new Button(200,150,60,30);
        b.setTitle("Negative");
        b.setTarget(this); b.setCommand("cmdNegative");
        mainRootView().addSubview(b);
    }

    /**
     *
     */
    public void performCommand(String command, Object arg) {

        if  (command.equals("cmdScale")) {

            Bitmap b = (Bitmap)img.image();
            img.setImage(null);
            img.setDirty(true);

            if (img.width()!=sz.width)
                img.sizeTo(sz.width,sz.height);
            else
                img.sizeTo(sz.width*2,sz.height*2);

            img.setImage(b); img.setDirty(true);
        }
        else if  (command.equals("cmdRotate") ||
command.equals("cmdNegative")) {

            boolean rotate = command.equals("cmdRotate");
            Bitmap b = (Bitmap)img.image();
            int buf[] = new int[b.width() * b.height()];

            if (!b.grabPixels(buf)) {
                System.out.println("grab failure"); return;
            }

            int rot[] = new int[b.width() * b.height()];

            //.. transpose matrix
            for(int y = 0; y < b.height(); y++) {
                for(int x = 0; x < b.width(); x++) {
                    if (rotate)
                        rot[((b.width()-x-1)*b.width())+y] =
```

```
buf[(y*b.width())+x];
                                    else {
                                        rot[(y*b.width())+x] = buf[(y*b.width())+x] &
0xff000000;
                                        rot[(y*b.width())+x] |= ~(buf[(y*b.width())+x] &
                                                                   0x00ffffff);
                                    }
                                }
                            }

                            img.setImage(new Bitmap(rot,b.width(),b.height()));
                        }
    }

    /**
     *      standard GUI application main() routine
     */
    public static void main(String args[]) {

        imageApp app = new imageApp();
        ExternalWindow win = new ExternalWindow();
        app.setMainRootView(win.rootView());

        Size size = win.windowSizeForContentSize(320, 200);
        win.sizeTo(size.width, size.height);
        win.setTitle("imageApp Example");
        win.show();

        app.run();
        System.exit(0);
    }
}
```

Notice that the `performCommand()` method, which does most of the work, handles the rotate and negative methods by using the `grabPixels()` method. It handles the scale operation by creating and setting a new image. Notice that the image must first be set to null because the `Image` class caches the image internally.

Graphics Class

The `Graphics` class provides a rich set of methods for implementing graphics operations. Besides providing methods for drawing and filling geometric shapes, it provides methods to control the clipping rectangle, the paint mode, and various other drawing-related operations.

NOTE AWT graphics can be mixed with IFC graphics using the `AWTCompatibility` class, which is examined in Chapter 11, "Advanced Topics.""

Listing 7.4 presents the code the defines the `Graphics` class.

Listing 7.4 ***Graphics* Class**

```
public class Graphics {
    public final static int CENTERED;
    public final static int LEFT_JUSTIFIED;
    public final static int RIGHT_JUSTIFIED;

    public Graphics(View);
    public Graphics(Bitmap);

    public void clearClipRect();                        //.. clipping
    public Rect clipRect();
    public void setClipRect(Rect, boolean);
    public void setClipRect(Rect);

    public void drawArc(Rect, int, int);                  //.. draw methods
    public void drawArc(int, int, int, int, int, int);
    public void drawBitmapAt(Bitmap, int, int);
    public void drawBitmapScaled(Bitmap, int, int, int, int);
    public void drawBytes(byte[], int, int, int, int);
    public void drawChars(char[], int, int, int, int);
    public void drawLine(int, int, int, int);
    public void drawOval(Rect);
    public void drawOval(int, int, int, int);
    public void drawPoint(int, int);
    public void drawPolygon(int[], int[], int);
    public void drawPolygon(Polygon);
    public void drawRect(Rect);
    public void drawRect(int, int, int, int);
    public void drawRoundedRect(Rect, int, int);
    public void drawRoundedRect(int, int, int, int, int, int);
    public void drawString(String, int, int);
    public void drawStringInRect(String, int, int, int, int, int);
    public void drawStringInRect(String, Rect, int);

    public void fillArc(Rect, int, int);                  //.. fill methods
    public void fillArc(int, int, int, int, int, int);
    public void fillOval(Rect);
    public void fillOval(int, int, int, int);
    public void fillPolygon(int[], int[], int);
    public void fillPolygon(Polygon);
    public void fillRect(Rect);
    public void fillRect(int, int, int, int);
    public void fillRoundedRect(Rect, int, int);
    public void fillRoundedRect(int, int, int, int, int, int);

    public void popState();                          //.. state
    public void pushState();

    public int debugOptions();                         //.. options
    public void setDebugOptions(int);
```

```
    public void setPaintMode();                           //.. mode
    public void setXORMode(Color);

    public void translate(int, int);                   //.. translation
    public Point translation();
    public int xTranslation();
    public int yTranslation();

    public Bitmap buffer();
    public boolean isDrawingBuffer();
    public Color color();
    public void setColor(Color);
    public Font font();
    public void setFont(Font);

    public void dispose();
    public void sync();
    public String toString();
}
```

DebugGraphics Class

The `DebugGraphics` class extends the `Graphics` class to implement debug versions of most of its methods. As its name suggests, the `DebugGraphics` class mainly serves debug graphics-intensive applications. The programmer seldom instantiates it, and the `View` class uses it internally, via the `setGraphicsDebugOptions()` method (see Lisitng 7.5).

Listing 7.5 *DebugGraphics* Class

```
public class DebugGraphics extends Graphics {

    public final static int BUFFERED_OPTION;
    public final static int FLASH_OPTION;
    public final static int LOG_OPTION;
    public final static int NONE_OPTION;

    public DebugGraphics(View);
    public DebugGraphics(Bitmap);

public static Color flashColor();
    public static int flashCount();
    public static int flashTime();
    public static PrintStream logStream();
    public static void setFlashColor(Color);
    public static void setFlashCount(int);
    public static void setFlashTime(int);
    public static void setLogStream(PrintStream);
```


continues

Listing 7.5 Continued

```
    public int debug();
    public int debugOptions();
    public void drawArc(int, int, int, int, int, int);
    public void drawBitmapAt(Bitmap, int, int);
    public void drawBitmapScaled(Bitmap, int, int, int, int);
    public void drawBytes(byte[], int, int, int, int);
    public void drawChars(char[], int, int, int, int);
    public void drawLine(int, int, int, int);
    public void drawOval(int, int, int, int);
    public void drawPoint(int, int);
    public void drawPolygon(int[], int[], int);
    public void drawRect(int, int, int, int);
    public void drawRoundedRect(int, int, int, int, int, int);
    public void drawString(String, int, int);

    public void fillArc(int, int, int, int, int, int);
    public void fillOval(int, int, int, int);
    public void fillPolygon(int[], int[], int);
    public void fillRect(int, int, int, int);
    public void fillRoundedRect(int, int, int, int, int, int);

    public void popState();
    public void pushState();
    public void setClipRect(Rect, boolean);
    public void setColor(Color);
    public void setDebugOptions(int);
    public void setFont(Font);
    public void setPaintMode();
    public void setXORMode(Color);
    public void translate(int, int);
}
```

Listing 7.6 shows a sample output of using the `DebugGraphics.LOG` option when debugging graphics for a `View` class. This listing gives you an idea of the detail available when using the `DebugGraphics` class.

Listing 7.6 *DebugGraphics* Sample Output

```
Graphics(1)——> Enabling debug
Graphics(1)——> Translating by: (0, 40) to: (0, 40)
Graphics(1)——> Setting clipRect: (0, 0, 320, 160) New clipRect: (0, 0, 320,
160)
Graphics(1)——> Setting color: netscape.application.Color (255, 255, 255)
Graphics(1)——> Filling rect: (0, 0, 320, 160)
Graphics(1)——> Setting color: netscape.application.Color (128, 128, 128)
Graphics(1)——> Drawing rect: (0, 0, 320, 160)
Graphics(1)——> <- state
Graphics(8)-> Enabling debug
Graphics(8)-> Setting color: netscape.application.Color (0, 0, 0)
Graphics(9)-> Enabling debug
```

```
Graphics(9)-> Setting color: netscape.application.Color (0, 0, 0)
Graphics(9)-> Drawing line: (29, 8, 29, 9)
Graphics(10)-> Enabling debug
Graphics(10)-> Setting color: netscape.application.Color (0, 0, 0)
```

Painting

Painting traditionally includes such operations as drawing shapes and filling them in with color. As shown in the preceding section, the `Graphics` class provides a number of useful methods for supporting such operations. In this section, the examples actually utilize some of these methods.

paintApp Example

The `paintApp` example uses some geometric drawing methods from the Graphics class to implement a simple drawing editor. Among the shapes and modes supported are freehand, line, rectangle, and oval (see Figure 7.2).

FIG. 7.2
`paintApp` example that shows custom drawing.

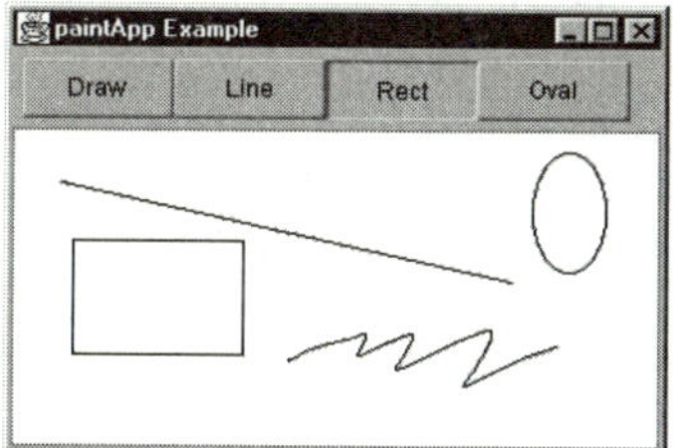

Listing 7.7 presents the code that generates the screen output shown in Figure 7.2.

Listing 7.7 paintApp.java: *paintApp* Example

```
import netscape.application.*;

/**
 *     Application which illustrates usage of Buttons
 */
public class paintApp extends Application implements Target {

     protected paintView panel;

     /**
      *
      */
     public void init() {
```

continues

Listing 7.7 Continued

```
        super.init();
            //.. set a light gray background
        mainRootView().setColor(Color.lightGray);

            //.. add a paintView object to fit the bounds()
        Rect r = mainRootView().bounds();
        panel = new paintView(r.x,r.y+40,r.width,r.height-40);
            //.. make it resizeable both ways
        panel.setHorizResizeInstruction(View.WIDTH_CAN_CHANGE);
        panel.setVertResizeInstruction(View.HEIGHT_CAN_CHANGE);
        mainRootView().addSubview(panel);

            //.. add buttons to control freehand, line, rect, oval drawing
        Button btn;
            btn = new Button(5,5,75,30);
            btn.setType(Button.RADIO_TYPE);
            btn.setTitle("Draw");
            btn.setTarget(this);
            btn.setCommand("cmdDraw");
        mainRootView().addSubview(btn);
            btn.click();  //.. select this button

        btn = new Button(80,5,75,30);
            btn.setType(Button.RADIO_TYPE);
        btn.setTitle("Line");
        btn.setTarget(this);
        btn.setCommand("cmdLine");
        mainRootView().addSubview(btn);

        btn = new Button(155,5,75,30);
        btn.setType(Button.RADIO_TYPE);
        btn.setTitle("Rect");
        btn.setTarget(this);
        btn.setCommand("cmdRect");
        mainRootView().addSubview(btn);

        btn = new Button(230,5,75,30);
        btn.setType(Button.RADIO_TYPE);
        btn.setTitle("Oval");
        btn.setTarget(this);
        btn.setCommand("cmdOval");
        mainRootView().addSubview(btn);
    }

    /**
     *
     */
    public void performCommand(String command, Object arg) {
            //.. set current drawing mode
        if (command.equals("cmdDraw")) panel.setMode(paintView.DRAW_MODE);
        else if (command.equals("cmdLine"))
panel.setMode(paintView.LINE_MODE);
        else if (command.equals("cmdRect"))
```

```
panel.setMode(paintView.RECT_MODE);
        else if (command.equals("cmdOval"))
panel.setMode(paintView.OVAL_MODE);
    }

    /**
     *     standard GUI application main() routine
     */
    public static void main(String args[]) {

        paintApp app = new paintApp();
        ExternalWindow win = new ExternalWindow();
        app.setMainRootView(win.rootView());

        Size size = win.windowSizeForContentSize(320, 200);
        win.sizeTo(size.width, size.height);
        win.setTitle("paintApp Example");
        win.show();

        app.run();
        System.exit(0);
    }
}

/**
 *  custom drawing view
 */
class paintView extends View {

    public static int DRAW_MODE     = 1;
    public static int LINE_MODE     = 2;
    public static int RECT_MODE     = 3;
    public static int OVAL_MODE     = 4;

    protected int x,y,px,py;
    protected int mode;

    /**
     *  constructor
     */
    public paintView(int x, int y, int w, int h) { super(x,y,w,h); }

    /**
     *  convenience methods
     */
    public int mode() { return mode; }
    public void setMode(int _mode) { mode = _mode; }
    public void clear() { setDirty(true); }

    /**
     *  drawView
     */
    public void drawView(Graphics g) {
            //.. fill the entire view with white
```


continues

Listing 7.7 Continued

```
        g.setColor(Color.white);
        g.fillRect(0,0,bounds().width,bounds.height);
            //.. draw a dark gray border around the view
        g.setColor(Color.gray);
        g.drawRect(0,0,bounds().width,bounds.height);
    }

    /**
     *  called when the mouse button is down
     */
    public boolean mouseDown(MouseEvent ev) {
          //.. save mouse click position
        px=x=ev.x; py=y=ev.y;
        return true;
    }

    /**
     *  called when the mouse button is up
     */
    public void mouseUp(MouseEvent ev) {

        Graphics g = createGraphics();
            g.setColor(Color.black);
        if (mode==LINE_MODE)
                  g.drawLine(x,y,ev.x,ev.y);
        else if (mode==RECT_MODE || mode==OVAL_MODE) {
            int w=ev.x-x, h=ev.y-y;
            if (ev.x<x) { w=x-ev.x; x=ev.x; }     //.. normalize
            if (ev.y<y) { h=y-ev.y; y=ev.y; }
            if (mode==RECT_MODE) g.drawRect(x,y,w,h);
            else if (mode==OVAL_MODE) g.drawOval(x,y,w,h);
        }
    }

    /**
     *  called when the mouse is dragged
     */
    public void mouseDragged(MouseEvent ev) {
        Graphics g = createGraphics();
        //.. do free hand drawing
        if (mode==DRAW_MODE) {
            g.setColor(Color.black);
            //.. draw from saved pt to this pt
            g.drawLine(x,y,ev.x,ev.y);
            x=ev.x; y=ev.y;      //.. save
        }
    }
}
```

As the program listing shows, the `paintView` subclass handles most of the drawing operations, while the `paintApp` class provides the controls to set the current drawing operation.

The mouseDragged() method handles only the freehand drawing, while the remaining operations, such as setting the drawing mode, are handled after the mouse is released (in the mouseUp() method).

textDrawApp Example

The textDrawApp example uses the drawString() method in the Graphics class to show how you can draw text on an IFC screen. The class also provides the drawStringInRect() method, which allows for a precise clipping rectangle and allows you to justify the string in that rectangle. Justification values are LEFT_JUSTIFIED, CENTERED, or RIGHT_JUSTIFIED, as defined in the Graphics class. Figure 7.3 shows the output of the textDrawApp example.

FIG. 7.3 textDrawApp example that demonstrates drawing text.

Listing 7.8 presents the program listing for the textDrawApp example that produces the output shown in Figure 7.3.

Listing 7.8 TEXTDRAWAPP.JAVA: *textDrawApp* Example

```
import netscape.application.*;

/**
 *      Application which illustrates usage of Graphics.drawString()
 */
public class textDrawApp extends Application {

     /**
      *
      */
     public void init() {

          super.init();

          mainRootView().setColor(Color.white);
          textDrawView view = new textDrawView(mainRootView().bounds());
          mainRootView().addSubview(view);
```

continues

Listing 7.8 Continued

```
    }

        /**
         *    standard GUI application main() routine
         */
        public static void main(String args[]) {

        textDrawApp app = new textDrawApp();
        ExternalWindow win = new ExternalWindow();
        app.setMainRootView(win.rootView());

        Size size = win.windowSizeForContentSize(320, 200);
        win.sizeTo(size.width, size.height);
        win.setTitle("textDrawApp");
        win.show();

        app.run();
        System.exit(0);
    }
}

/**
 *
 */
class textDrawView extends View {

    int x, y;

    public textDrawView(Rect r) { super(r); }

    public void drawView(Graphics g) {
        g.setColor(Color.white);      g.fillRect(bounds());
        g.setColor(Color.gray);     g.drawRect(bounds());
    }

    public boolean mouseDown(MouseEvent ev) {
        x=ev.x; y=ev.y;
        setDirty(true);
        return true;
    }

    public void mouseDragged(MouseEvent ev) {
        Graphics g = createGraphics();
        g.setFont(Font.fontNamed("Arial",Font.BOLD,24));

        g.setColor(Color.white); g.drawString("blurdybloop",x,y);

        g.setColor(Color.gray); g.drawString("blurdybloop",ev.x,ev.y);
        //.. draw from saved pt to this pt
        x=ev.x; y=ev.y;     //.. save
    }
}
```

The application uses the `textDrawView` subclass, which paints a text string while the user drags the mouse.

The `mouseDragged` routine *erases* the previously drawn text string, which was saved from the previous operation. The erase operation is performed by *writing* using the background color (white). The `setXORMode()` method of the `Graphics` class would also serve to accomplish the same effect.

Sound

Many programs benefit from some form of audio capability. Audio clips can denote events such as alarms and messages. Java provides rudimentary audio support in the `java.Applet` class.

NOTE Sound works only in applets. To use it in applications, you must use an external library, such as `sun.audio.*`, distributed with the JDK on solaris.

Currently, Java supports only one sound format: 8-bit, μlaw PCM, 8000 Hz, one-channel, AU files. More popular formats, such as the WAV file, must be converted using conversion tools.

NOTE Sun recently announced the Java Media Framework (JMF), which provides a more comprehensive multimedia framework. The latest info is available at the javasoft site at **www.javasoft.com**.

IFC wraps the audio support that Java provides into the `Sound` class along with a few convenience methods. Listing 7.9 presents the code that defines the `Sound` class.

Listing 7.9 *Sound* Class

```
public class Sound implements Codable {
     public Sound();

     public static Sound soundFromURL(URL);
     public static synchronized Sound soundNamed(String);

     public void describeClassInfo(ClassInfo);
     public void decode(Decoder);
     public void encode(Encoder);
     public void finishDecoding();

     public void setLoops(boolean);
     public boolean doesLoop();
```

continues

Listing 7.9 Continued

```
    public String name();
    public void play();
    public void stop();
    public String toString();
}
```

The class definition is quite straightforward and resembles the `java.Applet` support for sound. In addition, it contains static methods for loading sound files from the "sounds" sub-directory. Thus, the `soundNamed()` API would load the sound file from the *<codebase>*/sounds/ subdirectory, where *<codebase>* represents the current location of the applet/application. Note that the IFC application maintains a cache of named sound files that it checks first before loading.

CAUTION

IFC does not report any errors if the specified sound file does not exist or if the file is in the wrong format. The application must handle this condition.

In addition to using the `Sound.soundNamed()` method, you may specify a sound as an URL by using the static `soundFromURL()` method. For example:

```
Sound.soundFromURL(new URL("http;//foobar.com/sounds/foo.au"));
```

The `play()` and `stop()` methods start and stop the sound, respectively. The `Sound` class also supports the looping feature, via the `setLoops()` method.

soundApp Example

The `soundApp` example builds a simple applet/application to show the usage of the IFC's sound APIs. Figure 7.4 shows the output of the `soundApp` example.

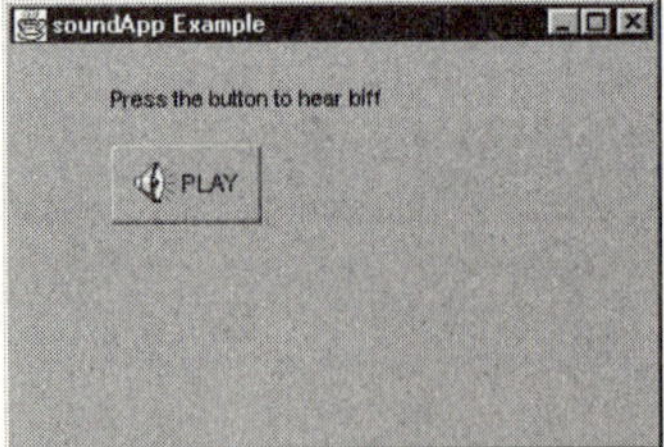

FIG. 7.4
soundApp example that shows usage of Sound class methods.

Listing 7.10 presents the code that generates the screen output shown in Figure 7.4.

Listing 7.10 soundApp.java: *soundApp* Example

```
import netscape.application.*;

/**
 *     Application which illustrates usage of Buttons
 */
public class soundApp extends Application implements Target {

     public Sound snd;

     public void init() {
          super.init();
               //.. set light gray background
          mainRootView().setColor(Color.lightGray);
                              //.. place a label descriptionTextField label =
TextField.createLabel("Press the button to hear biff",
                              Font.fontNamed("Arial", Font.PLAIN, 11));
          label.moveTo(50,20);
          mainRootView().addSubview(label);
               //.. place a button with PLAY/STOP titles
          Button btn = new Button(50,50,75,40);
          btn.setTitle("PLAY"); btn.setAltTitle("STOP");
               //.. speaker image on button
          btn.setImage(Bitmap.bitmapNamed("speaker.gif"));
               //.. set the Button's target/command/type
          btn.setCommand("cmdPlaySound"); btn.setTarget(this);
          btn.setType(Button.TOGGLE_TYPE);
          mainRootView().addSubview(btn);
               //.. create sound
          snd = Sound.soundNamed("oww.au");
          snd.setLoops(true);
     }

     public void performCommand(String command, Object arg) {

          if (command.equals("cmdPlaySound")) {
               Button b = (Button)arg;
                         //.. play/stop sound if button is down/up
               if (b.state()) snd.play(); else snd.stop();
          }
     }

     /**
      *     standard GUI application main() routine
      */
     public static void main(String args[]) {

          soundApo— pp = new soundApp();
          ExternalWindow win = new ExternalWindow();
          app.setMainRootView(win.rootView());

          Size size = win.windowSizeForContentSize(320, 200);
          win.sizeTo(size.width, size.height);
```

continues

Listing 7.10 Continued

```
        win.setTitle("soundApp Example");
        win.show();

        app.run();
        System.exit(0);
    }
}
```

The example implements an image button that plays an audio clip of a dog barking. The button is of the type `Button.TOGGLE_TYPE` and stops playing the sound when the user releases it. ●

CHAPTER 8

Drag and Drop

The ability to drag and drop visual objects has gained importance in most modern platforms as an intuitive way to perform tasks. The ability to drag an object on the screen with the mouse and drop it to an accepting object accomplishes tasks such as the moving and copying of data, launching of applications, and so on. For example, in some operating systems, dropping a data file onto an accepting application launches it with that data file already opened.

IFC provides the Java platform with a drag and drop framework, albeit one that works only inside IFC applications. ■

See the big picture

Overview of the drag and drop framework in IFC.

Learn about draggable objects

See how to build objects that may be dragged.

See how to use droppable objects

Learn and implement objects that accept dragged items.

Look into drag and drop objects

See how to implement both interfaces to construct objects that are draggable and droppable.

Drag and Drop Overview

IFC implements the drag and drop framework with the help of the following interfaces and classes:

- `DragSource` interface

  Implemented by objects that may be dragged

- `DragDestination` interface

  Implemented by objects that accept dragged items

- `DragSession` class

  Encapsulation of a drag and drop session

There can be only one drag and drop session active at any given time, which is represented by the `DragSession` object. A drag and drop session is started when the user clicks a `DragSource` object and starts to drag the mouse. Figure 8.1 shows an overview of a drag and drop session in the IFC environment.

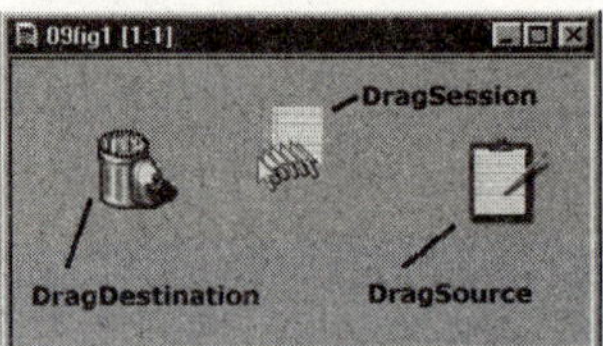

FIG. 8.1
Overview of the IFC Drag and Drop framework.

At this point, a `DragSession` object is created that manages the session by:

- Following the mouse pointer with an icon.
- As the mouse is dragged over various views along with the draggable object, each view is queried to see if it will accept the object being dragged.
- Returning results back to the `DragSource` object.
- Optionally animating the icon back to the `DragSource` if the object is not accepted.

While the `DragSource` object is being dragged, views under the mouse pointers are queried to see if they will accept the object. When the user releases the mouse button, the session ends and the object is released on the current view. The result of this operation, whether acceptance or rejection, is communicated back to the `DragSource` object. Often a rejected `DragSource` object's icon animates back to the source.

DragSession Class

The `DragSession` class represents a single drag and drop session and contains all methods and data to manage it. Usually it is created by the `DragSource` object in the `mouseDown()` or `mouseDragged()` methods. Listing 8.1 gives its class definition.

Listing 8.1 *DragSession* Class

```
public class DragSession {
      public final static int ALT_MASK;
      public final static int CONTROL_MASK;
      public final static int META_MASK;
      public final static int SHIFT_MASK;

      public DragSession(DragSource, Image, int, int, int, int, String, Object);

      public Rect absoluteBounds();
      public Point absoluteMousePoint();
      public Object data();
      public String dataType();
      public DragDestination destination();
      public Rect destinationBounds();
      public Point destinationMousePoint();
      public View destinationView();
      public int dragModifiers();
      public boolean isAltKeyDown();
      public boolean isControlKeyDown();
      public boolean isMetaKeyDown();
      public boolean isShiftKeyDown();
      public void setData(Object);
      public void setDataType(String);
      public DragSource source();
}
```

Besides containing methods to maintain a drag session, the `DragSession` class also has methods to query if any special key is pressed while the session is in progress.

In Java 1.1, the Meta Key is mapped onto the right button of a two-button mouse.

DragSource

The `DragSource` interface is implemented by classes that can be dragged and contains the methods shown in Listing 8.2.

Listing 8.2 *DragSource* Interface

```
public interface DragSource {
      public abstract View sourceView(DragSession);
      public abstract void dragWasAccepted(DragSession);
      public abstract boolean dragWasRejected(DragSession);
}
```

The `sourceView()` class tells the caller where the `DragSession` originated. Normally it will return itself via the `this` operator. The `dragWasAccepted()` method gets called whenever the session completes successfully—in other words, when the dragged object is accepted by a `DragDestination` object. Lastly, the `drawWasRejected()` method is called when the user drops the dragged object and it is not accepted. Returning `true` causes the icon to animate back to the origin of the `DragSource` object.

DragWell Class

IFC provides a `DragWell` class as a convenient `DragSource` subclass for use in many common scenarios. Listing 8.3 shows the class definition.

Listing 8.3 *DragWell* Class

```
public class DragWell extends View implements DragSource {

      public DragWell();
      public DragWell(Rect);
      public DragWell(int, int, int, int);

      public Border border();
      public Object data();
      public String dataType();
      public void decode(Decoder);
      public void describeClassInfo(ClassInfo);
      public void dragWasAccepted(DragSession);
      public boolean dragWasRejected(DragSession);
      public void drawView(Graphics);
      public void encode(Encoder);
      public Image image();
      public boolean isEnabled();
      public boolean isTransparent();
      public boolean mouseDown(MouseEvent);
      public void setBorder(Border);
      public void setData(Object);
      public void setDataType(String);
      public void setEnabled(boolean);
      public void setImage(Image);
      public View sourceView(DragSession);
}
```

The class has many capabilities of the `ContainerView` class along with `DragSource` support. The user may associate an image and data with this object by using the `setImage()` and `setData()` methods, respectively. The same data and image are used for each drag session.

dragApp Example

The `dragApp` example implements the `dragView` class, which implements the `DragSource` interface. This view class is used to construct an application that lets users drag objects from a clipboard object, as shown in Figure 8.2.

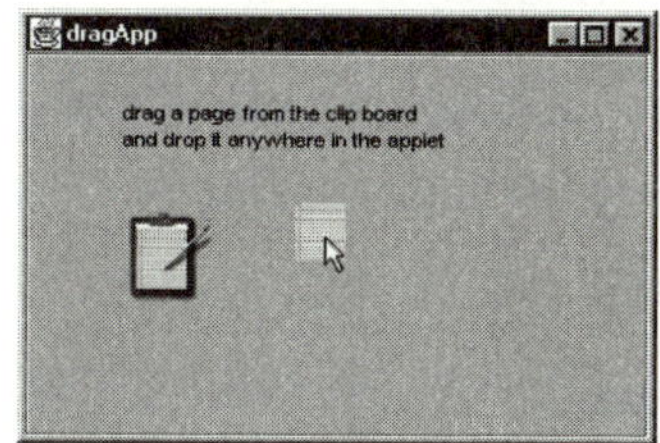

FIG. 8.2
dragApp example that implements a draggable object.

We have associated a static icon to this view, which looks like a sheet from the clip board. This icon is used with the `DragSession` to follow the mouse pointer. We also have assigned a static name that may be interrogated by the `DragDestination` object. Listing 8.4 shows the program listing for the `dragApp` example.

Listing 8.4 dragApp.java—*dragApp* Example

```
import netscape.application.*;

/**
 * Application demonstrating the DragSource interface
 */
public class dragApp extends Application {

      public void init() {
            super.init();

            mainRootView().setColor(Color.white);     //.. set background color

            //.. add a resizable panel
            ContainerView panel = new ContainerView(mainRootView().bounds());
            panel.setHorizResizeInstruction(View.WIDTH_CAN_CHANGE);
            panel.setVertResizeInstruction(View.HEIGHT_CAN_CHANGE);

            //.. add a dragView object
            dragView pad = new dragView(50,75,50,60);
```

continues

Listing 8.4 Continued

```
            pad.setImage(Bitmap.bitmapNamed("wpad.gif"));

            //.. add a multiline label
            TextField label = TextField.createLabel("drag a page from the clip
➥board\n"
                            +"and drop it anywhere in the applet",
                                Font.fontNamed("Arial", Font.PLAIN, 11));
            label.moveTo(50,20); label.sizeTo(200,35);
            label.setWrapsContents(true);
            panel.addSubview(label);

            panel.addSubview(pad);
            mainRootView().addSubview(panel);
        }

        /**
         *     standard GUI application main() routine
         */
        public static void main(String args[]) {

            dragApp app = new dragApp();
            ExternalWindow win = new ExternalWindow();
            app.setMainRootView(win.rootView());

            Size size = win.windowSizeForContentSize(320, 200);
            win.sizeTo(size.width, size.height);
            win.setTitle("dragApp");
            win.show();

            app.run();
            System.exit(0);
        }
}

/**
 * ContainerView subclass which implements the DragSource interface
 */
class dragView extends ContainerView implements DragSource {

        public static Image ICON = Bitmap.bitmapNamed("page.gif");
        public static String NAME = "dragPanel";

        protected DragSession drag;

        /**
         *
         */
        public dragView(int x, int y, int w, int h) {
            super(x,y,w,h);
            setBorder(null);
```

```
            setTransparent(true);
        }

        /**
         *     DragSource destination
         */
        public void dragWasAccepted(DragSession session) {
            System.out.println("dragPanel was accepted");
            drag=null;
        }

        public boolean dragWasRejected(DragSession session) {
            System.out.println("dragPanel was rejected");
            drag=null;
            return true;
        }

        public View sourceView(DragSession session) { return this; }

        /**
         *     override mouse methods
         */
        public boolean mouseDown(MouseEvent event) {
           //.. return true so that subsequent mouseDragged() events are generated
            return true;
        }

        public void mouseDragged(MouseEvent ev) {
            super.mouseDragged(ev);
            if (drag != null) return;   //.. only 1 session should be started
            //.. create a new dragSession with our own icon
            drag = new DragSession(this, ICON, ev.x-16, ev.y-16, ev.x, ev.y, NAME,
this);
        }
}
```

Notice that we could have used the `DragWell` class to implement the preceding example.

DragDestination

This interface is implemented by objects that accept `DragSource` objects. The interface methods are called at various stages of the drag and drop session. Most methods return true if they will accept the `DragSession` object passed in as a parameter.

The interface definition is as shown in Listing 8.5.

Listing 8.5 *DragDestination* Interface

```
public interface DragDestination {
        public abstract boolean dragDropped(DragSession);
        public abstract boolean dragEntered(DragSession);
        public abstract void dragExited(DragSession);
        public abstract boolean dragMoved(DragSession);
}
```

As the mouse moves over different views, each view's `acceptsDrag()` method is queried. By default this returns null, and interested `DragDestination` objects must override this method.

dropApp Example

The `dropApp` example, as shown in Figure 8.3, implements a `DragDestination` interface in the `dropView` class, which for the sake of simplicity accepts all `DragSource` objects. Place this `View` along with the `dragView` object created earlier to create a drag and drop application.

FIG. 8.3
`dropApp` example that shows implementation of a droppable object.

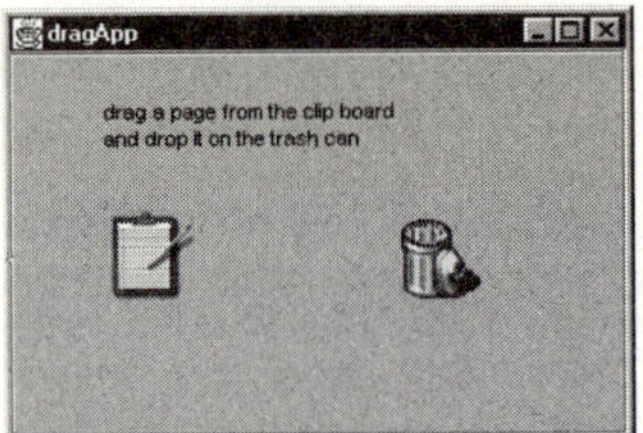

The user can drag pages from the clipboard and drop them onto the trash can. Listing 8.6 shows the source code for this example.

Listing 8.6 dropApp.java—*dropApp* Example

```
import netscape.application.*;

/**
 *      Application demonstrating the DragDestination interface
 */
public class dropApp extends Application {

        /**
         *
         */
        public void init() {
```

```
        super.init();

        mainRootView().setColor(Color.white);     //.. set background color

        //.. create a resizeable panel
        ContainerView panel = new ContainerView(mainRootView().bounds());
        panel.setHorizResizeInstruction(View.WIDTH_CAN_CHANGE);
        panel.setVertResizeInstruction(View.HEIGHT_CAN_CHANGE);

        //.. attach  a dragPanel object
        dragView pad = new dragView(50,75,50,60);
        pad.setImage(Bitmap.bitmapNamed("wpad.gif"));
        panel.addSubview(pad);

        //.. add a multiline label
        TextField label = TextField.createLabel("drag a page from the clip
➥board\n"
                             +"and drop it on the trash can",
                                 Font.fontNamed("Arial", Font.PLAIN, 11));
        label.moveTo(50,20); label.sizeTo(200,35);
        label.setWrapsContents(true);
        panel.addSubview(label);

        //.. attach  a dragPanel object
        dropView drop = new dropView(200,80,50,60);
        drop.setImage(Bitmap.bitmapNamed("trashcan.gif"));
        panel.addSubview(drop);

        mainRootView().addSubview(panel);
    }

    /**
     *     standard GUI application main() routine
     */
    public static void main(String args[]) {

        dropApp app = new dropApp();
        ExternalWindow win = new ExternalWindow();
        app.setMainRootView(win.rootView());

        Size size = win.windowSizeForContentSize(320, 200);
        win.sizeTo(size.width, size.height);
        win.setTitle("dragApp");
        win.show();

        app.run();
        System.exit(0);
}
}

/**
 *
 */
```

continues

Listing 8.6 Continued

```
class dropView extends ContainerView implements DragDestination {

      /**
       *
       */
      public dropView(int x, int y, int w, int h) {
            super(x,y,w,h); setBorder(null); setTransparent(true);
      }

      /**
       *     override View.acceptsDrag()
       */
      public DragDestination acceptsDrag(DragSession sess, int x, int y) {
➥return this;
}

      /**
       *     DragDestination methods
       */
      public boolean dragEntered(DragSession sess) { return true; }
      public void dragExited(DragSession sess)       { }

      public boolean dragMoved(DragSession sess) {
            if (sess.data()==this) return false;
            return true;
      }

      public boolean dragDropped(DragSession sess) { return true;     }
}
```

Drag and Drop Example

In some situations, objects would need to exhibit both `DragSource` and `DragDestination` behavior. To look into this special case, we will build the `dndApp` example, which subclasses the `dragView` `DragSource` object implemented earlier.

dndApp Example

Our example displays two computer systems; the user may drag a diskette icon between the two. Each computer system represents an object that can drag and accept dragged items as shown in Figure 8.4. A real application would do some useful work in the appropriate `DragSource` and `DragDestination` methods.

The application sets the static icon and name fields of the `dragView` class. The `dndView` class, which is a subclass of the `dragView` class, is an implementation similar to the `dropView` class implemented earlier. The `dndApp` program listing is given in Listing 8.7.

FIG. 8.4
dndApp example that demonstrates the drag and drop capabilities of IFC.

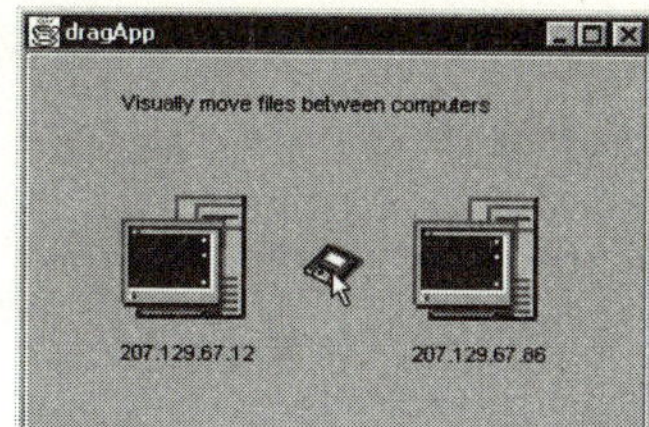

Listing 8.7 dndApp.java—Drag and Drop Example

```
import netscape.application.*;

/**
 * Application demonstrating Drag & Drop Objects
 */
public class dndApp extends Application {

      public void init() {
            super.init();

            mainRootView().setColor(Color.white);     //.. set background color

            //.. add a resizable panel
            ContainerView panel = new ContainerView(mainRootView().bounds());
            panel.setHorizResizeInstruction(View.WIDTH_CAN_CHANGE);
            panel.setVertResizeInstruction(View.HEIGHT_CAN_CHANGE);

            //.. add a drag & drop panel
            dndPanel.ICON = Bitmap.bitmapNamed("floppy.gif");
            dndPanel pad = new dndPanel(50,75,64,64);
            pad.setImage(Bitmap.bitmapNamed("computer.gif"));
            panel.addSubview(pad);

            pad = new dndPanel(200,75,64,64);
            pad.setImage(Bitmap.bitmapNamed("computer.gif"));
            panel.addSubview(pad);

            //.. add a labels
            TextField label = TextField.createLabel("Visually move files between
computers",
                              Font.fontNamed("Arial", Font.PLAIN, 11));
            label.moveTo(50,20);
            panel.addSubview(label);

            label = TextField.createLabel("207.129.67.12",
Font.fontNamed("Arial", Font.PLAIN, 11));
            label.moveTo(50,150); panel.addSubview(label);
            label = TextField.createLabel("207.129.67.86",
Font.fontNamed("Arial", Font.PLAIN, 11));
            label.moveTo(200,150); panel.addSubview(label);
```

continues

Listing 8.7 Continued

```
        mainRootView().addSubview(panel);
    }

    /**
     *     standard GUI application main() routine
     */
    public static void main(String args[]) {

        dndApp app = new dndApp();
        ExternalWindow win = new ExternalWindow();
        app.setMainRootView(win.rootView());

        Size size = win.windowSizeForContentSize(320, 200);
        win.sizeTo(size.width, size.height);
        win.setTitle("dragApp");
        win.show();

        app.run();
        System.exit(0);
    }
}

/**
 *     ContainerView subclass which is both draggable and droppable
 */
class dndView extends dragPanel implements DragDestination {

    public dndPanel(int x, int y, int w, int h) {
        super(x,y,w,h); setBorder(null); setTransparent(true);
        }

        /**
         *     override View.acceptsDrag()
         */
        public DragDestination acceptsDrag(DragSession sess, int x, int y) {
return this;
}

    /**
     *     DragDestination methods
     */
    public boolean dragEntered(DragSession sess) { return true; }
    public void dragExited(DragSession sess)      { }

    public boolean dragMoved(DragSession sess) {
        if (sess.data()==this) return false;
        return true;
    }

    public boolean dragDropped(DragSession sess) {
        return true;
    }
}
```

PART III

Advanced Techniques

CHAPTER 9

Persistence

Basics and foundations of object persistence

Background on the various concepts of persistence and the terminology used.

Overview of IFC persistence

An overview of how IFC implements persistence.

A simple example

Illustrates the minimal persistent application using standard data types and objects.

A networked GUI persistent application

A more complex persistent application that uses GUI and networking concepts.

Security issues relating to persistent objects

Addresses the various security issues that affect the usage of persistent objects in real-world applications.

Object Persistence refers to the capability of an object to be stored outside the program environment and be restored at a later time without loss of critical information. It has attracted great interest in recent times, especially since the advent of the Java environment. This can be attributed partially to the availability of open standards and tools and to the increased popularity of networking technologies.

With the advent of networking and stream-based technologies, persistent objects increasingly are being used to pass cooked data between remote processes. ■

Background

With context to the Java environment, objects and data members do not live outside a program's lifetime. Resources used by these data and objects are reused by the Java Virtual Machine (JVM) for other tasks. In fact, the garbage collector makes sure that the object does not live beyond its scope. So, in order to maintain objects outside the JVM, persistence mechanisms need to be used.

Before we go into the specifics of persistent technology and techniques, let's briefly touch upon some of the concepts, procedures, and terminology used in regard to persistence:

- Orthogonal persistence
- Persistence via reachability
- Marshalling
- Versioning
- Transient data

Orthogonal Persistence

Orthogonal persistence refers to the concept of isolating the persistent function from the object. Therefore, it's up to the serializing process to make persistent any objects it encounters. This approach is more generic and does not involve any changes to existing objects and data.

Persistence via Reachability

As opposed to orthogonal persistence, persistence via reachability works on the basis of a root object that is specified as persistent. The serializing process serializes it and all objects reachable from it, thereby creating a graph of serialized objects.

The benefits offered by this approach include:

- Performance

  The serialization process does not have to process each object, so performance is enhanced.

- Customization

  A persistent object may serialize only portions.

- Control

  At runtime, persistent objects can determine action that affects the persistent behavior.

- Security

  Since the objects get a chance to serialize and deserialize, they can implement custom encryption processing.

IFC takes this approach to persistence and uses a Hashtable mechanism to store persistent data.

Marshalling

Marshalling refers to the access of the data members that make up a persistent object and can be either:

- Meta Structured

  This is usually referred to the schematized approach to marshalling and separates out the schema definition from the actual serialization process.

  A significant advantage offered by this approach is that it becomes possible to write different storage mechanisms for the same encoding API.

- Free Form

  In this approach, the persistent object is given total control over its serialization. The serialization framework implemented in Java is of this type and implements the `Serializable` and `Externalizable` interfaces to achieve this.

Versioning

The ability to perform operations on persistent objects based on the version information stored is referred to as *versioning.*

As reusability and maintenance become key ingredients of software products, versioning takes up an increasingly important role by providing features such as backward-compatibility to older versions of data.

Transient Data

Transient data refers to the data members that are runtime-dependent and should not be serialized. For example, in the Java environment, `FileDescriptor` objects would be transient data because their values would not make sense to other processes.

A process consists of persistent, non-persistent, and transient objects, as shown in Figure 9.1.

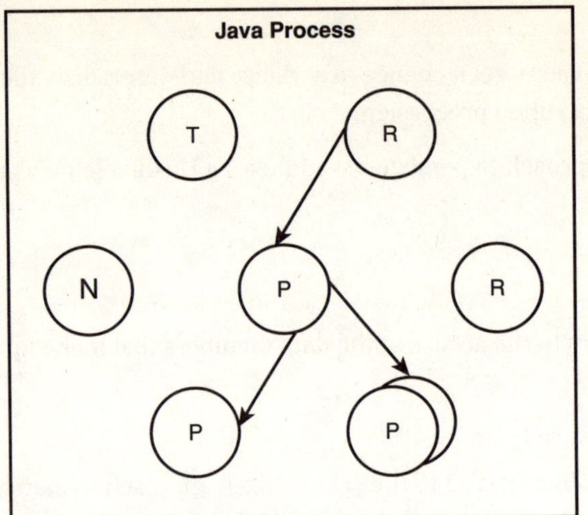

FIG. 9.1
Objects in a Java Process.

Persistent objects are serialized by their *root* reference, and it is the responsibility of the object to ensure that transient data is managed properly.

Overview

The IFC persistent framework is implemented using objects and interfaces to support the encoding/decoding process and data storage.

We will cover the following concepts:

- Codable Interface

  Interface implemented by persistent objects
- Encoding Process

  Overview of the encoding/decoding process
- `Archive`

  The container that holds the persistent objects

This is illustrated in Figure 9.2.

As can be seen from the figure, the `Archive` holds encoded persistent objects in a `ClassTable` that may be saved or restored to a stream. The `Archiver` and `Unarchiver` are responsible for converting to and from a codable object.

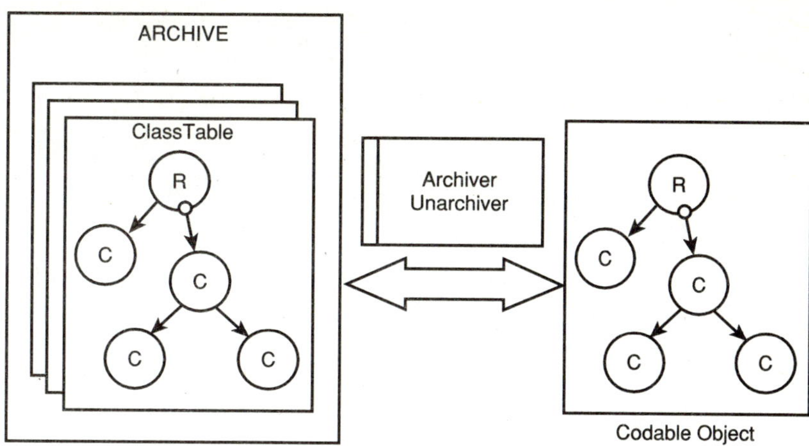

FIG. 9.2 Overview of IFC persistence.

Codable

Persistent objects implement the codable interface, which defines the methods needed to support the IFC persistence framework. The serialization and deserialization processes call methods in these objects to implement persistence.

NOTE Many IFC classes themselves implement the codable interface, making them persistent.

The codable interface is as shown in Listing 9.1.

Listing 9.1 Codable Interface

```
public interface Codable {
      public void describeClassInfo(ClassInfo info);
      public void encode(Encoder encoder) throws CodingException;
      public void decode(Decoder decoder) throws CodingException;
      public void finishDecoding() throws CodingException;
}
```

`describeClassInfo()` gives classes a way to declare their schema and can be thought of as a *registration* phase.

Taking this approach makes the design robust and efficient by providing a fixed schema upon which the persistence mechanism can operate, while enhancing performance.

Another major benefit is that because the schema has been segregated from the actual processing, implementing different storage and transport mechanisms becomes easy because they have a chance to *examine* the object and act appropriately before processing actually begins.

`encode()` is the place where the object actually encodes its registered fields. It is called when the `Archiver` is encoding the Object graph and throws a `CodingException` when the specified field is not found.

`decode()` is called during the deserialization process and is where the individual fields are decoded. It is called when the `Unarchiver` is decoding the Object graph, and throws a `CodingException` when the specified field is not found.

`finishDecoding()` gives the object a chance to do any cleanup operations that may be required before the serialization or deserialization process ends.

NOTE For security reasons, codable objects must be public and must implement a public empty constructor. Otherwise an `IllegalAccessException` is thrown.

Encoding

Persistent objects are encoded into a canonical form and stored in an `Archive` object.

The application starts the encoding process that first calls the `describeClassInfo()` and processes the schema for the object. The schema is passed to the back-end stream-based mechanism, which can optionally take action based on this information. This includes the class, version, and field identifiers.

After this, the object's `encode()` method is called, which returns its fields through a `Encoder` object. The `Encoder` class itself implements methods to encode most data types and also the generic `encodeObject()` method. It also contains methods to process arrays of data and objects, as shown in Listing 9.2.

Listing 9.2 ***Encoder* Interface**

```
public interface Encoder {
      public abstract void encodeBoolean(String, boolean);
      public abstract void encodeBooleanArray(String, boolean[], int, int);
      public abstract void encodeByte(String, byte);
      public abstract void encodeByteArray(String, byte[], int, int);
      public abstract void encodeChar(String, char);
      public abstract void encodeCharArray(String, char[], int, int);
      public abstract void encodeDouble(String, double);
      public abstract void encodeDoubleArray(String, double[], int, int);
      public abstract void encodeFloat(String, float);
      public abstract void encodeFloatArray(String, float[], int, int);
      public abstract void encodeInt(String, int);
      public abstract void encodeIntArray(String, int[], int, int);
      public abstract void encodeLong(String, long);
      public abstract void encodeLongArray(String, long[], int, int);
      public abstract void encodeObject(String, Object);
      public abstract void encodeObjectArray(String, Object[], int, int);
```

```
        public abstract void encodeShort(String, short);
        public abstract void encodeShortArray(String, short[], int, int);
        public abstract void encodeString(String, String);
        public abstract void encodeStringArray(String, String[], int, int);
}
```

The decoding process occurs using the `decode()` method of the object. Data to be decoded is passed in via a `Decoder` object that contains corresponding decoding methods. The `Decoder` interface is defined in Listing 9.3.

Listing 9.3 *Decoder* Interface

```
public interface Encoder {
        public abstract boolean decodeBoolean(String);
        public abstract boolean[] decodeBooleanArray(String);
        public abstract byte decodeByte(String);
        public abstract byte[] decodeByteArray(String);
        public abstract char decodeChar(String);
        public abstract char[] decodeCharArray(String);
        public abstract double decodeDouble(String);
        public abstract double[] decodeDoubleArray(String);
        public abstract float decodeFloat(String);
        public abstract float[] decodeFloatArray(String);
        public abstract int decodeInt(String);
        public abstract int[] decodeIntArray(String);
        public abstract long decodeLong(String);
        public abstract long[] decodeLongArray(String);
        public abstract Object decodeObject(String);
        public abstract Object[] decodeObjectArray(String);
        public abstract short decodeShort(String);
        public abstract short[] decodeShortArray(String);
        public abstract String decodeString(String);
        public abstract String[] decodeStringArray(String);
        public abstract void replaceObject(Object);
        public abstract int versionForClassName(String);
}
```

Archive

Objects are streamed to a data structure called an *archive*, essentially a container that holds them. Each object is stored in a `ClassTable` data structure with a `rootIdentifier`, from which all its reachable objects may be accessed. There can be multiple objects in an archive, each with its own `rootIdentifier`.

`Archives` come in two varieties:

- Text archive

  The objects are stored as a stream of text strings. You may make an archive more readable by using the "pretty" feature.

Even more control may be exercised by using the `FormattingSerializer` object, which allows manipulation of the ASCII generated by the Serializer. For example, you can insert comments in the archive.

- Binary archive

  A more compact form where data is stored in binary form.

CAUTION

Don't confuse the IFC Archive with the Java Archive (`jar`) of Java 1.1. These represent two totally different concepts and functions. Whereas the IFC Archive holds the encoded state of codable objects, `jar` represents a compressed aggregation of many files.

The `Archive` class definition is given in Listing 9.4.

Listing 9.4 *Archive* Class

```
public class Archive {
      public void addClassTable(ClassTable);
      public ClassTable classTableForIdentifier(int);
      public ClassTable classTableForName(String);
      public boolean removeRootIdentifier(int);
      public int[] rootIdentifiers();
      public void addRootIdentifier(int);
      public int rowForIdentifier(int);
      public int identifierCount();
      public int mapIdentifier(ClassTable, int);
      public void read(InputStream);
      public void write(OutputStream);
      public void readASCII(InputStream);
      public void writeASCII(OutputStream, boolean);
}
```

Methods in this class deal with `ClassTable` objects, Identifiers, and I/O operations.

NOTE Most programs do not deal directly with archives and instead work with them through Archivers and Unarchivers. ■

Each class in an `Archive` is stored as a table with each row representing an object in that class. Each object is allocated an identifier or *handle* that is used for its reference, with the starting object called the root object and its identifier being the `rootIdentifier` for that object.

The I/O operations include reading and writing to streams, and implementing the `read()` and `readASCII()` methods to read from streams and the corresponding `write()` and `writeASCII()` methods to write.

Mechanics of IFC Persistence

We will cover the following aspects of IFC persistence:

- `ClassTable`
- `Serializer`
- `Archiver`
- `Deserializer`
- `Unarchiver`
- `FormattingSerializer`

CAUTION

IFC1.0 BUG: Strings containing "@" are not being quoted properly in ASCII serializations.

ClassTable

As described earlier, each class in an `Archive` has a `ClassTable` that holds the data for instances of that class. The data in a `ClassTable` is accessed by row and column index, with a row corresponding to an instance of the class and a column corresponding to a field of that class.

NOTE Most programs do not deal directly with `ClassTables` and instead work with them through Archivers and Unarchivers.

The `ClassTable` class definition is given in Listing 9.5.

Listing 9.5 *ClassTable* Class

```
public class Archive {
      public Archive archive();
      public boolean[] booleanArrayAt(int, int);
      public boolean booleanAt(int, int);
      public byte[] byteArrayAt(int, int);
      public byte byteAt(int, int);
      public char[] charArrayAt(int, int);
      public char charAt(int, int);
      public String className();
      public String[] classNames();
      public int columnForField(String);
      public double[] doubleArrayAt(int, int);
      public double doubleAt(int, int);
      public float[] floatArrayAt(int, int);
```

continues

Listing 9.5 Continued

```
        public float floatAt(int, int);
        public int[] identifierArrayAt(int, int);
        public int identifierAt(int, int);
        public int[] intArrayAt(int, int);
        public int intAt(int, int);
        public long[] longArrayAt(int, int);
        public long longAt(int, int);
        public int newIdentifier();
        public void readData(InputStream);
        public void readInfo(InputStream);
        public int rowCount();
        public int rowForIdentifier(int);
        public void setBooleanArrayAt(int, int, boolean[]);
        public void setBooleanAt(int, int, boolean);
        public void setByteArrayAt(int, int, byte[]);
        public void setByteAt(int, int, byte);
        public void setCharArrayAt(int, int, char[]);
        public void setCharAt(int, int, char);
        public void setDoubleArrayAt(int, int, double[]);
        public void setDoubleAt(int, int, double);
        public void setFloatArrayAt(int, int, float[]);
        public void setFloatAt(int, int, float);
        public void setIdentifierArrayAt(int, int, int[]);
        public void setIdentifierAt(int, int, int);
        public void setIntArrayAt(int, int, int[]);
        public void setIntAt(int, int, int);
        public void setLongArrayAt(int, int, long[]);
        public void setLongAt(int, int, long);
        public void setShortArrayAt(int, int, short[]);
        public void setShortAt(int, int, short);
        public void setStringArrayAt(int, int, String[]);
        public void setStringAt(int, int, String);
        public short[] shortArrayAt(int, int);
        public short shortAt(int, int);
        public String[] stringArrayAt(int, int);
        public String stringAt(int, int);
        public int versionForClassName(String);
        public void writeData(OutputStream);
        public void writeInfo(OutputStream);
}
```

Serializer

This class serializes a fixed set of data types (Dictionaries, Arrays, Vectors, and Strings) to an ASCII stream. For other object types, the object's `toString()` method is used.

Strings with non-alphanumeric characters are quoted and special characters are escaped to maintain consistency.

The `Serializer` class definition is given in Listing 9.6.

Listing 9.6 *Serializer* Class Definition

```
public class Serializer {
      public static String serializeObject(Object);
      public static boolean writeObject(OutputStream, Object);
      public void flush();
      public void writeObject(Object);
}
```


Deserializer

This is a subclass of the `java.io.FilterInputStream` class, and it deserializes a fixed set of objects that include Hashtables, Vectors, Arrays, and Strings. It handles input only from an ASCII stream, processing quoted and escaped characters during the deserialization process.

The `Deserializer` class definition is given in Listing 9.7.

Listing 9.7 *Deserializer* Class

```
public class Deserializer {
      public static Object deserializeObject(String);
      public static Object readObject(InputStream);
      public Object readObject();
}
```

Archiver

Most programs manage `Archive` objects through this object, which is a subclass of the `Encoder` class. After initializing it with an `Archive` object, the `archiveRootObject()` method is usually used to stream a codable object.

This is shown in the Listing 9.8, which uses an Archiver to write the `persistObject` object to the `System.out` stream.

Listing 9.8 Using the *Archiver*

```
archiver = new Archiver(new Archive());
archiver.archiveRootObject(persistObject);
archiver.archive().writeASCII(System.out, true);
```

Unarchiver

Most programs deserialize objects using this object, which, as expected, is a subclass of the `Decoder` class. After initializing it with a valid `Archive` object, the `unarchiveIdentifier()` method is used to deserialize a codable object by its `rootIdentifier`.

This is shown in Listing 9.9, which uses an `Unarchiver` to read in a codable object from the `System.in` stream.

Listing 9.9 Using the *Unarchiver*

```
archive = new Archive();
archive.readASCII(System.in)
rootIdentifiers = archive.rootIdentifiers();
unarchiver = new Unarchiver(archive);
rootObject = unarchiver.unarchiveIdentifier(rootIdentifiers[0]);
```

FormattingSerializer

This class is used to format ASCII `Archive` objects as they are generated. It extends the `Serializer` class and by default formats and indents the ASCII stream. It may be subclassed to provide features like insertion of comments in the archive, translation to other national languages, etc.

NOTE Notice that this is an `Output` object. Objects created using this class can be deserialized using the standard `Deserializer` object.

The `FormattingSerializer` class definition is given in Listing 9.10.

Listing 9.10 *FormattingSerializer* Class

```
public class FormattingSerializer {
      public static byte[] formatBytes(byte[]);
      public static String serializeObject(Object);
      public static boolean writeObject(OutputStream, Object);
      public int indentationLength();
      public void setIndentationLength(int);
      public void writeComment(String, boolean);
      public void writeObject(Object);
}
```

A Simple Persistent Application

Let's look at an example application using some of the concepts that we have covered. The `persistApp` application is broken into two programs for clarity. These are the *data* part and the *control* part. The classes implemented are:

- `persistObject`

  This represents the *data* part of the application and holds some data types and objects.

- `persistApp`

  This implements the *control* portion of the application and manipulates the `persistObject`.

persistObject

The `persistObject` class implements a simple object with three data members of type `int`, `String` and `Vector`. This object is serialized and deserialized by the `persistApp` class, which acts like the control application.

The `persistObject` class starts with the import statement and class definition. As we have discussed, since this is intended to be a persistent class, it must implement the codable interface.

```
import netscape.util.*;
public class persistObject implements Codable {
```

We now define the data members of this object. These are the actual members that are serialized and represent the data portion of the object.

```
protected int i;
protected String str;
protected Vector vect;
```

Next we define the constructors. As noted earlier, a persistent class must implement at least one public constructor with no parameters. We will implement an additional constructor that accepts values to initialize its data members.

```
    public persistObject() {  }
    public persistObject(int i, String str, Vector vect) {
this.i=i; this.str=str; this.vect = vect;
}
```

The `describeClassInfo()` method comes next and defines the schema for representation of this object. Values are passed back to the caller via the `ClassInfo` object passed in. The class should define a name and a version that are associated with the class itself. Then we define names and values for all the fields that we would like to make persistent.

In this example we associate the name "persistobject" with the class and have hardcoded the version with a value of 1. We use the name of the field itself as the name to associate with the field. The second parameter of the `addField` method accepts the data type of the field.

```
public void describeClassInfo(ClassInfo info) {
info.addClass("persistObject",1);
info.addField("i",INT_TYPE);
info.addField("str",STRING_TYPE);
info.addField("vect",OBJECT_TYPE);
}
```

The `encode()` method is the place where encoding or serialization actually occurs. We have already associated the names of our three fields and specified the data types for each of them, so now we use the appropriate `encode` method to serialize each of the fields. As is apparent, the data type must match the encode function being called. If the encode method finds an incorrect name (the first parameter), it throws a `CodingException`.

```
public void encode(Encoder encoder) throws CodingException {
encoder.encodeInt("i",i);
encoder.encodeString("str",str);
encoder.encodeObject("vect",vect);
}
```

The `decode()` method does the opposite and deserializes the object to restore the fields from the decoder object passed in as a parameter. We use the appropriate `decode` method with the correct data type to restore each field. As can be seen, the decode methods take the field name as the parameter. This is the same name that was used to store the Object in the first place. If you pass an invalid name, it will throw a `CodingException`.

```
public void decode(Decoder decoder) throws CodingException {
i = decoder.decodeInt("i");
str = decoder.decodeString("str");
vect = (Vector)decoder.decodeObject("vect");
}
```

Note that the `decodeObject()` returns the generic `Object` class, so it must be cast to the proper field type during the deserialization process. If the cast is invalid, a `ClassCastException` exception is thrown.

Lastly, we leave the `finishDecoding()` empty because we have no cleanup operations to perform.

```
public void finishDecoding() throws CodingException { }
```

We also implement a `toString()` method for debugging purposes.

Unless space is a constraint and/or the object representation is too complex or large, it's a good idea to define a `toString()` method for debugging purposes.

The entire `persistObject` class is reproduced in Listing 9.11 for reference.

Listing 9.11 *persistObject.java*: *persistObject* Class

```
import netscape.util.*;
public class persistObject implements Codable {
     protected int i;
     protected String str;
     protected Vector vect;

     public persistObject() {  }
     public persistObject(int i, String str, Vector vect) {
this.i=i; this.str=str; this.vect = vect;
}
public void describeClassInfo(ClassInfo info) {
info.addClass("persistObject",1);
info.addField("i",INT_TYPE);
info.addField("str",STRING_TYPE);
info.addField("vect",OBJECT_TYPE);
}
public void encode(Encoder encoder) throws CodingException {
encoder.encodeInt("i",i);
encoder.encodeString("str",str);
encoder.encodeObject("vect",vect);
}
public void decode(Decoder decoder) throws CodingException {
i = decoder.decodeInt("i");
str = decoder.decodeString("str");
vect = (Vector)decoder.decodeObject("vect");
}
public void finishDecoding() throws CodingException { }
public String toString() {
          return "i="+i+", str="+str+", vect["+vect.size()+"]";
}
}
```

This is the "data" part of the application. Now you also need a "control" part that handles these data objects. Let's examine the "control" part of the example.

persistApp

We begin with the usual `import` statement and `class` definition. Note that the `persistApp` class is stand-alone and neither extends any class nor implements any interface.

```
import netscape.util.*;
public class persistApp {
```

Next, we define the `persistObject` data and a constructor that accepts values to initialize it. The constructor then builds a `persistObject`.

```
public persistObject data;
public persistApp(int i, String str, Vector vect) {
     data = new persistObject(i,str,vect);
}
```

The `save()` method handles serialization of the `persistObject` to a file, whose name is passed in as a parameter. It starts by creating a new (and empty) archive and passing it to an `Archiver` object. The archiver is then instructed to start the serialization process with the `persistObject` data to be the root. It goes through the `persistObject` class and serializes it by calling its `describeClassInfo()` and `encode()` method. By the time it returns, it has created the `Archive` object that holds the serialized data object. Lastly, that `Archive` object is stored to a newly created file stream in ASCII form, with the "pretty" option turned on for easy readability.

```
public void save(String filename) throws CodingException, IOException {
Archiver archiver = new Archiver(new Archive());
          archiver.archiveRootObject(data);
archiver.archive().writeASCII(new FileOutputStream(filename),true);
}
```

The `load()` method handles deserialization of the `persistObject` from a file, whose name is specified as a parameter. It throws all the exceptions thrown by the file operations, as well as those by the deserialization process.

It creates a stream for the file specified and passes it to a newly created `Archive` object. As we discussed earlier, this is the procedure for the deserialization process. The file is then read in using the `readASCII()` method, which initializes the `Archive` object. The `Archive` object is then passed to an `Unarchiver` object. The `persistObject` is finally recreated by asking the `Unarchiver` to recreate the first (and only) `rootObject` in the `Archive`.

```
public void load(String filename) throws IOException,
CodingException, DeserializationException
{
          FileInputStream is = new FileInputStream(filename);
          Archive archive = new Archive();
          archive.readASCII(is);
          int[] rootIds = archive.rootIdentifiers();
          Unarchiver unarchiver = new Unarchiver(archive);
          data = (persistObject)unarchiver.unarchiveIdentifier(rootIds[0]);
}
```

Note that the `persistObject` must be cast to the proper type as the `unarchiveIdentifier()` method returns the generic `Object` class.

The `main()` routine starts with the creation of a `persistApp` object from some random values, which are used by it to construct a `persistObject`.

```
public static void main(String args[]) {
     Vector v = new Vector();
     v.addElement("first");
     v.addElement("second");
     persistApp app = new persistApp(123, "abc", v);
```

To actually manipulate the `persistObject`, it must handle all the exceptions thrown by the methods. Therefore, we put a try/catch block around all these operations.

The `save()` method is called to serialize the `persistObject` to a file called `persist.dat`.

```
try {
     System.out.println(app.data.toString());
     app.save("persist.dat");
```

To ensure that we read in the real serialized object from disk, we deallocate the `persistObject` data by assigning *null* to it and then calling the `load()` method to actually deserialize it.

```
app.data=null;
app.load("persist.dat");
System.out.println(app.data.toString());
```


The `catch` statement catches all exceptions and prints the program stack trace leading up to that exception. If you have debugging options on, you also see the line numbers in the stack trace.

```
          } catch (Exception e) {
               System.out.println(e.getMessage());
          }
     }
```

When you run the program, the `System.out.println` statements produce the output shown in Listing 9.12.

Listing 9.12 Output from the *persistApp* Program

```
i=123, str=abc, vect[2]
vect[0]=first
vect[1]=second
i=123, str=abc, vect[2]
vect[0]=first
vect[1]=second
```

As expected, the first set of results match the second, which tells us that we successfully serialized the `persistObject` object to a disk file called `persist.dat` and deserialized it back to re-create an equivalent object.

The `persist.dat` file produced from our exercise is shown in Listing 9.13.

Listing 9.13 *persist.dat*: *persistApp* Output

```
{
    archiveVersion = 1;
    classTables = {
        java.lang.String = {
            classNames = [ java.lang.String ];
            classVersions = [ 1 ];
            fieldNames = [ value ];
```

continues

Listing 9.13 Continued

```
            fieldTypes = [ java.lang.String ];
            instances = { String-0 = { value = first;}; String-1 = { value =
➥second;};};
        };
        netscape.util.Vector = {
            classNames = [ netscape.util.Vector ];
            classVersions = [ 1 ];
            fieldNames = [ array ];
            fieldTypes = [ "java.lang.Object[]" ];
            instances = { Vector-0 = { array = [ String-0, String-1 ];};};
        };
        persistObject = {
            classNames = [ persistObject ];
            classVersions = [ 1 ];
            fieldNames = [ i, str, vect ];
            fieldTypes = [ int, java.lang.String, java.lang.Object ];
            instances = { persistObject-0 = { i = 123;  str = abc; vect =
Vector-0;};};
        };
    };
    rootInstances = [ persistObject-0 ];
}
```

Discussion of the preceding is beyond the scope of this book. For the inquisitive, it might be worth looking at the source code of IFC itself to get a better understanding of the serialization process.

The entire `persistApp` class is reproduced in Listing 9.14 for reference.

Listing 9.14 *persistApp.java*: *persistApp* Class

```
public class persistApp {
     public persistObject data;
     public persistApp(int i, String str, Vector vect) {
          data = new persistObject(i,str,vect);
     }
public void save(String filename) throws CodingException, IOException {
Archiver archiver = new Archiver(new Archive());
          archiver.archiveRootObject(data);
archiver.archive().writeASCII(new FileOutputStream(filename),true);
}
public void load(String filename) throws IOException, CodingException,
DeserializationException
{
          FileInputStream is = new FileInputStream(filename);
          Archive archive = new Archive();
          archive.readASCII(is);
          int[] rootIds = archive.rootIdentifiers();
          Unarchiver unarchiver = new Unarchiver(archive);
          data = (persistObject)unarchiver.unarchiveIdentifier(rootIds[0]);
}
```

```
        public static void main(String args[]) {
            Vector v = new Vector();
            v.addElement("first");
            v.addElement("second");
            persistApp app = new persistApp(123, "abc", v);
            try {
                // before storage
                System.out.println(app.data.toString());
                // save to file
                app.save("persist.dat");
                // just to make sure
                app.data=null;
                // load from file
                app.load("persist.dat");
                // after storage and retrieval
                System.out.println(app.data.toString());
            } catch (Exception e) {
                System.out.println(e.getMessage());
            }
        }
    }
```

NOTE Because the serialization classes are stream-oriented, it's not possible to write to a random access file at this time.

You can use the Java 1.1 `jar` facilities to compress/decompress data on-the-fly.

A Networked Persistent GUI Application

Let's look at a more advanced sample application. We will combine our GUI skills with our networking skills to produce a persistent GUI object that is accessed over the network.

The object is first created with some test values, saved to a network `HTTP` server, and retrieved using the `HTTP/1.0 GET` method, which is used widely to fetch documents over the Web. To save the object back to the server, the new `HTTP/1.1 PUT` method is used. `HTTP/1.1` is defined in `RFC 2068`. As this book goes to press, a number of Web server vendors are supporting this new standard.

To make things more interesting, we will dynamically manipulate the serialization process at runtime by checking versions and the time of day to do some "intelligent" processing.

The application consists of three programs:

- `persistButton`

  A persistent version of the `Button` class that stores only the title and image associated with a button. Other attributes are ignored.

- `persistInternalWindow`

  A persistent version of `InternalWindow` that stores only a few attributes and contains a collection of `persistButton` objects.

- `persistNetGUI`

  The "control" portion of the application that stores the `persistInternalWindow` object and manages network resources, etc.

CAUTION

IFC1.0 BUG: There are still a few minor bugs remaining in the serialization of GUI objects such as TextView and Button. Please see the list of known bugs at the IFC site at **http://developer.netscape.com/library/ifc/index.html**.

persistButton

The `persistButton` starts with the standard import statements and the class definition. As is evident from the class declaration, we are extending the `Button` class and making this class persistent by implementing the codable interface.

```
import netscape.application.*;
import netscape.util.*;
public class persistButton extends Button implements Codable {
```

The version is controlled by a `public static` variable, which can be directly manipulated. The fields of interest to us, the button title and image, are declared next.

```
public static int VERSION = 1;
protected String text;
protected Bitmap icon;
```

The constructors include the necessary public empty constructor and one that takes the position and dimension of the button as parameters.

```
public persistButton() { }
public persistButton(int x, int y, int w, int h) {
     super(x,y,w,h);
}
```

`describeClassInfo()` uses its own name by calling the `getName()`. The version passed is the static `VERSION` variable. Next it uses the field names as the names to associate with the fields.

```
public void describeClassInfo(ClassInfo info) {
     super.describeClassInfo(info);
     info.addClass(getClass().getName(),VERSION);
     info.addField("text",STRING_TYPE);
     info.addField("icon",OBJECT_TYPE);
}
```

Notice the `super.describeClassInfo()`. This is an extremely important step and ensures that the rest of the persistent graph is also serialized. In this case, we are inheriting from the `View` class, which is codable.

NOTE As a rule of thumb, always call the parent method first when inheriting from codable classes. This ensures that all "higher" level classes are serialized/deserialized first. This may become especially important when doing runtime processing during the serialization/deserialization process.

The `encode()` method first calls its parent's `encode()` method. It then serializes the relevant fields after initializing them with values from the base class.

```
public void encode(Encoder encoder) throws CodingException {
     super.encode(encoder);
     text = title(); icon = (Bitmap)image();
     encoder.encodeString("text",text);
     encoder.encodeObject("icon",icon);
}
```

The `decode()` method does the opposite of the `encode()` method and sets the parent's attributes with the deserialized values. Again, the parent's method is called first.

```
public void decode(Decoder decoder) throws CodingException {
     super.decode(decoder);
     text = decoder.decodeString("text");
     icon = (Bitmap)decoder.decodeObject("icon");
     setTitle(text); setImage(icon);
}
```

Lastly, the `finishDecoding()` method is implemented with just a call to its parent.

```
public void finishDecoding() throws CodingException {
     super.finishDecoding();
}
```

The entire `persistApp` class is reproduced in Listing 9.15 for reference.

Listing 9.15 ***persistButton.java*: *persistButton* Class**

```
import netscape.application.*;
import netscape.util.*;
/**
 *
```

continues

Listing 9.15 Continued

```
 */
public class persistButton extends Button implements Codable {
     public static int VERSION = 1;
     protected String text;
     protected Bitmap icon;
     /**
      *     constructor
      */
     public persistButton() { }
     public persistButton(int x, int y, int w, int h) {
          super(x,y,w,h);
     }
     /**
      *     Codable Interface
      */
     public void describeClassInfo(ClassInfo info) {
          super.describeClassInfo(info);
          info.addClass(getClass().getName(),VERSION);
          info.addField("text",STRING_TYPE);
          info.addField("icon",OBJECT_TYPE);
     }

     public void encode(Encoder encoder) throws CodingException {
          super.encode(encoder);
          text = title(); icon = (Bitmap)image();
          encoder.encodeString("text",text);
          encoder.encodeObject("icon",icon);
     }
     public void decode(Decoder decoder) throws CodingException {
          super.decode(decoder);
          text = decoder.decodeString("text");
          icon = (Bitmap)decoder.decodeObject("icon");
          setTitle(text); setImage(icon);
     }
     public void finishDecoding() throws CodingException {
          super.finishDecoding();
     }
}
```

persistInternalWindow

The `persistInternalWindow` starts with the import statement for the `java.util.Date` class, besides the usual import statements.

```
import java.util.Date;
import netscape.application.*;
import netscape.util.*;
public class persistInternalWindow extends InternalWindow implements Codable
{
```

CAUTION

Some classes of IFC have the same names as their java counterparts, such as Vector, HashTable, etc. This may sometimes lead to erratic errors and messages from some compilers.

Next the data members and version are stored. In this example, we are only concerned about the `InternalWindow`'s title, closeability, and resizability. We ignore the rest of the `InternalWindow` attributes. Notice that we are maintaining an array of `persistButton` objects.

```
public static int VERSION = 1;
protected String title;
protected boolean closeable,resizable;
protected persistButton[] buttons;
```

The constructors include the standard public constructor with no parameters and one that accepts the position and dimensions of the `InternalWindow`.

```
public persistInternalWindow() {
}
public persistInternalWindow(int x, int y, int w, int h) {
super(x,y,w,h);
}
```

A helper method is defined next to set the array of `persistButton` objects from the outside.

```
public void setButtons(persistButton[] btns) { buttons=btns; }
```

The `show()` method is overridden to call its ancestor after adding its collection of `persistButtons`, if applicable. This ensures that the `InternalWindow` is always updated with the `persistButtons` before being shown.

```
public void show() {
     if (buttons!=null) {
          for (int i=0;i<buttons.length;i++)
               addSubview(buttons[i]);
     }
     super.show();
}
```

`describeClassInfo()` calls its parent before registering itself with its own name and version. Then, all its data fields are declared using their own names. Notice the buttons are stored as an `OBJECT_ARRAY_TYPE`. IFC serialization has the ability to store arrays as conveniently as scalar types.

```
public void describeClassInfo(ClassInfo info) {
     super.describeClassInfo(info);
     info.addClass(getClass().getName(),VERSION);
     info.addField("title",STRING_TYPE);
```

```
info.addField("closeable",BOOLEAN_TYPE);
info.addField("resizable",BOOLEAN_TYPE);
info.addField("buttons",OBJECT_ARRAY_TYPE);
}
```

The `encode()` method calls its parent and then checks the time. Depending on the time, it will store "Day Shift" or "Night Shift" as the title of the `InternalWindow`. It then serializes its closeable and resizable fields. Lastly, it serializes its buttons array, if applicable. This means that if there are no buttons, they won't be stored at all.

```
public void encode(Encoder encoder) throws CodingException {
     super.encode(encoder);
     Date d = new Date();
     title = (d.getHours()<12) ? "Day Shift" : "Night Shift";
     encoder.encodeString("title",title);
     encoder.encodeBoolean("closeable",closeable);
     encoder.encodeBoolean("resizable",resizable);
     if (buttons!=null)
          encoder.encodeObjectArray("buttons",buttons,0,buttons.length);
}
```

The `decode()` method does some more runtime processing. It first queries the version number and forces the title to be "Day Shift" if the version is less than 2. Otherwise, it deserializes the title field from the decoder. Then it deserializes the two Boolean fields.

Next, it tries to deserialize the `buttons` field. Since there is a possibility that such a field does not exist (see `encode()` above), `decodeObjectArray()` might throw a `CodingException`. Hence, we surround this section with a try/catch statement and ignore any `CodingException` thrown during this operation.

In case `buttons` did exist, it is returned as an `Object[]` array and must be manually copied onto the `buttons` array. This is because in Java, you cannot cast an array of objects to another type.

```
public void decode(Decoder decoder) throws CodingException {
     super.decode(decoder);
     int ver = decoder.versionForClassName(getClass().getName());
     title = (ver < 2) ? "Day Shift" : decoder.decodeString("title");
     closeable  = decoder.decodeBoolean("closeable");
     resizable = decoder.decodeBoolean("resizable");
     //.. ignore this exception
     try {
         Object[] o = decoder.decodeObjectArray("buttons");
         buttons = new persistButton[o.length];
         for (int i=0;i<o.length;i++)
              buttons[i]=(persistButton)o[i];
     }
     catch (CodingException e) { }
     }
```

And lastly, the `finishDecoding()` method is implemented with a call to its parent.

```
    public void finishDecoding() throws CodingException {
         super.finishDecoding();
    }
```

The entire `persistInternalWindow` class is reproduced in Listing 9.16 for reference.

Listing 9.16 ***persistInternalWindow.java: persistInternalWindow* Class**

```
import java.util.Date;
import netscape.application.*;
import netscape.util.*;
/**
 *
 */
public class persistInternalWindow extends InternalWindow implements Codable {
     public static int VERSION = 1;
     protected String title;
     protected boolean closeable,resizable;
     protected persistButton[] buttons;

     /**
      *     constructor
      */
     public persistInternalWindow() { }

     public persistInternalWindow(int x, int y, int w, int h) {
          super(x,y,w,h);
     }

     public void setButtons(persistButton[] btns) { buttons=btns; }

     public void show() {
      //.. if buttons are available, add them to the rootview
          if (buttons!=null) {
               for (int i=0;i<buttons.length;i++)
                    addSubview(buttons[i]);
          }
          super.show();
     }

     /**
      *     Codable Interface
      */
     public void describeClassInfo(ClassInfo info) {
      // call the parents method first to ensure its objects are serialized
          super.describeClassInfo(info);
           info.addClass(getClass().getName(),VERSION);      //.. add the class
➥definition
           info.addField("title",STRING_TYPE);            //.. add the instance
➥variables
          info.addField("closeable",BOOLEAN_TYPE);
          info.addField("resizable",BOOLEAN_TYPE);
          info.addField("buttons",OBJECT_ARRAY_TYPE);
     }
```

continues

Listing 9.16 Continued

```
    public void encode(Encoder encoder) throws CodingException {
        super.encode(encoder);
        Date d = new Date();
        title = (d.getHours()<12) ? "Day Shift" : "Night Shift";
        encoder.encodeString("title",title);     //.. encode instance
➥variables
        encoder.encodeBoolean("closeable",closeable);
        encoder.encodeBoolean("resizable",resizable);
        if (buttons!=null)           //.. encode buttons only if available
            encoder.encodeObjectArray("buttons",buttons,0,buttons.length);
    }

    public void decode(Decoder decoder) throws CodingException {
// call the parents method first to ensure its objects are serialized
super.decode(decoder);
     //.. get the version number
        int ver = decoder.versionForClassName(getClass().getName());
        title = (ver < 2) ? "Day Shift" : decoder.decodeString("title");
     //.. decode instance variables
        closeable  = decoder.decodeBoolean("closeable");
        resizable = decoder.decodeBoolean("resizable");
        //..  decode buttons, ignoring exceptions

        try {
            Object[] o = decoder.decodeObjectArray("buttons");
            buttons = new persistButton[o.length];
            for (int i=0;i<o.length;i++)
                buttons[i]=(persistButton)o[i];
        }
        catch (CodingException e) { }     }

    public void finishDecoding() throws CodingException {
        super.finishDecoding();
    }
}
```

persistNetGUI

Now that we have the data classes ready, let's take a look at the application that actually manipulates them. This is a GUI application, so we will need to extend the `Application` class and have an Event Queue, etc.

We begin with the usual import statements and class declaration, and define the `persistInternalWindow` object as data.

```
    import java.io.*;
    import java.net.*;
    import netscape.application.*;
    import netscape.util.*;
    public class persistNetGUI extends Application {
        protected persistInternalWindow data;
```

The `create()` method creates a `persistInternalWindow` with some test values. We create three buttons with a title and bitmap associated with each of them. They are arranged in a single column at a position 30 pixels to the right of the left margin. The `buttons` member of the `persistInternalWindow` is then set to this array.

```
/**
*     create()
*/
public void create() {
     data = new persistInternalWindow(50,50,300,200);
     data.setTitle("Day Shift");
     data.setCloseable(true);
     data.setResizable(true);
     String[] teams = { "Packers", "Cowboys", "Broncos" };
     persistButton[] buttons = new persistButton[teams.length];
    for (int i=0;i<teams.length;i++) {
         buttons[i] = new persistButton(30,30+i*45,100,40);
         buttons[i].setTitle(teams[i]);
         buttons[i].setImage(Bitmap.bitmapNamed(teams[i]+".gif"));
   }
data.setButtons(buttons);
}
```

Next, we define the `show()` method to create a place to associate the `rootView` to the `persistInternalWindow`. This is to ensure that no matter where the `InternalWindow` is created—either the `create()` method or from the deserialization stream—it will always have a `rootView` before it shows.

```
public void show() {
     if (data.rootView()!=mainRootView())
          mainRootView().addSubview(data);
     data.show();
}
```

The `save()` method uses the `HTTP/1.1 PUT` method to store data to a Web server.

NOTE The remote Web server must be properly configured to accept `PUT` requests.

The program starts by opening a socket connection to the hostname specified in the parameter and extracting the `InputStream` and `OutputStream`, which are used to create a corresponding `DataInputStream` and `DataOutputStream`.

```
     public void save(String hostname) throws CodingException, IOException {
          Socket sock = new Socket(hostname,80);
          DataInputStream  is = new DataInputStream(sock.getInputStream());
          DataOutputStream os = new
DataOutputStream(sock.getOutputStream());
```

Next, we ask the Archiver to `write()` the serialized object to a `ByteArrayOutputStream` object that holds the result.

```
    Archiver archiver = new Archiver(new Archive());
  archiver.archiveRootObject(data);
  ByteArrayOutputStream buf = new ByteArrayOutputStream();
  archiver.archive().write(buf);
```

NOTE There's no way of knowing beforehand how big the archive is going to be. The destination stream must accept any data written to it. If this poses a problem, you may subclass the `OutputStream` to handle splitting the data into manageable blocks.

Now that we have the serialized object stored in `buf`, we can determine its `size()` and send it over to the server. To do this we need to send the following `HTTP/1.1` stream, which includes `HTTP/1.1` headers such as `Content-type:` and `Content-length:`. Finally, as per the `HTTP/1.1` protocol, we end the `HTTP` header with a blank line and then send in the data.

```
          os.writeBytes("PUT /~foo/gui.dat HTTP/1.1\n");
          os.writeBytes("Hostname: foo.bar.comn");
          os.writeBytes("Content-type: application/octect-stream\n");
          os.writeBytes("Content-length: "+buf.size()+"\n");
          os.writeBytes("\n");
          buf.writeTo(os);
  }
```

The `load()` method connects to the hostname specified in the parameter, and the `InputStream` and `OutputStream` are extracted from the Socket and used to create a corresponding `DataInputStream` and `DataOutputStream`. We issue a `HTTP/1.0` GET command to fetch the `gui.dat` file from the remote server. The inputstream is then passed to the `Archive`, which reads the stream and initializes itself. This is then passed to the `Unarchiver` object, which creates the `persistInternalWindow` object. We then close the network connection.

```
      public void load(String hostname) throws IOException,
                    CodingException, DeserializationException
      {
            Socket sock = new Socket(hostname,80);
            DataInputStream  is = new DataInputStream();
            DataOutputStream os = new
  DataOutputStream(sock.getOutputStream());
            os.writeBytes("GET /~foo/gui.dat\n");
            Archive archive = new Archive();
            archive.read(is);
            int[] rootIds = archive.rootIdentifiers();
            Unarchiver unarchiver = new Unarchiver(archive);
            data =
  (persistInternalWindow)unarchiver.unarchiveIdentifier(rootIds[0]);
            sock.close();
      }
```

The `main()` method is implemented by first creating the `persistNetGUI` object and associating a newly created `ExternalWindow` with it.

```
        public static void main(String args[]) {
    persistNetGUI app = new persistNetGUI();
    ExternalWindow win = new ExternalWindow();
    app.setMainRootView(win.rootView());
```

The `create()` method then creates the `persistInternalWindow` and the associated `persistButton` objects. The objects are stored on the Web server at **www.foobar.com** using the `save()` method. We then recreate the `persistInternalWindow` from the same server by calling the `load()` method.

```
    app.create();
              //.. get data
              try {
                   app.save("www.foobar.com");
                   app.load("www.foobar.com");
              }
              catch (Exception e) {
                   e.printStackTrace(System.err);
              }
```

Notice that the `save()` and `load()` methods are enclosed in a try-catch block to catch any interceptions thrown by them. By this time, we should have a `persistInternalWindow` object after it has been recreated from the server. By calling its `show()` method, it should be visible on the screen. This happens only after the `win ExternalWindow` is shown. Before that, it's resized to a width of 400 pixels and a height of 300 pixels. Its title is also set.

```
              app.show();
    Size size = win.windowSizeForContentSize(400, 300);
    win.sizeTo(size.width, size.height);
    win.setTitle("persistNetGUI Example"); win.show();
```

Last but not least, the event processing for the `Application` is started by calling its `run()` method, which returns only when the program exits.

```
    app.run();
         }
    }
```

The entire `persistNetGUI` class is reproduced in Listing 9.17 for reference and the result is shown in Figure 9.3.

Listing 9.17 ***persistNetGUI.java: persistNetGUI* Application**

```
import java.io.*;
import java.net.*;
import netscape.application.*;
import netscape.util.*;
/**
 *
 */
public class persistNetGUI extends Application {
```

continues

Listing 9.17 Continued

```
protected persistInternalWindow data;
/**
 *     constructor
 */
public persistNetGUI() {
     data = new persistInternalWindow();
}
/**
 *     create()
 */
public void create() {
     data = new persistInternalWindow(50,50,300,200);
     data.setTitle("Day Shift");
     data.setCloseable(true);
     data.setResizable(true);

     String[] teams = { "Packers", "Cowboys", "Broncos" };
     persistButton[] buttons = new persistButton[teams.length];
     for (int i=0;i<teams.length;i++) {
          buttons[i] = new persistButton(30,30+i*45,100,40);
          buttons[i].setTitle(teams[i]);
          buttons[i].setImage(Bitmap.bitmapNamed(teams[i]+".gif"));
     }
     data.setButtons(buttons);
}
public void show() {
     if (data.rootView()!=mainRootView())
          mainRootView().addSubview(data);
     data.show();
}
/**
 *     save() test only on apache 1.2b6 (for illustration purposes)
 */
public void save(String hostname) throws CodingException, IOException {
     Socket sock = new Socket(hostname,80);
     DataInputStream  is = new DataInputStream(sock.getInputStream());
     DataOutputStream os = new DataOutputStream(sock.getOutputStream());
        Archiver archiver = new Archiver(new Archive());
     archiver.archiveRootObject(data);
     ByteArrayOutputStream buf = new ByteArrayOutputStream();
     archiver.archive().write(buf);
     os.writeBytes("PUT /~foo/gui.dat HTTP/1.1\n");
     os.writeBytes("Hostname: foo.bar.comn");
     os.writeBytes("Content-type: application/octect-stream\n");
     os.writeBytes("Content-length: "+buf.size()+"\n");
```

```
            os.writeBytes("\n");
            buf.writeTo(os);
}
      /**
       *     load()
       */
      public void load(String hostname) throws IOException,
                     CodingException, DeserializationException
      {
            Socket sock = new Socket(hostname,80);
            DataInputStream  is = new DataInputStream(sock.getInputStream());
            DataOutputStream os = new DataOutputStream(sock.getOutputStream());
            os.writeBytes("GET /~foo/gui.dat\n");
            Archive archive = new Archive();
            archive.read(is);
            int[] rootIds = archive.rootIdentifiers();
            Unarchiver unarchiver = new Unarchiver(archive);
            data =
(persistInternalWindow)unarchiver.unarchiveIdentifier(rootIds[0]);
            sock.close();
      }
      /**
       *     main()
       */
      public static void main(String args[]) {
persistNetGUI app = new persistNetGUI();
ExternalWindow win = new ExternalWindow();
app.setMainRootView(win.rootView());
app.create();
            //.. get data
            try {
                  app.load("www.foobar.com");
                  app.save("www.foobar.com");
            }
            catch (Exception e) {
                  e.printStackTrace(System.err);
            }
            app.show();
         Size size = win.windowSizeForContentSize(400, 300);
         win.sizeTo(size.width, size.height);
         win.setTitle("persistNetGUI Example"); win.show();
         app.run();
      }
}
```

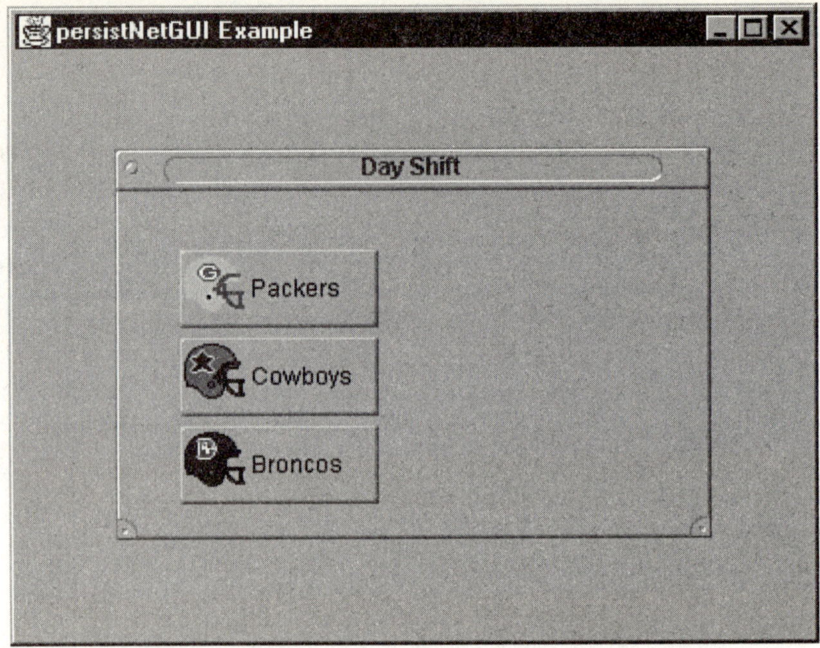

FIG. 9.3
Screen output of `persistNetGUI` example.

Archives and DataBases

The `Archive` object is a data structure, not a storage mechanism, meaning that it does not dictate how its contents are stored in a file or other storage medium. Because it's not a storage mechanism, an `Archive`'s data can be easily mapped to a relational database, binary data stream, or any other storage device. The `Archive` provides methods that write and read its data using the `AsciiSerializer` and `AsciiDeserializer`. The Archive's database-like structure, combined with the human-readable nature of `AsciiSerializer` output, makes hand-editing of serialized archives very easy. The `Archive` also provides a more compact binary storage format.

Security Issues

The IFC 1.0 persistent framework delegates most data-related functionality to the objects themselves and focuses mainly on the serialization/deserialization process itself. This means that the persistent classes themselves need to implement a security framework to ensure security.

Some issues of concern are:

- Access control

  In a multiuser environment, if the persistent object needs to be shared among different users, an access control mechanism needs to be implemented. This can be accomplished by maintaining access control lists (ACL) with each object.

  Java 1.1 provides a powerful framework for implementing access control to resources by managing principals and associated access permissions.

- Executable data

  The usual security manager restrictions apply to persistent data. If you were to store actual classes as data and then use the ClassLoader mechanism to run them at a later time, you would have implemented a "live" object mechanism. Extra precautions must be exercised when venturing into this dangerous territory. If you must do this, then ensure that the "live" persistent object is indeed the intended one by using a digital signature or other technique.

- Encrypted data

  There are various approaches to managing data that is secured using some form of encryption/decryption process. Popular techniques include PGP.

- Authentication

  Digital signatures, including X.509 certificates, ensure that the referenced object has been "signed" by the signature owner.

- Secure streams

  The most prevalent form for secure communication channels seems to be the Secure Socket Layer (SSL).

Enhancements

As this book goes to press, Netscape has stated the overall structure of the persistent framework will remain unchanged for the near future and that only minor changes have been planned.

Enhancements planned include such features as automatic encoding/decoding based on the reflection API of Java 1.1. Another enhancement under consideration is making the `ExternalCoder` class public. This is the API for encoding external objects, ones that do not implement the codable interface. ●

CHAPTER 10

Utilities

The reusablility of software components has become important in recent times, especially since the advent of object-oriented methodologies. Java, being object-oriented from the outset, has emphasized this notion by providing a feature-rich set of utilities, most of which are bundled together in the `java.util.*` package.

IFC enhances and complements these utilities with its own set of functions. This chapter gives the programmer a better feel for these functions and covers them in four broad categories.

GUI-based utilities

Commonly used GUI operations like file selection and message boxes can be carried out by using the Choosers and Alerts provided by IFC.

Timer-based

IFC provides a rich set of timer-based utility classes, including animation sequences.

Container classes

Containers, like `HashTable` and `Vector`, have been enhanced and made persistent.

Sorting

We look into the sorting routines provided by IFC.

GUI Utilities

The GUI-based utility functions of IFC, or ***helpers,*** are designed to help the programmer implement such functionality as managing message boxes, handling file selection from local disk, and so on.

Some of these utility functions that we cover are:

- `Alerts`

  Helps the programmer present messages to the user and accept limited responses
- `ColorChooser`

  Query box for the user to select a color (supports drag-and-drop)
- `FileChooser`

  Graphical selection to load and save files to local disk
- `FontChooser`

  Selection of a font based on various characteristics, such as name, size, and style

Alert

This class displays messages in a modal fashion and consists solely of *static* members. Here is a sample usage:

```
int result = Alert.runAlertExternally(Bitmap.bitmapNamed("Packers.gif"),
     "Packers", "Do you like the Packers ?", "Yes", "No", "Maybe");
```

The `Alert` blocks until the user has pressed a key and returns a result that reflects the button pressed. The values returned can take a value `Alert.DEFAULT_OPTION`, `Alert.SECOND_OPTION`, or `Alert.THIRD_OPTION`. An example Alert message is shown in Figure 10.1.

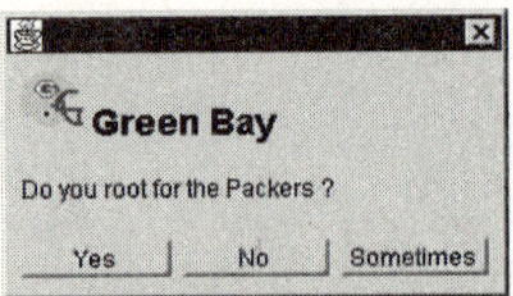

FIG. 10.1
Alert example.

The Alert title is shown in a bold font with the icon showing at the top left. The message consists of a single line and determines the width of the Alert window.

NOTE Keep the length of the Alert message short, typically 50 characters, or the Alert will appear too wide.

The Alert class definition is given in Listing 10.1.

Listing 10.1 ***Alert*** **Class**

```
public class Alert {
public final static int DEFAULT_OPTION;
public final static int SECOND_OPTION;
public final static int THIRD_OPTION;
public static Image notificationImage();
public static Image questionImage();
public static Image warningImage();
public static int runAlertExternally(String, String, String, String, String);
public static int runAlertExternally(Image, String, String, String, String,
String);
public static int runAlertInternally(String, String, String, String, String);
public static int runAlertInternally(Image, String, String, String, String,
String);
}
```


Alerts are shown using the `runAlert()` methods and can be shown either inside an `ExternalWindow` or an `InternalWindow`. Results are returned when the user clicks one of the selection buttons. The maximum number of selections offered is three, such as the *Yes, No,* and *Sometimes* buttons shown in Figure 10.1. Fewer buttons can be displayed by setting the remainder button parameters to `null`.

The class defines the `DEFAULT_OPTION`, `SECOND_OPTION`, and `THIRD_OPTION` values, which reflect the return values of the `runAlert()` methods.

The `Alert` class also provides a set of *standard* images to handle notification, question, and warning messages, via the `notificationImage()`, `questionImage()`, and `warningImage()` APIs. These may be used in the `Alert` as follows:

```
Alert.runAlertInternally(Alert.warningImage(), "Warning",
"Your Hard disk is running low on free space", "OK", null, null);
```

This brings up the warning dialog box shown in Figure 10.2.

FIG. 10.2
Warning alert.

Notice that Alerts running inside an `InternalWindow` show a striped title border. This has been internally set and may be changed by subclassing the Alert class to implement custom drawing methods.

ColorChooser

Giving the user a choice of color in an interactive and intuitive manner is important to most GUI-based applications. IFC provides the `ColorChooser` class to make this task easier.

The `ColorChooser` works by presenting the user with a standard dialog box that can be used to construct a 24-bit color. The box presents three Slider controls, which are used to control the Red, Green, and Blue components of the color and can take a value from 0 to 255.

The box also provides text fields that can be used to directly enter the RGB component values from the keyboard.

Let's study the ColorChooser API, as shown in Listing 10.2, more closely.

Listing 10.2 *ColorChooser* Class

```
public class ColorChooser implements Target, TextFieldOwner {
public ColorChooser();
public View contentView();
public void performCommand(String, Object);
public Color color();
public void setColor(Color);
public void textEditingDidBegin(TextField);
public void textEditingDidEnd(TextField, int, boolean);
public boolean textEditingWillEnd(TextField, int, boolean);
public void textWasModified(TextField);
public void show();
public void hide();
public void setWindow(Window);
public Window window();
}
```

The `ColorChooser` can be used in two ways:

- Inside a Window

  When the `ColorChooser` needs to have its own Window.

- `ColorChooser` as a View

  When the `ColorChooser` needs to be put directly into the view hierarchy.

***ColorChooser* Used Inside a Window** For use inside a Window (`InternalWindow` or `ExternalWindow`), use the `setWindow()` to set and `window()` to query the current Window associated with the `ColorChooser`.

The `show()` and `hide()` methods are used to show or hide the Window that contains it.

Here's an example that illustrates this usage:

```
ColorChooser clr = new ColorChooser();
     InternalWindow w = new InternalWindow();
clr.setWindow(w);
clr.show();
```

Notice that we aren't setting the size or any other attributes for our window. This is because the `ColorChooser` object directly set the size, title, and other characteristics of the Window.

NOTE To control the location of the `ColorChooser` window, specify it in the `InternalWindow` constructor. For example:

```
InternalWindow w = new InternalWindow(50,50,0,0);
```

The ColorChooser window is shown in Figure 10.3.

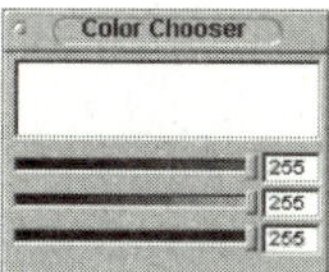

FIG. 10.3
ColorChooser.

***ColorChooser* Used as a View** When the view is being used directly, the `contentView()` method is used to *get* the internal view component. Here is an example illustrating this usage.

```
ColorChooser clr = new ColorChooser();
     mainRootView().addSubview(clr.contentView());
```

Here, we have directly added the `ColorChooser` to the `mainRootView` of the application.

The `ColorChooser` class also implements the `TextFieldOwner` interface for applications interested in events relating to the RGB `TextField` entries of the `ColorChooser`. Interested classes must subclass ColorChooser and implement appropriate routines to handle the various events.

Another feature of the `ColorChooser` class relates to the use of drag-and-drop. Notice that you can actually drag the current color from the `ColorChooser`. This can be dropped onto an Object that implements the standard `DragDestination` interface.

IFC provides one such class that accepts color objects dropped from the `ColorChooser` class. This is the `ColorWell` class and has been covered in Chapter 5, "Widgets."

FileChooser

The `FileChooser` class provides a convenient way to load and save files from the local disk. As most native platforms handle this operation, the `FileChooser` class calls the native method that opens a native window to handle this operation.

NOTE Due to the Applet security restrictions in the Java Virtual Machine, the FileChooser works only in standalone applications. ■

Listing 10.3 shows the usage of the `FileChooser` class.

Listing 10.3 Using *FileChooser*

```
FileChooser fc = new FileChooser(mainRootView(),
"Select Signature", FileChooser.LOAD_TYPE);
fc.showModally();
if (fc.file()!=null)
System.out.println("selected: "+ new String(fc.directory()+fc.file()));
```

The `FileChooser` object is constructed by passing the `rootView` in which to show the window. The constructor also accepts the title to display and a parameter specifying the operation being performed. It's shown using the `showModally()` method and does not return until a file is selected or the operation is cancelled. Results can be checked by calling the `directory()` and `file()` methods.

If the operation is cancelled, the `file()` and `directory()` methods return `null`.

On a Win32 platform, the above example would show the `FileSelect` dialog shown in Figure 10.4.

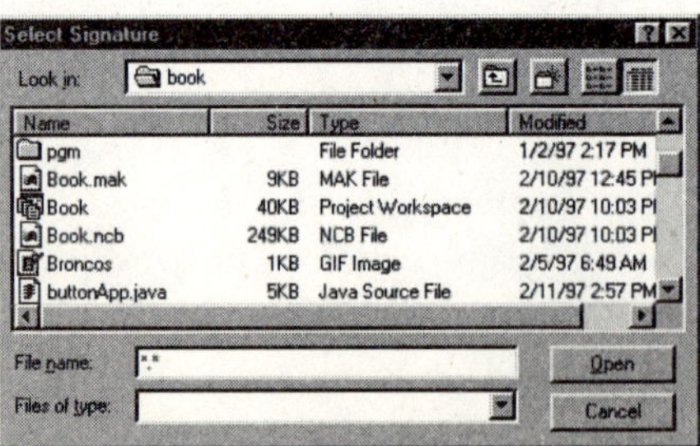

FIG. 10.4
Win32 FileChooser.

Let's examine the rest of the API. The class definition is shown in Listing 10.4.

Listing 10.4 *FileChooser*

```
public class FileChooser {
public final static int LOAD_TYPE;
public final static int SAVE_TYPE;
public FileChooser(RootView, String, int);
public String directory();
public String file();
public FilenameFilter filenameFilter();
public void setDirectory(String);
public void setFile(String);
public void setFilenameFilter(FilenameFilter);
public void setTitle(String);
public void showModally();
public String title();
public int type();
}
```


The `FileChooser` class also allows the programmer to set the `FilenameFilter`, which determines the kinds of files that will display in the `FileChooser` window when it is first displayed.

CAUTION

Due to a bug in the Win32 implementation of Java 1.0.2, the `FilenameFilter` feature does not work.

The `FilenameFilter` feature of `FileChooser` can be used by implementing a `FilenameFilter` class, such as the `InternetFilesFilter` class shown in the following code, which handles files with the extension *.java, *.html only, rejecting others. An instance of this class can be used with the `setFilenameFilter()` method of the `FileChooser` class to set this filter.

```
class InternetFilesFilter implements FilenameFilter {
     public boolean accept(File  dir, String  name) {
          return name.endsWith(".java") || name.endsWith(".html");
     }
}
```

FontChooser

The `FontChooser` class presents a convenient way for the user to select a font based on such characteristics as font name, size, and style.

Here is a simple example that illustrates how it is used.

```
FontChooser fc = new FontChooser();
     InternalWindow w = new InternalWindow();
     fc.setWindow(w);
     fc.show();
```

This displays the window shown in Figure 10.5.

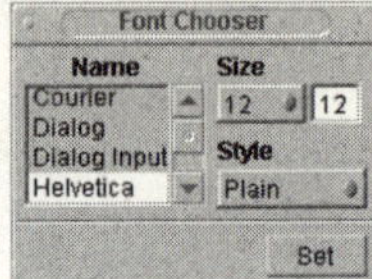

FIG. 10.5
FontChooser.

Using the `FontChooser` is quite similar to the `ColorChooser` class, covered earlier in the section "`ColorChooser`," in the sense that it can be used either inside a window, as shown in Figure 10.5, or by manipulating the View portion directly.

Listing 10.5 *FontChooser* Class

```
public class FontChooser implements Target {
     /* Constructors
      */
     public FontChooser();
     /* Methods
      */
     public View contentView();
     public Font font();
     public void hide();
     public void performCommand(String, Object);
     public void setFont(Font);
     public void setWindow(Window);
     public void show();
     public Window window();
}
```

When the user presses the Set button, an `ExtendedTarget.SET_FONT` command is put into the application event queue and thus is handled by the first target in the Target Chain that can perform the command.

Timers and Animation

Many programs require action to be taken on a time-based activity. This includes such applications as alarms, animation, and so on. To assist such applications, IFC provides the programmer with a set of useful tools:

- `Timer`

  Basic timer class with many configurable parameters

- `DrawingSequence`

  Foundation class for IFC animation

- `ImageSequence`

  A `DrawingSequence` subclass that specializes in handling Image Objects

Timer

Timers provide a convenient way to use timed events, either in a single occurrence or as a repetitive occurrence.

The underlying mechanism is based on the Event-Target model that is common to IFC. The `Timer` object sends events to the target along with a user-defined object.

The IFC `Timer` class enables you to specify a Target, either in the constructor or by the `setTarget()` API, and also the Object to send, using the `setData()` method.

An event queue may be specified in the alternate constructor, which causes events to be sent to that queue. Some parameters used with the Timer class are shown in Figure 10.6.

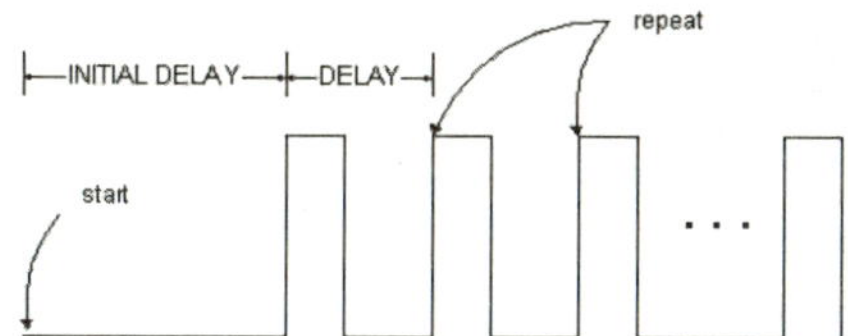

FIG. 10.6
`Timer` Parameters.

The following is a simple example showing usage of the `Timer` class.

```
public class timerApp extends Application implements Target {
          :
     timer = new Timer(this, "tick", 1000);
          timer.setCoalesce(true);
     timer.setInitialDelay(3000);
          :
public void performCommand(String command, Object arg) {
     if (command.equals("tick")) {
     :
```

The `timerApp` class creates a `Timer` object with the command "tick" and specifies itself as the target, along with a periodicity of 1,000 milliseconds. The `Timer` repeats by default, so the `Timer` object will send a "tick" command every second, which may be processed in the `performCommand()` method.

Let's methodically study the Timer class, which is shown in Listing 10.6.

Listing 10.6 *Timer* Class

```
public class Timer extends java.lang.Object implements EventProcessor,
EventFilter {
public Timer(EventLoop, Target, String, int);
public Timer(Target, String, int);
public EventLoop eventLoop();
public String command();
public void setCommand(String);
public Target target();
public void setTarget(Target);
public Object data();
public void setData(Object);
public int delay();
public void setDelay(int);
public boolean doesCoalesce();
public void setCoalesce(boolean);
public int initialDelay();
public void setInitialDelay(int);
public boolean repeats();
public void setRepeats(boolean);
public void start();
public void stop();
public boolean isRunning();
public long timeStamp();
public void processEvent(Event);
public Object filterEvents(Vector);
public String toString();
}
```

The constructors allow you to specify a target, command, periodicity, and, optionally, an alternate event queue that can be queried by the `eventLoop()` method.

The next few methods `get` and `set` `Timer` properties such as:

- command: The command sent to the Target
- target: The target to which commands are sent
- data: The object sent as the argument to the Target
- delay: The periodicity value
- coalescence: Whether multiple events should be coalesced together (for busy applications)
- initial delay: Timer starts after this
- repeatablity: Whether the timer should repeat at all

Methods relating to starting, stopping, and querying the state of the Timer are shown next. The `timeStamp()` returns the timestamp of the last event generated. This timestamp is the number of seconds since Jan. 1, 1970, that day also being called the ***epoch***.

The `processEvent()` method is the implementation of the `EventProcessor` interface and should not be called. Similarly, the `filterEvents()` method implements the `EventFilter` interface and should not be called.

Finally, as all good classes do, the `toString()` method is implemented.

DrawingSequence

The `DrawingSequence` class is the basis for Animation in IFC. It provides most of the functionality required to implement sophisticated animation.

The model underlying the `DrawingSequence` class is that of a finite sequence of frames that are animated in a particular order. To this effect, the class implements methods to set the number of frames, the animation direction, and the type and delay between frames, among other things.

NOTE The Aquarium example that comes with the IFC SDK makes excellent use of the `DrawingSequence` class.

The different kinds of playback modes include:

- Forward/Backward direction with and without looping
- Bounce or Oscillate modes

Because it is an abstract class, you must subclass it and support the abstract methods to use this class. Let's take a closer look at the class definition, as given in Listing 10.7.

Listing 10.7 *DrawingSequence* Class

```
public abstract class DrawingSequence extends Image implements Target, Codable {
public final static int BACKWARD;
public final static int BACKWARD_LOOP;
public final static int BOUNCE;
public final static int FORWARD;
public final static int FORWARD_LOOP;
public final static java.lang.String NEXT_FRAME;
public final static java.lang.String START;
public final static java.lang.String STOP;
public DrawingSequence();                           //.. constructors
public DrawingSequence(DrawingSequenceOwner);
public int currentFrameNumber();                      //.. status
public void setCurrentFrameNumber(int);
public boolean isAnimating();
public boolean nextFrame();
public boolean doesLoop();
public abstract int width();                           //.. abstract
public abstract int height();
```

continues

Listing 10.7 Continued

```
public abstract void drawAt(Graphics, int, int);
public void describeClassInfo(ClassInfo);              //.. persistence
public void encode(Encoder);
public void decode(Decoder);
public void finishDecoding();
public int playbackMode();                         //.. operating mode
public void setPlaybackMode(int);
public int frameCount();                          //.. total frames
public void setFrameCount(int);
public int frameRate();                          //.. periodicity
public void setFrameRate(int);
public String name();                              //.. name
public void setName(String);
public void setOwner(DrawingSequenceOwner);              //.. owner
public DrawingSequenceOwner owner();
public void performCommand(String, Object);              //.. internal
public boolean doesResetOnStart();                   //.. start/stop
public void setResetOnStart(boolean);
public boolean doesResetOnStop();
public void setResetOnStop(boolean);
public void reset();
public void start();
public void stop();
}
```

The class defines a number of useful static values, or *constants*, that are used by its methods. The constructor also accepts a `DrawingSequenceOwner` that is discussed later. Methods are available to check status-related values, abstract methods (discussed later), persistence support, operating mode, total frame, periodicity, name, owner, and start/stop operations.

A detailed discussion of each API can be found in the IFC reference documentation.

yelRectApp Example

Let's use some of these concepts in a simple example consisting of two classes: `yelRect`, a subclass of `DrawingSequence`, and `yelRectApp`, which is the main Application.

The `yelRect` class implements the abstract methods of `DrawingSequence`—`width()`, `height()`, and `drawAt()`—and accepts the width and height parameters in its constructor.

The `drawAt()` method, which is called for each frame of the animation, draws a yellow rectangle that grows from the top-left corner down to the bottom-right corner as the animation progresses. (See Listing 10.8.)

Listing 10.8 yelRectApp.java: *yelRectApp* Example

```
class yelRect extends DrawingSequence {
      protected int wd, ht;
      public yelRect(int wd, int ht) { this.wd=wd; this.ht=ht; }
      public int width()  { return wd; }
      public int height() { return ht; }
      public void drawAt(Graphics g, int x, int y) {
            g.setColor(Color.yellow);
            g.fillRect(0,0,currentFrameNumber()*(wd/frameCount()),
currentFrameNumber()*(ht/frameCount()));
      }
}

public class yelRectApp extends Application {
      protected yelRect panel;
      public void init() {
            super.init();
            panel = new yelRect(100,100);
            panel.setFrameRate(100);
            panel.setFrameCount(10);
            panel.setPlaybackMode(DrawingSequence.FORWARD_LOOP);
            Button btn = new Button(100,100,100,100);
            btn.setImage(panel);
            btn.setBuffered(true);
            mainRootView().addSubview(btn);
            panel.start();
      }

      public static void main(String[] args) {
      yelRectApp app = new yelRectApp();
      ExternalWindow win = new ExternalWindow();
      app.setMainRootView(win.rootView());
      Size size = win.windowSizeForContentSize(640, 480);
      win.sizeTo(size.width, size.height);
      win.show();
      app.run();
      }
}
```

The `yelRectApp` class creates a `yelRect` instance of size (100,100) and sets it with a frame rate of 100 milliseconds, a frame count of 10, and the playback mode set to a forward looping type.

This instance, which is an `Image` subclass, is added to a `Button` object, which is itself added to the view hierarchy, before starting the animation.

The `main()` routine starts the entire application.

When you run the application you will notice that the `drawAt()` method of `yelRect` gets called every 100 milliseconds and causes it to repaint the yellow rectangle.

A more complex application will implement a `DrawingSequenceOwner` interface and pass it to the `DrawingSequence` object in its constructor. The interface definition of the `DrawingSequenceOwner` is given below:

```
public interface DrawingSequenceOwner {
      public abstract void drawingSequenceCompleted(DrawingSequence);
      public abstract void drawingSequenceFrameChanged(DrawingSequence);
}
```

This will cause the `drawingSequenceFrameChanged()` method to be called whenever there is a frame change taking place. Thus, an application can get more control over how the animation is actually constructed.

ImageSequences

Using multiple image frames is one of the more common animation techniques. IFC provides a convenient way of doing this using the `ImageSequence` class, which provides a flexible way to handle image animations.

The `ImageSequence` class is a subclass of the `DrawingSequence` class and specializes in handling images. It's self-contained, doesn't need to be subclassed, and may be directly manipulated as a view.

The procedure for implementing image sequences in IFC is to create an `ImageSequence` Object, assign images to it, set parameters (such as frame rate, playback direction, and so on), and start the animation.

The `ImageSequence` class definition is shown in Listing 10.9.

Listing 10.9 *ImageSequence* Class

```
public class ImageSequence extends DrawingSequence {
public ImageSequence();                       //.. constructor
public ImageSequence(DrawingSequenceOwner);
public void addImage(Image);                      //.. addi images
public void addImagesFromName(String, int);
public void removeAllImages();                //.. remove images
public void removeImage(Image);
public Image currentImage();                      //.. query/access
public int imageCount();
public Vector images();
public void setCurrentImageNumber(int);
public void drawAt(Graphics, int, int);             //..drawing
public void drawScaled(Graphics, int, int, int, int);
public void describeClassInfo(ClassInfo);               //.. persistence
public void encode(Encoder);
public void decode(Decoder);
public int frameHeight();                      //.. image strip
public int frameWidth();
```

```
public Image imageStrip();
public void setImageStrip(Image);
public void setFrameHeight(int);
public void setFrameWidth(int);
public int width();                          //.. dimensions
public int height();
public Size maxSize();
}
```

Examining the class definition, notice that the methods can be broadly categorized to handle adding and deleting images from the sequence, querying and accessing images stored in the sequence, drawing methods that may be used in subclasses to do custom drawing, persistence functionality, image strip handling, and dimension-related methods.

Part III Ch 10

NOTE An image strip is a single image that consists of multiple animation frames.

A detailed discussion of each API can be found in the IFC reference documentation.

fishSequenceApp Example

Let's look at an example to test these concepts. The `fishSequenceApp` example animates a fish swimming inside a toggle button. The animation can be started and stopped by pressing the button. The animation screen appears in Figure 10.7. See also Listing 10.10.

FIG. 10.7
`fishSequenceApp` example screen.

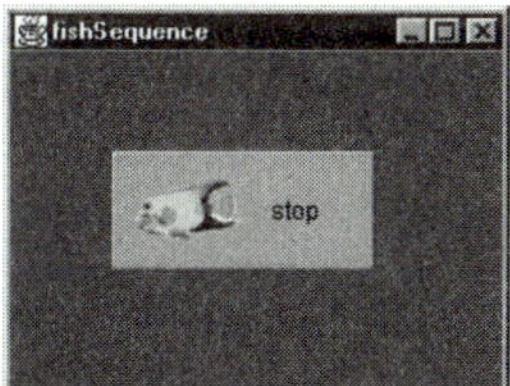

The step-by-step example is explained below:

1. We start by defining the `fishSequenceApp Application` class that implements the `Target` interface. This will be used to accept events generated by a Button.
2. We define an `ImageSequence` Object called *fish*, which uses an image strip from the file `fish.gif` and consists of five frames.
3. We set the `ImageSequence` to this strip and specify the frame width, rate, and playback mode.
4. Next, we construct a Toggle Button to hold this image on the left and some title text on the right. We set the command and target for the button and turn on the buffered drawing mode. We then add the button to the view hierarchy and start the animation.

Listing 10.10 *fishSequenceApp.java: ImageSequence* Example

```
public class fishSequenceApp extends Application implements Target {
      protected ImageSequence fish;
      protected Button btn;
      public void init() {
            super.init();

            //.. create a new image sequence
      fish = new ImageSequence();
      fish.setImageStrip(Bitmap.bitmapNamed("fish.gif"));
                  //.. set its image strip
            //.. set its frame count, width, rate, modefish.setFrameCount(5);
            fish.setFrameWidth(74);
            fish.setFrameRate(200);
            fish.setPlaybackMode(DrawingSequence.BOUNCE);

            //.. create a toggle button
            btn  = new Button(100,100,110,40); btn.setImage(fish);
            btn.setType(Button.TOGGLE_TYPE);
            btn.setImagePosition(Button.IMAGE_ON_LEFT);
            btn.setTitle("stop");
            btn.setAltTitle("start");
            btn.setTarget(this);
            btn.setCommand("cmdButton");
            btn.setBuffered(true);mainRootView().addSubview(btn);

            //.. start the sequence
            fish.start();
}

      public void performCommand(String command, Object arg) {
            //.. start/stop the sequence depending on the toggle button's state
            if (command.equals("cmdButton")) {
                  if (btn.state())
                        fish.stop();
                  else
                        fish.start();
            }
      }

      /**
       *      standard GUI application main() routine
       */
      public static void main(String[] args) {
      fishSequenceApp app = new fishSequenceApp();
      ExternalWindow win = new ExternalWindow();
            app.setMainRootView(win.rootView());
            Size size = win.windowSizeForContentSize(640, 480);
            win.sizeTo(size.width, size.height);
      win.show();
            app.run();
      }
}
```

When the user presses the "Stop" button, the animation stops and the title changes to "Start." These actions are handled in the `performCommand()` routine above.

The `main()` function actually starts this application.

Containers

IFC implements persistent versions of two very useful `Container` classes, `Hashtable` and `Vector`. These classes are implemented from the ground up and have been optimized for use in a non-threaded environment. Needless to say, they also work in a multithreaded application.

- `Hashtable`

  Container that holds (key, value) pairs
- `Vector`

  A dynamic array of objects

Hashtable

The `Hashtable` is an extremely useful persistent container class that is used to store (key, data) pairs. Data is queried and retrieved with the key used to store it. The key must implement the `hashcode()` and `equals()` methods. A hashtable grows and shrinks in fixed increments to accommodate data.

The `Hashtable` class definition is given in Listing 10.11.

Listing 10.11 *Hashtable* Class

```
public class Hashtable extends java.lang.Object implements Cloneable, Codable {
public Hashtable();                              //.. Constructors
public Hashtable(int);
public Object clone();
public void describeClassInfo(ClassInfo);             //.. Codable Interface
public void encode(Encoder);
public void decode(Decoder);
public void finishDecoding();
public Enumeration elements();                    //.. access elements
public Object[] elementsArray();
public Vector elementsVector();
public boolean contains(Object);                    //.. add, query data
public boolean containsKey(Object);
public Object get(Object);
public Object put(Object, Object);
public Enumeration keys();                          //.. retrieve keys
```

continues

Listing 10.11 Continued

```
public Object[] keysArray();
public Vector keysVector();
public void clear();                                    //.. delete
public Object remove(Object);
public boolean isEmpty();                               //.. quantity
public int count();
public int size();
public String toString();
}
```

Upon examining Listing 10.11, we see that the `Hashtable` class has methods to support the Codable interface, clone itself, access elements, add and query data, retrieve keys, delete one or all objects, check quantity and capacity values, and return a string representation of the hash table.

A simple example showing the use of Hashtable is shown in Listing 10.12.

Listing 10.12 *Hashtable* Example

```
public class Fruit {
public String name;
public String comment;
public Fruit(String n, String c) {
name=n; comment=c;
}
public String toString() {
             return (name + " " +comment);
}

     public static void main(String[] args) {
Hashtable basket = new Hashtable(10);

basket.put("apple", new Fruit("Apple", "Delicious red fruit"));
             basket.put("orange", new Fruit("Orange", "Florida has the best"));
        // Make a copy of it
             Hashtable trash = (Hashtable)basket.clone();
        // find houndDog in jukebox
             System.out.println("looking for apple: " + basket.get("apple"));
        System.out.println("removing it: " + basket.remove("apple"));
             System.out.println("looking for it again: " + basket.get("apple"));
        // find houndDog in oldies (should still be there)
             System.out.println("looking for apple in trash: "
+trash.get("apple"));
     }
}
```

Here we have implemented a class, called `Fruit`, that holds a name and description String. The main routine stores two instances of this class with the keys "apple" and "orange" in a hashtable called *basket*. We clone a copy to another hashtable called *trash*.

Next we delete the "apple" entry from the *basket* hashtable and query it again, and lastly, we check our *trash* hashtable for the "apple" entry.

As predicted, the following is the result:

```
looking for apple: Apple - Delicious red fruit
removing it: Apple - Delicious red fruit
looking for it again: null
looking for apple in trash: Apple - Delicious red fruit
```


Vector

The `Vector` class implements a dynamic array of objects that can grow or shrink as needed to accommodate data. Elements can be accessed using an integer index.

Storage management is optimized by growing and shrinking by a fixed increment size that can be specified.

The IFC `Vector` class provides the methods shown in Listing 10.13.

Listing 10.13 *Vector* Class

```
public class Vector implements Cloneable, Codable {
public Vector();
public Vector(int);
public void addElement(Object);               //.. adding
public void addElementIfAbsent(Object);
public void addElements(Vector);
public void addElementsIfAbsent(Vector);
public Object clone();                         //.. clone
public void copyInto(Object[]);               //.. output
public void describeClassInfo(ClassInfo);          //.. Codable interface
public void encode(Encoder);
public void decode(Decoder);
public void finishDecoding();
public boolean contains(Object);               //.. query
public boolean containsIdentical(Object);
public Object[] elementArray();
public Object elementAt(int);
public Enumeration elements();
public Enumeration elements(int);
public Object firstElement();
public Object lastElement();
public int indexOf(Object);
public int indexOf(Object, int);
public int indexOfIdentical(Object, int);
```

continues

Listing 10.13 Continued

```
public int indexOfIdentical(Object);
public int lastIndexOf(Object);
public int lastIndexOf(Object, int);
public int count();                              //.. capacity
public int capacity();
public void ensureCapacity(int);
public boolean isEmpty();
public int size();
public void trimToSize();
public boolean insertElementAfter(Object, Object);     //.. insert
public void insertElementAt(Object, int);
public boolean insertElementBefore(Object, Object);
public void removeAll(Object);                   //.. remove
public void removeAllElements();
public boolean removeElement(Object);
public Object removeElementAt(int);
public boolean removeElementIdentical(Object);
public Object removeFirstElement();
public Object removeLastElement();
public Object replaceElementAt(int, Object);           //.. replace
         public void setElementAt(Object, int);
public void sort(boolean);                        //.. sort
public void sortStrings(boolean, boolean);
public String toString();                        //.. toString
}
```

We see that methods of the `Vector` class can be broadly classified into the following categories: adding, cloning, output, persistence, query, capacity, insert, remove, replace, sort, and a `toString()` method. Details can be found in the IFC reference documentation.

This is a fundamental container class that has been covered in numerous books and documents, so we'll skip any examples of its usage.

Sorting

IFC implements the Quick Sort algorithm by C.A.R. Hoare and provides two static `Sort` functions.

```
public static void sort(Object array[], Object other[], int begin, int
count,
boolean ascending)
```

This accepts Comparable objects or String objects. The alternate function is:

```
public static void sortStrings(Object strings[], int begin, int count,
boolean ascending, boolean ignoreCase)
```

This accepts Strings and Comparable objects, and provides an additional case-sensitivity control parameter.

Here are the above methods in a simple example:

```
public class sortSample {
     public static void main(String args[]) {
          String[] data = {  "gamma", "alpha", "epsilon",  "omega", "beta",
"kappa"  ;
          System.out.println("Before Sort:");
          for (int i=0;i<data.length-1;i++)
               System.out.print(data[i]+", ");

          System.out.println(data[data.length-1]);     //.. last element w/o
','
          System.out.println("Sorting...");
          Sort.sortStrings(data,0,data.length,true,true);

          System.out.println("After Sort:");
          for (int i=0;i<data.length-1;i++)
               System.out.print(data[i]+", ");
          System.out.println(data[data.length-1]);
     }
}
```

The output is shown in Listing 10.14.

Listing 10.14 *sortSample* Output

```
Before Sort:
gamma, alpha, epsilon, omega, beta, kappa
Sorting...
After Sort:
alpha, beta, gamma, kappa, omega, epsilon
```

CAUTION

IFC 1.0 Bug: `Sort.sortStrings()` will throw a `null` pointer exception when doing a case-insensitive sort and the array contains a `null` element (even outside the range of the array being sorted). A workaround is to trim the array to exactly the number of non-null elements.

CHAPTER 11

Advanced Topics

Learn about the IFC application class

The main class for all IFC applications that controls and supports many application-level features.

Look into IFC compatibility with AWT

We learn to translate between AWT and IFC entities and embed AWT components inside IFC applications.

Learn to process HTML

The `TextView` class allows display of HTML documents along with handling of embedded hyperlinks.

Discover how IFC interfaces with JavaScript

We see how IFC programs can interact with Javascript objects on an HTML page inside a browser.

Learn about the Keyboard UI

IFC allows applications to be built that can be controlled entirely with the keyboard.

You have now come to the part of the book that deals with topics thus far not covered. Many of these topics should prove of interest to intermediate and advanced programmers. As has been the case in the rest of the book, concepts are illustrated by simple examples. ■

Application Class

The `Application` class represents the overall IFC-based Java application and is an essential part of any IFC program. Common services and features for the entire application are provided in the `Application` class. It also maintains application-wide state information and manages access to resources and services. Some of the important features and functions of the `Application` class are:

- Interface to the `Applet` instance
- Access to Clipboard
- Event processing
- Resources and services
- Keyboard UI

Listing 11.1 presents the code that defines the `Application` class, which includes the `Application` class methods (including those related to the preceding list of features and functions).

Listing 11.1 ***Application*** **Class**

```
public class netscape.application.Application extends java.lang.Object
    implements java.lang.Runnable,  netscape.application.EventProcessor
{
        /* Fields
         */
        public final static int BOTTOM_LEFT_POSITION;
        public final static int BOTTOM_RIGHT_POSITION;
        public final static int TOP_LEFT_POSITION;
        public final static int TOP_RIGHT_POSITION;

        /* Constructors
         */
        public Application();
        public Application(Applet);

        /* Methods
         */
        public static Application application();
          public static String clipboardText();
        public static String releaseName();
        public static void setClipboardText(String);

        public void addObserver(ApplicationObserver);
        public void appletStarted();
        public void appletStopped();
```

```
        public void chooseNextCurrentDocumentWindow(Window);
        public void cleanup();
        public java.net.URL codeBase();
        protected FoundationApplet createApplet();
        public Window currentDocumentWindow();
        public void didProcessEvent(Event);
        public EventLoop eventLoop();
        public Vector externalWindows();
        public void init();
        public boolean isApplet();
        public boolean isKeyboardUIEnabled();
        public boolean isPaused();
        public boolean isRunning();
        public void keyDown(KeyEvent);
        public void keyUp(KeyEvent);
        public Point keyboardArrowHotSpot(int);
        public Image keyboardArrowImage(int);
        public Point keyboardArrowLocation(View, int);
        public int keyboardArrowPosition(View);
        public RootView mainRootView();
        public void makeCurrentDocumentWindow(Window);
        public View modalView();
        public String parameterNamed(String);
        public void performCommandAndWait(Target, String, Object);
        public void performCommandLater(Target, String, Object, boolean);
        public void performCommandLater(Target, String, Object);
        public void processEvent(Event);
        public void removeObserver(ApplicationObserver);
        public Vector rootViews();
        public void run();
        public void setKeyboardUIEnabled(boolean);
        public void setMainRootView(RootView);
        public void stopRunning();
        public void willProcessEvent(Event);
}
```

The `Application` class provides a rich set of features, including the ability to control the application solely from the keyboard. The section "Keyboard UI," later in the chapter, looks into this specific feature.

The `addObserver()` method allows the application itself to send certain messages to the observer. The *observer* is an object that implements the `ApplicationObserver` interface.

The `ApplicationObserver` interface allows IFC applications to be monitored by an external IFC program by providing event notifications for important state changes. These include starting and stopping the IFC application.

Listing 11.2 presents the code that defines the `ApplicationObserver` interface.

Listing 11.2 *ApplicationObserver* Interface

```
public interface netscape.application.ApplicationObserver {
      /* Methods
       */
      public abstract void applicationDidPause(Application);
      public abstract void applicationDidResume(Application);
      public abstract void applicationDidStart(Application);
      public abstract void applicationDidStop(Application);
      public abstract void currentDocumentDidChange(Application, Window);
      public abstract void focusDidChange(Application, View);
}
```

You use this feature in the following `appObserverApp` example.

appObserverApp Example

The `appObserverApp` example demonstrates some methods of the `Application` class in use. Results of these method calls are displayed in the `TextView`, as shown in Figure 11.1.

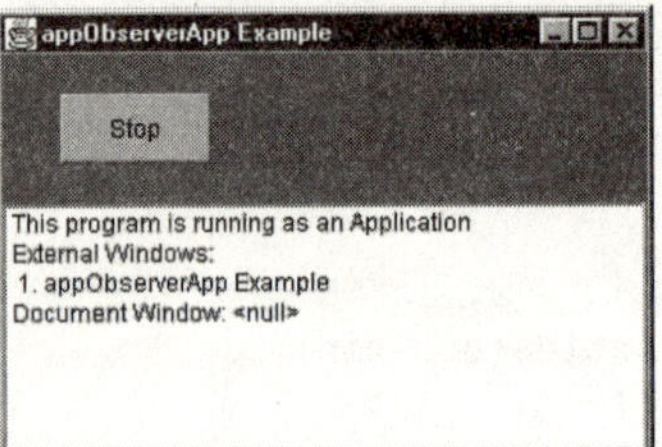

FIG. 11.1 `appObserverApp` example that illustrates the `ApplicationObserver` interface.

Clicking the Stop button generates a call to the `stopRunning()` method, which halts the application. Listing 11.3 presents the code for the `appObserverApp` example.

Listing 11.3 appObserverApp.java: *appObserverApp* Example

```
import netscape.application.*;
import netscape.util.*;

/**
 *      Example which shows some features of the Application class
 */
public class appObserverApp extends Application implements Target,
➥ApplicationObserver {

      public void init() {

      //.. add a button
      Button b;
      mainRootView().addSubview(b = new Button(30,20,75,35));
```

```
        b.setTitle("Stop");
        b.setCommand("cmdStop"); b.setTarget(this);

        //.. create a white ScrollGroup item
        ScrollGroup sg = new ScrollGroup(0,75,320,125);
        sg.setBackgroundColor(Color.white);

        //.. add it to the background
        mainRootView().addSubview(sg);

        //.. create a TextView item
        TextView tv=new TextView(sg.bounds());
        tv.setTransparent(true);
        tv.setEditable(false);

        //.. attach the TextView to the ScrollGroup
        sg.setContentView(tv);

             tv.appendString("This program is running as an
"+(isApplet()?"Applet":"Application")
                                     +"\n");
              //.. enumerate external windows
              Vector v = externalWindows();
              tv.appendString("External Windows:\n");
              for (int i=0;i<v.size();i++) {
                    tv.appendString(" "+(i+1)+".
"+((ExternalWindow)v.elementAt(i)).title()+"\n");
              }

            //.. display the document window, if any
            Window w = currentDocumentWindow();
            tv.appendString("Document Window:
            ➥"+((w==null)?"<null>":w.title())+"\n");
        }

       public void performCommand(String command, Object arg) {
            //.. if the button was pressed, stop the application
            if (command.equals("cmdStop")) {
                 stopRunning();
            }
       }

        public void applicationDidPause(Application a) { }
        public void applicationDidResume(Application a) { }
        public void currentDocumentDidChange(Application a, Window w) {     }
        public void focusDidChange(Application a, View v) { }

        //.. display message when the following events are received
        public void applicationDidStart(Application a) {
              System.out.println("applicationDidStart");
        }
        public void applicationDidStop(Application a) {
              System.out.println("applicationDidStop");
```

continues

Listing 11.3 Continued

```
    }

    /**
     *     standard GUI application main() routine
     */
     public static void main(String args[]) {

     appObserverApp app = new appObserverApp();
            ExternalWindow win = new ExternalWindow();
            app.setMainRootView(win.rootView());

            Size size = win.windowSizeForContentSize(320,200);
            win.sizeTo(size.width, size.height);
            win.setTitle("appObserverApp Example");
            win.show();

            app.addObserver(app);
            app.run();
            System.exit(1);
     }
}
```

The example illustrates various parameters, such as run state, list of external windows, and the current document window. Notice that the application implements the `ApplicationObserver` interface and that the observer is set explicitly using the `addObserver()` method in the `main()` routine. This allows the `applicationDidStart()` method to get called, which would not happen if the `addObserver()` method had been inside the `init()` method.

Compatibility with AWT

IFC enables you to interact with the underlying AWT system by means of the `AWTCompatibility` and `AWTComponentView` classes. These classes allow you to translate values and use AWT components inside IFC, respectively.

Besides these classes, IFC also provides the `FoundationApplet` and `FoundationPanel` classes, which map directly to the underlying `java.applet.Applet` and `java.awt.Panel` classes, respectively. Most IFC programs would not use these classes directly.

AWTCompatibility Class

IFC is built on top of AWT, and even though it hides most AWT operations from the IFC programmer, situations might arise in which IFC applications need to access AWT objects.

The `AWTCompatibility` class takes care of these potential situations by providing a number of static methods for conversion and access of various objects between the AWT and IFC systems. Listing 11.4 presents the code that defines the `AWTCompatibility` class.

Listing 11.4 ***AWTCompatibility* Class**

```
public class netscape.application.AWTCompatibility extends java.lang.Object {
      /* Methods
       */
      public static java.applet.Applet awtApplet();
      public static java.applet.AudioClip awtAudioClipForSound(Sound);
      public static java.awt.Color awtColorForColor(Color);
      public static java.awt.FileDialog
      ➥awtFileDialogForFileChooser(FileChooser);
      public static java.awt.Font awtFontForFont(Font);
      public static java.awt.FontMetrics
      ➥awtFontMetricsForFontMetrics(FontMetrics);
      public static java.awt.Frame awtFrameForRootView(RootView);
      public static java.awt.Graphics awtGraphicsForGraphics(Graphics);
      public static java.awt.Image awtImageForBitmap(Bitmap);
      public static java.awt.image.ImageProducer
      ➥awtImageProducerForBitmap(Bitmap);
      public static java.awt.MenuBar awtMenuBarForMenu(Menu);
      public static java.awt.Menu awtMenuForMenu(Menu);
      public static java.awt.MenuItem awtMenuItemForMenuItem(MenuItem);
      public static java.awt.Panel awtPanelForRootView(RootView);
      public static java.awt.Toolkit awtToolkit();
      public static java.awt.Window awtWindowForExternalWindow(ExternalWindow);
      public static Bitmap bitmapForAWTImage(Image);
      public static Bitmap bitmapForAWTImageProducer(ImageProducer);
      public static Color colorForAWTColor(Color);
      public static Font fontForAWTFont(Font);
      public static FontMetrics fontMetricsForAWTFontMetrics(FontMetrics);
      public static Graphics graphicsForAWTGraphics(Graphics);
      public static Sound soundForAWTAudioClip(AudioClip);
}
```


Most of the methods shown in Listing 11.4 have self-explanatory names. You can find details in the reference.

AWTComponentView Class

Being the *de facto* standard for Java user interfaces, AWT has had the support of the Java community from its inception. Consequently, a large number of components have been built using the AWT framework. IFC allows you to use these AWT components inside an IFC application by way of the `AWTComponentView` class. Listing 11.5 presents the definition of the `AWTComponentView` class.

Listing 11.5 *AWTComponentView* Class

```
public class AWTComponentView extends netscape.application.View {

      /* Constructors
       */
      public AWTComponentView();
      public AWTComponentView(Rect);
      public AWTComponentView(int, int, int, int);

      /* Methods
       */
      protected void ancestorWasAddedToViewHierarchy(View);
      protected void ancestorWillRemoveFromViewHierarchy(View);
      public java.awt.Component awtComponent();
      public void setAWTComponent(Component);
}
```

AWT components may be used inside an IFC application by containing them inside an `AWTComponentView` object. Note that the AWT component will not be clipped by other IFC views, causing the AWT component to always be drawn over all IFC views. IFC ignores all AWT events; the base AWT system handles them directly. The following `ifcAWTApp` example illustrates this point.

ifcAWTApp Example

The `ifcAWTApp` example shows you how to embed AWT components in an IFC application and illustrates the visual interaction between the two types of components. The example places the AWT button alongside an IFC button, as shown in Figure 11.2. It also displays an Internal Window below the buttons.

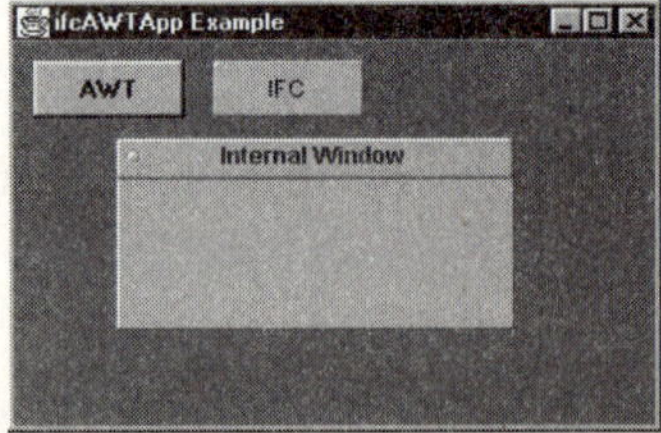

FIG. 11.2
`ifcAWTApp` example shows embedding AWT components inside an IFC application.

Moving the window over the AWT component shows the interaction between IFC and AWT components. The AWT button always displays on top and does not get clipped by the Internal Window, even if you set the layer to `POPUP_LAYER` (which is the topmost layer allowed for an internal window). Listing 11.6 presents the code for the `ifcAWTApp` example.

Listing 11.6 ifcAWTApp.java: *ifcAWTApp* Example

```
import netscape.application.*;

/**
 * Application which displays AWT and IFC together
 */
public class ifcAWTApp extends Application {

      public void init() {

            //.. all AWT components must be held in an AWTComponentView
            AWTComponentView c = new AWTComponentView(10,10,75,30);

            //.. add an AWT button to it
            c.setAWTComponent(new java.awt.Button("AWT"));

            //.. attach it to the background
            mainRootView().addSubview(c);

            //.. create and attach an IFC Button
            Button b = new Button(100,10,75,30); b.setTitle("IFC");
            mainRootView().addSubview(b);

            //.. create and display an IFC Internal Window
            InternalWindow w = new InternalWindow(50,50,200,100);
            w.setTitle("Internal Window"); w.setCloseable(true);
            w.show();
      }


      /**
       *     standard GUI application main() routine
       */
      public static void main(String args[]) {

            ifcAWTApp app = new ifcAWTApp();
            ExternalWindow win = new ExternalWindow();
            app.setMainRootView(win.rootView());

            Size size = win.windowSizeForContentSize(320,200);
            win.sizeTo(size.width, size.height);
            win.setTitle("ifcAWTApp Example");
            win.show();

            app.run();
      }
}
```

Processing HTML

The `TextView` component provides the powerful capability to display HTML documents and handle links embedded within them. Presently, `TextView` supports most of the HTML 1.0 standard and provides a framework to support additional tags. The list of supported HTML tags can be found in the IFC documentation. Parsing rules for some HTML tags may also be changed by using the `TextView.setHTMLParsingRules()` method along with the `HTMLParsingRules` class.

HTML documents are loaded into the `TextView` by using the `importHTMLInRange()` and `importHTMLFromURLString()` methods, which accept HTML data from an `InputStream` and an URL, respectively. For your reference, Listing 11.7 presents methods in `TextView` that are related to HTML processing.

Listing 11.7 HTML-Related Methods in *TextView*

```
public java.net.URL baseURL();
public String formElementText();
public HTMLParsingRules htmlParsingRules();
public void importHTMLFromURLString(String);
public void importHTMLInRange(InputStream, Range, URL);
public void importHTMLInRange(InputStream, Range, URL, Hashtable);
public void insertHTMLElementsInRange(Vector, Range, Hashtable);
public Range runWithLinkDestinationNamed(String);
public void setHTMLParsingRules(HTMLParsingRules);
```

After the HTML document loads, the `TextView` treats its data as multi-font data and you can use the appropriate methods to manipulate individual elements and ranges.

The `TextViewOwner` interface handles links by providing the `linkWasSelected()` method. When the user clicks an HTML link within a `TextView`, the `linkWasSelected()` method is called and passed the `TextView` object, the range of the link in the `TextView` object, and URL of the link. We use this mechanism to implement a mini-HTML browser in the following `htmlBrowseApp` example.

htmlBrowseApp Example

The `htmlBrowseApp` example loads an HTML file from the current directory and displays it in a `TextView` object. The HTML document contains some basic HTML tags and an embedded image. It also contains a hyperlink that points to another file in the same directory. The user can click the link to jump to this other HTML page. Figure 11.3 shows the end product of the `htmlBrowseApp` example.

FIG. 11.3
`htmlBrowseApp` example implements a mini HTML browser.

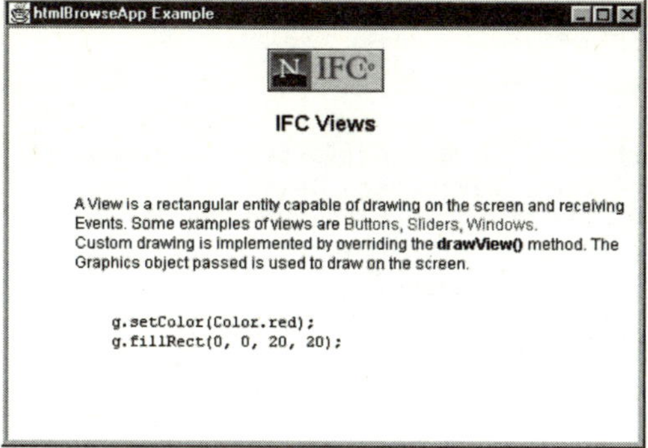

The example displays the document shown in Figure 11.3 by loading, first, the `index.html` file, and then, when the user clicks the hyperlink, the `views.html` file. Listing 11.8 presents the code for the `htmlBrowseApp` example.

Listing 11.8 htmlBrowseApp.java: *htmlBrowseApp* Example

```
import netscape.application.*;

/**
 *     A simple application which loads an HTML 1.0 page displays it
 *     page contains some HTML tags, an image, and a hyperlink that
 *     loads and displays another page
 */
public class htmlBrowseApp extends Application implements TextViewOwner {

      public void init() {

            //.. create a white ScrollGroup item
            ScrollGroup sg = new ScrollGroup(mainRootView().bounds());
            sg.setBackgroundColor(Color.white);

            //.. create a TextView item
            TextView tv=new TextView(sg.bounds());
            tv.setOwner(this);
            tv.setTransparent(true);
            tv.setEditable(false);

            //..read in the index.html from the base directory
            tv.importHTMLFromURLString(codeBase()+"index.html");

            //.. attach the TextView to the ScrollGroup
            sg.setContentView(tv);

            //.. add it to the background
            mainRootView().addSubview(sg);
      }

      /**
```

continues

Listing 11.8 Continued

```
     *     TextViewOwner Methods
     */
    public void attributesDidChange(TextView t, Range r)            { }
    public void attributesWillChange(TextView t, Range r)       { }
    public void selectionDidChange(TextView t)                  { }
    public void textDidChange(TextView t, Range r)              { }
    public void textEditingDidBegin(TextView t)                   { }
    public void textEditingDidEnd(TextView t)                   { }
    public void textWillChange(TextView t, Range r)             { }

    //.. gets called when the user clicks an HTML 'anchor' link
    public void linkWasSelected(TextView t, Range r, String url) {
          //.. load and display the requested URL
          t.importHTMLFromURLString(codeBase()+url);
    }

    /**
     *     standard GUI application main() routine
     */
    public static void main(String args[]) {

          htmlBrowseApp app = new htmlBrowseApp();
          ExternalWindow win = new ExternalWindow();
          app.setMainRootView(win.rootView());

          Size size = win.windowSizeForContentSize(480,320);
          win.sizeTo(size.width, size.height);
          win.setTitle("htmlBrowseApp Example");
          win.show();

          app.run();
    }
}
```

The `htmlBrowseApp` example implements the `TextViewOwner` interface and handles link activation in the `linkWasSelected()` method, as shown in Listing 11.8. The `init()` method places a `TextView` object inside a `ScrollGroup` object and loads the `index.html` document. When the user clicks a hyperlink, the `htmlBrowseApp` loads the `TextView` object with the document pointed to by the clicked URL.

Interfacing to JavaScript

JavaScript is a high-level scripting language originally implemented as a scripting companion for HTML. It has gained popularity for its ease of use and power when combined with HTML and, more recently, in style sheets and dynamic HTML.

Allowing Java applets to talk to JavaScript objects on an HTML page adds useful capabilities to a browser document. To this end, Netscape offers classes to interact with JavaScript as part of its LiveWire Pro SDK.

The main JavaScript interface class is `JSObject`, the definition of which is given in Listing 11.9.

Listing 11.9 ***netscape.javascript.JSObject*** **Class**

```
public class netscape.javascript.JSObject {
       call(String, Object[]);
       eval(String);
       finalize();
       getMember(String);
       getSlot(int);
       getWindow(Applet);
       removeMember(String);
       setMember(String, Object);
       setSlot(int, Object);
       toString();
}
```


`JSObject` allows Java to manipulate objects that are defined in JavaScript. Values passed from Java to JavaScript are converted as follows:

- `JSObject` is converted to the original JavaScript object.
- Any other Java object is converted to a JavaScript wrapper, which can be used to access methods and fields of the Java object.
- Java arrays are wrapped with a JavaScript object that understands `array.length` and `array[index]`.
- A Java Boolean is converted to a JavaScript Boolean.
- Java `byte`, `char`, `short`, `int`, `long`, `float`, and `double` are converted to JavaScript numbers.

Values passed from JavaScript to Java are converted as follows:

- Objects that are wrappers around Java objects are unwrapped.
- Other objects are wrapped with a `JSObject`.
- Strings, numbers, and Booleans are converted to `String`, `Float`, and `Boolean` objects, respectively.

This means that all JavaScript values show up as some kind of `java.lang.Object` in Java. Before you can make much use of them, you must cast them to the appropriate subclass. The next section looks into doing just that, in the `jscriptApp` example.

jscriptApp Example

The `jscriptApp` example demonstrates communication between a Java applet and a JavaScript object on the same HTML page in a JavaScript-enabled browser. The example HTML document contains both a Java applet and a JavaScript-enabled form that contains a text input field. Figure 11.4 shows the way the document appears when it displays.

FIG. 11.4
`jscriptApp` example shows interfacing IFC with Javascript.

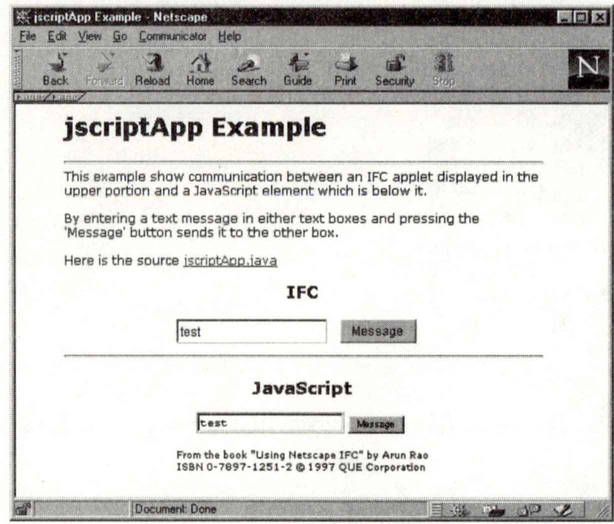

To see communication between the two text fields, enter any text in either text field and press the associated *message* button. Notice that the text transfers over to the other text field. Listing 11.10 presents the program code for the `jscriptApp` example.

CAUTION

Due to differences in implementation of Javascript, this example might not work under Internet Explorer.

Listing 11.10 jscriptApp.java: *jscriptApp* Example

```
import netscape.application.*;
import netscape.javascript.*;

/**
 *     Example which shows communication between a Java applet
 *     and a Javascript object
 */
public class jscriptApp extends Application implements Target {
```

```
        JSObject message;       //.. our javascript objects
        TextField text;

        public void init() {
              super.init();

              //.. white applet background
              mainRootView().setColor(Color.white);

              //.. add a TextField
              text = new TextField(2,4,150,24);
              mainRootView().addSubview(text);

              //.. add a Button which would send the TextField's contents
              //      to the javascript object
              Button b = new Button(165,4,75,24);
              b.setTitle("Message"); b.setCommand("cmdSend"); b.setTarget(this);
              mainRootView().addSubview(b);

              //.. get the JSObject 'handle' for the 'message' text field
              JSObject jso = JSObject.getWindow(AWTCompatibility.awtApplet());
              jso = (JSObject)jso.getMember("document");
              jso = (JSObject)jso.getMember("form");
              message = (JSObject)jso.getMember("message");
      }

       //.. public method called by the javascript object
       public void setValue(String value) {
              text.setStringValue(value);
       }

      //.. Target interface
      public void performCommand(String command, Object arg) {
           //.. if button with "cmdSend" ws pressed
           if (command.equals("cmdSend")) {
                //.. assign value to javascript text field
                try {
                     message.eval("message.value=\""+text.stringValue()+"\"");
                }
                catch(Exception e) {
                     Alert.runAlertExternally("JavaScript Exception",
                           e.getMessage(),"OK",null,null);
                }
           }
      }
}
```

The pure applet example places a `TextField` object and a `Button` object on the background after setting its color to white. It then stores the JSObject reference of the *message* member of the Javascript-enabled HTML page. When the user clicks the button, the contents of the textfield are sent over to the saved JSObject reference.

The public `setValue()` method allows JavaScript to set the value of the `TextField` object.

Keyboard UI

IFC 1.1 introduces a new feature that enables you to control applications from just the keyboard. This feature is useful in designing data entry applications such as cash registers.

The user accesses on-screen components by using the Tab and Shift-Tab keys for forward and backward motion. The user moves among these components in the direction in which they were laid out.

A green arrow at the top-left corner of the view denotes the current focus. You can change both the bitmap and the position by subclassing the `Application` class and overriding the `keyboardArrowImage()` and `keyboardArrowPosition()` methods.

By default, all IFC applications have the keyboard UI enabled. You can control whether the keyboard UI is enabled, however, by using the `setKeyboardUIEnabled()` method.

The `kbdUIApp` example, discussed next, takes a closer look at the keyboard UI in IFC.

kbdUIApp Example

The `kbdUIApp` example shows some of the capabilities of the keyboard user interface in IFC 1.1. The example places three controls and lets you change focus between them by pressing the Tab and Shift-Tab keys, as shown in Figure 11.5.

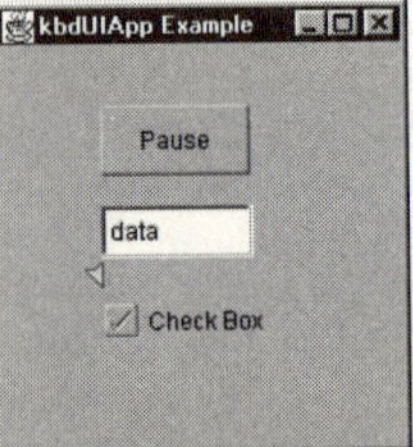

FIG. 11.5
`kbdUIApp` example uses the keyboard to control an IFC application.

Pressing the spacebar when the focus is on the check box causes the event mechanism to send the associated command to the check box. Listing 11.11 presents the code for the `kbdUIApp` example.

Listing 11.11 kbdUIApp.java: *kbdUIApp* Example

```
import netscape.application.*;

/**
 *     Example which shows the Keyboard feature of IFC
```

```
 */
public class kbdUIApp extends Application {

      public void init() {

            mainRootView().setColor(Color.lightGray);

            //.. place a button
           Button b;
            mainRootView().addSubview(b = new Button(50,30,75,35));
            b.setTitle("Button");

            //.. place a text field
            TextField t;
            mainRootView().addSubview(t = new TextField(50,80,75,25));

            //.. place a checkbox
            mainRootView().addSubview(b =
Button.createCheckButton(50,120,90,35));
            b.setTitle(" Check Box");
            //.. cause the spacebar key to send button a command
            b.setCommandForKey(Button.SEND_COMMAND,' ',View.WHEN_SELECTED);
      }

      /**
      *     standard GUI application main() routine
      */
      public static void main(String args[]) {

            kbdUIApp app = new kbdUIApp();
            ExternalWindow win = new ExternalWindow();
            app.setMainRootView(win.rootView());

            Size size = win.windowSizeForContentSize(200,200);
            win.sizeTo(size.width, size.height);
            win.setTitle("kbdUIApp Example");
            win.show();

            app.run();
      }
}
```

Note the `setCommandForKey()` method, which binds the spacebar with the check button. Therefore, pressing the spacebar causes the check button to toggle. ●

CHAPTER 12

IFC Tools and Applications

Many software vendors have embraced IFC and are providing applications and developer toolkits based on it. These range from developer toolkits and libraries to full-blown applications. Future releases of IFC will support the JavaBeans framework, increasing support manyfold.

Netscape has also released a development tool called Constructor, an advance prototype and build tool for rapid IFC application development.

Look at some IFC Toolkits

Explore some the popular third-party developer toolkits available for use with IFC.

Learn about Netscape Constructor

A unique IFC application tool that builds, tests, and saves IFC projects.

See sample IFC Applications

Look at some IFC-based products from leading vendors.

Developer Toolkits

Tool vendors have been quick to provide support to IFC by porting their existing toolkits and developer products to the IFC platform and also creating new ones. Many compiler manufacturers now bundle IFC libraries along with their products and include guidelines on using them. A number of vendors provide libraries of user interface components to aid in rapid application development.

MicroLine Toolkit

Company: Neuron Data, Inc.

http://www.neurondata.com/

The MicroLine View Toolkit (MVT) provides a powerful set of user-interface objects for IFC. The toolkit extends classes contained in IFC to implement many useful widgets.

Some of these powerful components are:

***MlGridView* Component** The `GridView` provides an editable grid displaying text or images in cells and is useful for creating high-performance tables, forms, and multi-column lists. From colors and fonts on a row, column, or cell basis to individual borders on the top, bottom, left, and right of cells, the `GridView` allows you to fine-tune your display to present an optimal interface. Some capabilities of the `MlGridView` component are shown in Figure 12.1.

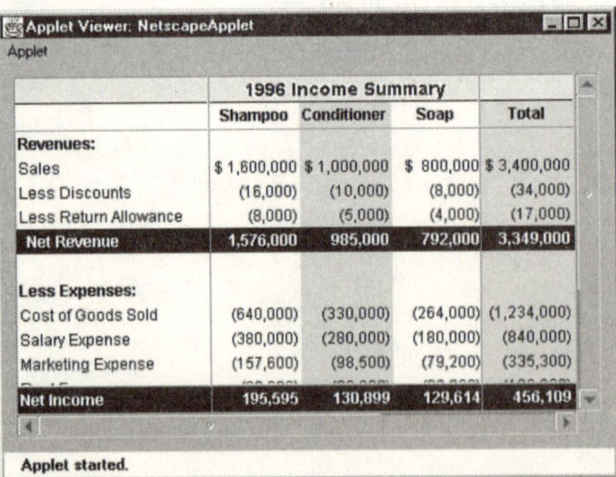

	1996 Income Summary			
	Shampoo	Conditioner	Soap	Total
Revenues:				
Sales	$ 1,600,000	$ 1,000,000	$ 800,000	$ 3,400,000
Less Discounts	(16,000)	(10,000)	(8,000)	(34,000)
Less Return Allowance	(8,000)	(5,000)	(4,000)	(17,000)
Net Revenue	1,576,000	985,000	792,000	3,349,000
Less Expenses:				
Cost of Goods Sold	(640,000)	(330,000)	(264,000)	(1,234,000)
Salary Expense	(380,000)	(280,000)	(180,000)	(840,000)
Marketing Expense	(157,600)	(98,500)	(79,200)	(335,300)
Net Income	195,595	130,899	129,614	456,109

FIG. 12.1 Sample table created using the `MlGridView` component.

Setting and getting values for rows, columns, and cells is accomplished by using a single resource mechanism shared by all views in the toolkit. The `GridView` allows a user to traverse and edit cells and can traverse across the grid with the arrow and page keys.

***MlTreeView* Component** The `TreeView` provides a hierarchical list supporting multiple columns, fixed rows and columns on any side, a number of selection policies, and intuitive expansion and collapse of nodes. Figure 12.2 displays a sample `MlTreeView` component. You have pinpoint control over the `TreeView`'s appearance through resources that allow you to set fonts, colors, borders, margins, and spacing on a row, column, or cell basis.

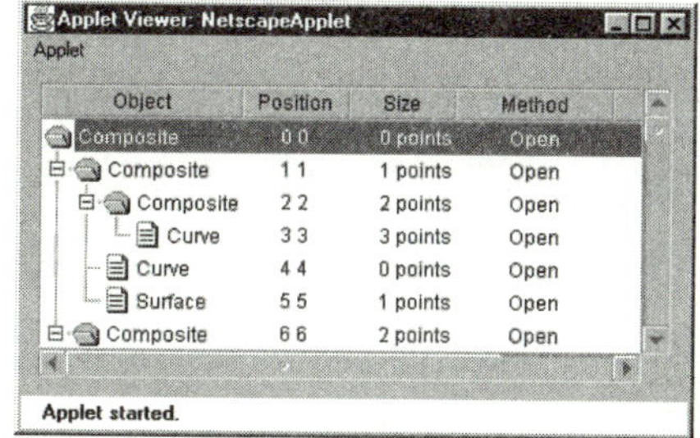

FIG. 12.2 A tree and table combo created using the `MlTreeView` component.

For those who require the display of large amounts of hierarchical data, the `TreeView` provides an interface that allows dynamic addition and removal of nodes.

***MlTabView* Component** The `TabView` displays an interface with single or multiple rows of tabs along its top, bottom, left, or right, and a page area managed by its tabs in the center. The `TabView` can flip views placed in the page area as tabs are selected, or a single view may be added to the `TabView` and its contents may be changed as tabs are selected. A sample `MlTabView` component is shown in Figure 12.3.

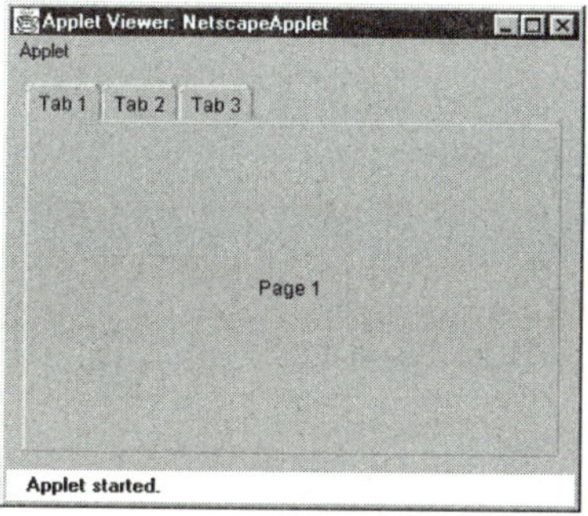

FIG. 12.3 `MlTabView` component used to create a Tabbed folder.

The interface presented can be fine-tuned through resources that control spacing, margins, dimensions, colors, and fonts for the `TabView` as a whole or for individual tabs.

***MlProgressView* Component** The `Progress` view displays a progress bar showing a level of process completion as shown in Figure 12.4. Features include choice of meter styles, full control over bar colors, fonts, shadows, and an optional percentage complete" indicator.

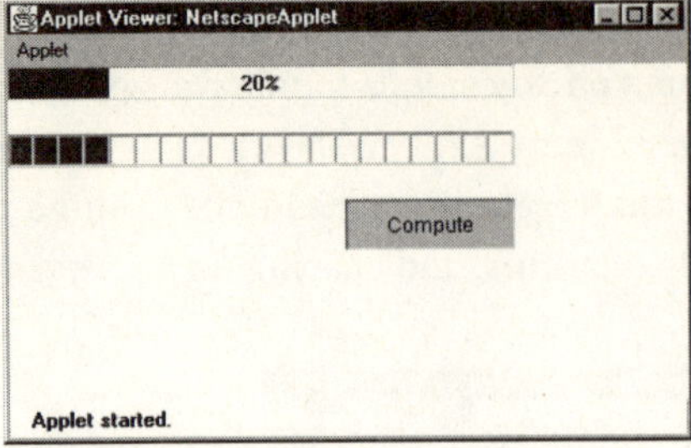

FIG. 12.4 Two types of progress bars using the `MlProgressView` component.

The Progress view also supports the display of elapsed and estimated time to completion.

Indius Components

Company: Indius, Inc.

http://www.indius.com/

The Indius Java component packages are based on, and extend the capabilities of, IFC to provide a variety of high-quality visual components. The APIs promote the use of a programming style very much in keeping with IFC itself. The underlying design philosophy has been to maintain a clean separation between the data models and the views wherever possible.

The library includes the following packages:

Base Package The Indius BASE package (`indius.base`) is a Java class library that augments the capabilities found in Netscape IFC library. It contains a number of useful utility classes and view classes, including the Tab component shown in Figure 12.5. Some other components provided include Border and Splitter views.

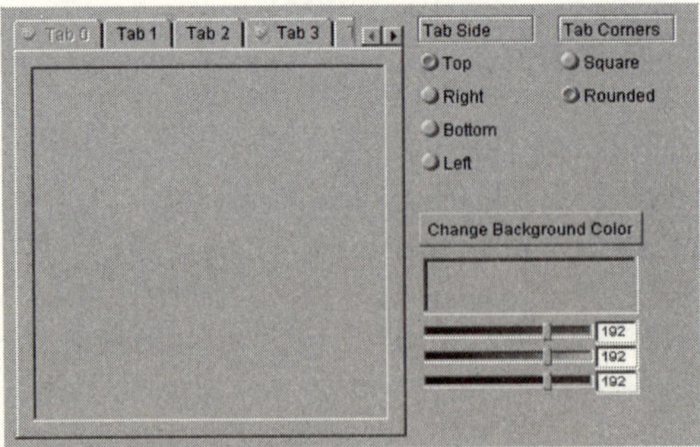

FIG. 12.5 Tab component with associated control features.

This package also provides the necessary support for some of the higher-level Indius packages (e.g., GRID, TREE, EXPLORER, CALENDAR, etc.).

Grid Package The Indius GRID package (`indius.grid`) is a Java class library that provides a family of grid views, featuring a variety of drawing, interaction, selection, and editing policies. A sample grid view is shown in Figure 12.6. The views are driven by a conceptually simple grid data model interface (IGrid).

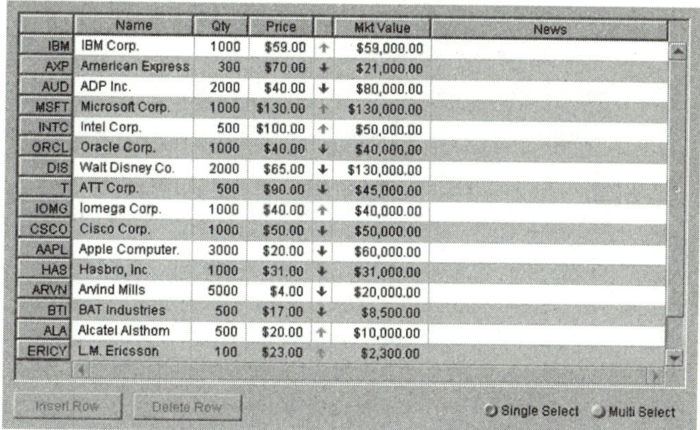

	Name	Qty	Price		Mkt Value	News
IBM	IBM Corp.	1000	$59.00	↑	$59,000.00	
AXP	American Express	300	$70.00	↓	$21,000.00	
AUD	ADP Inc.	2000	$40.00	↓	$80,000.00	
MSFT	Microsoft Corp.	1000	$130.00	↑	$130,000.00	
INTC	Intel Corp.	500	$100.00	↑	$50,000.00	
ORCL	Oracle Corp.	1000	$40.00	↓	$40,000.00	
DIS	Walt Disney Co.	2000	$65.00	↓	$130,000.00	
T	ATT Corp.	500	$90.00	↓	$45,000.00	
IOMG	Iomega Corp.	1000	$40.00	↑	$40,000.00	
CSCO	Cisco Corp.	1000	$50.00	↓	$50,000.00	
AAPL	Apple Computer.	3000	$20.00	↓	$60,000.00	
HAS	Hasbro, Inc.	1000	$31.00	↓	$31,000.00	
ARVN	Arvind Mills	5000	$4.00	↓	$20,000.00	
BTI	BAT Industries	500	$17.00	↓	$8,500.00	
ALA	Alcatel Alsthom	500	$20.00	↑	$10,000.00	
ERICY	L.M. Ericsson	100	$23.00	↑	$2,300.00	

FIG. 12.6 Grid component used to implement a table.

Some of the capabilities provided include row labels and column labels, flexible row and column sizing, in-place editing of cells, and complete control over tabbing policy.

Tree Package The Indius TREE package (`indius.grid`) is a Java class library that provides a simple tree data model and an easily customizable tree view, as shown in Figure 12.7.

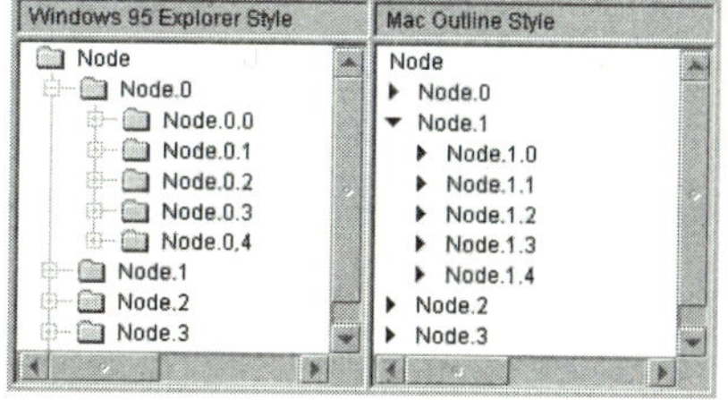

FIG. 12.7 Two different tree layouts using the Tree component.

The view includes buttons that allow portions of the outline to be expanded and collapsed. It also contains lines that illustrate the hierarchical relationships. There is support for optionally including icons with the text label of each item (or node) in the tree.

Calendar Package The Indius CALENDAR package (`com.indius.calendar`) is a Java class library that contains a number of views related to calendars (day view, week view, month view, etc.) A sample calendar view is shown in Figure 12.8.

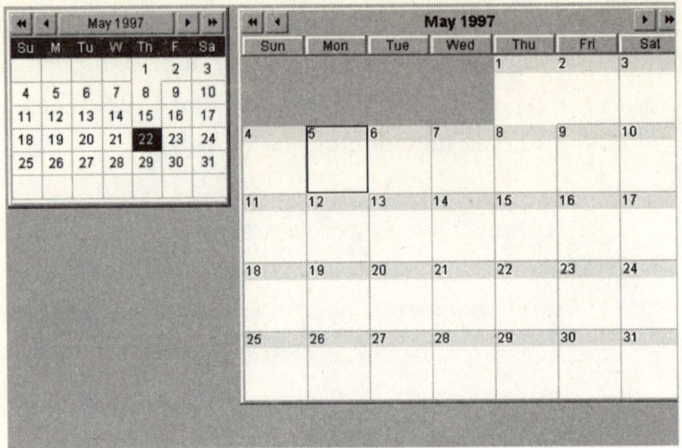

FIG. 12.8
Calendar components used to create different calendars.

All these classes are built around an industrial-strength date class, and depend fairly heavily on the concepts and classes defined in the GRID package (`com.indius.grid`).

Visual Numerics Libraries

Company: Visual Numerics, Inc.

http://www.vni.com/

Visual Numerics provides tools for data analysis and presentation and provides many Java libraries for developing network applications.

JWave Library The JWave components allow you to create visual and numerical analysis applications written entirely in Java. It provides access to data analysis and visualization techniques from a server running the PV-WAVE product. Sample output from a program using JWave components is shown in Figure 12.9.

JWAVE classes support plots, histograms, images, contours, surfaces, pie charts, bar charts, and VRML output. The JWAVE custom classes allow you to create any type of plot available from PV-WAVE. You can also tap into the power of PV-WAVE to perform complex numerical calculations.

SmartTable Library SmartTable converts basic Excel worksheets into Java applets. A sample SmartTable applet is shown in Figure 12.10. With the SmartTable converter, you can create custom calculators for such applications as expense reports, mortgage calculations, budgets, project tracking, and inventory analysis.

By embedding these SmartTable applets into an HTML page, you can distribute your spreadsheet applications across your intranet, extranet, or the Internet. Data is stored on a server that contains the latest version of the spreadsheet application, and changes are reflected to all applets as soon as data is changed.

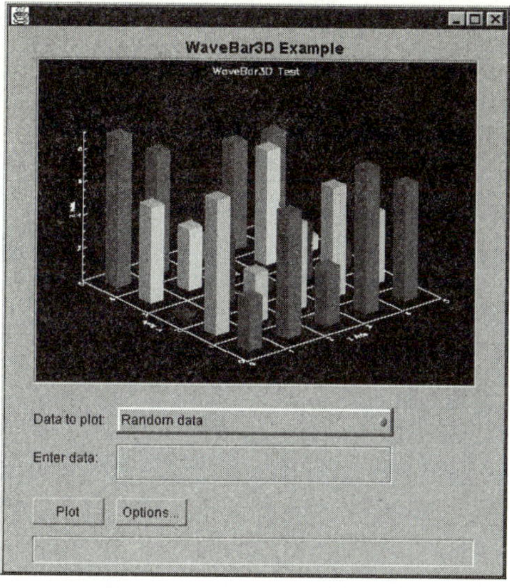

FIG. 12.9
Sample 3-D graph created using the JWave library.

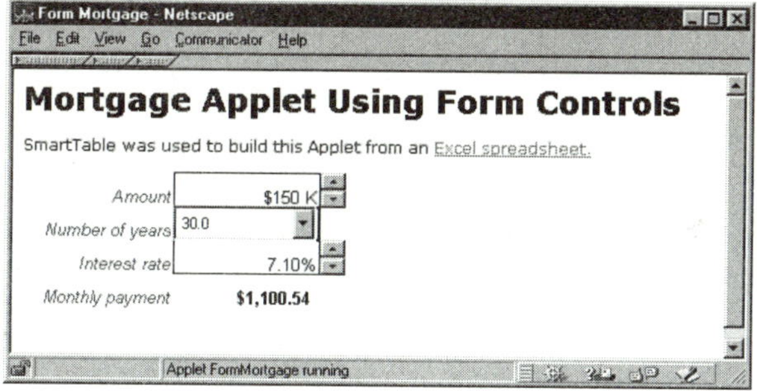

FIG. 12.10
Mortgage calculator applet using the SmartTable.

Netscape Constructor

Company: Netscape Communications Corporation

http://home.netscape.com/

Netscape Constructor for IFC is an all-Java visual design tool that allows IFC/Java developers to rapidly lay out graphical elements of their application's user interface, as well as assign target actions between UI objects and then test their intended behavior. It does not generate Java code, but instead stores the project in data files. A screenshot of Netscape Constructor is shown in Figure 12.11.

Constructor's file format provides the option of saving user interface projects as simple ASCII or IFC Archive/Binary files called Plan files. These contain IFC-specific information that is mapped to a Java program's objects prior to compilation of your Java program.

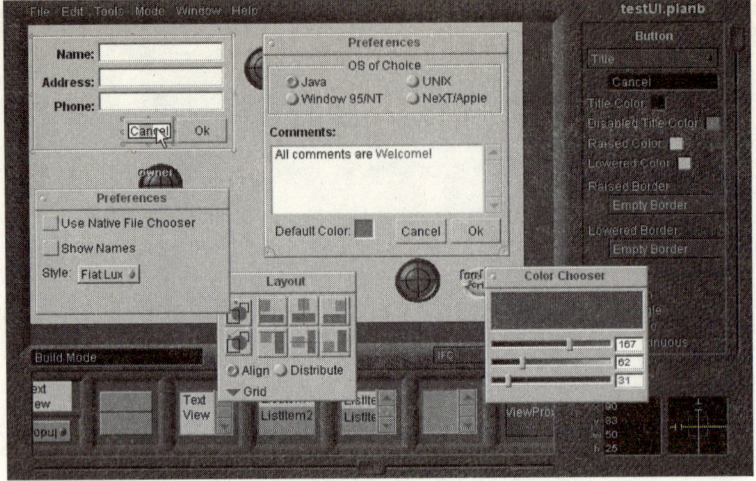

FIG. 12.11
Netscape Constructor screen shot showing various features.

Constructor provides an interactive environment that uses IFC's drag-and-drop support extensively, and is itself written using IFC technology. It is intended to be used by experienced Java programmers who are using IFC to prototype and design more advanced application user interfaces in less time.

By using prebuilt software building blocks, the Netscape Constructor application simplifies the task of arranging them in the creation of an application user interface. It also provides IFC developers with API support for adding/loading their own custom widgets and UI components.

Future versions of Constructor will be able to read and write JavaBeans.

Applications

IFC has enabled Java programmers to build and deploy network-centric, platform-independent applications, and the number of companies who are using IFC has increased at a rapid pace. Many commercial and non-commercial products have been announced in recent months. In addition, there are a number of IFC-based projects that are being implemented by organizations for internal use. The official IFC site at **http://developer.netscape.com/library/ifc/index.html** also contains some useful applications that demonstrate IFC capabilities. Here are some of these applications:

Netmosphere Actionplan

Company: Netmosphere, Inc.

http://www.netmosphere.com/

Netmosphere's ActionPlan product, shown in Figure 12.12, enables distributed IT workgroups to plan and effectively execute complex business projects. It offers a level of information-sharing across the enterprise found previously only in client/server products.

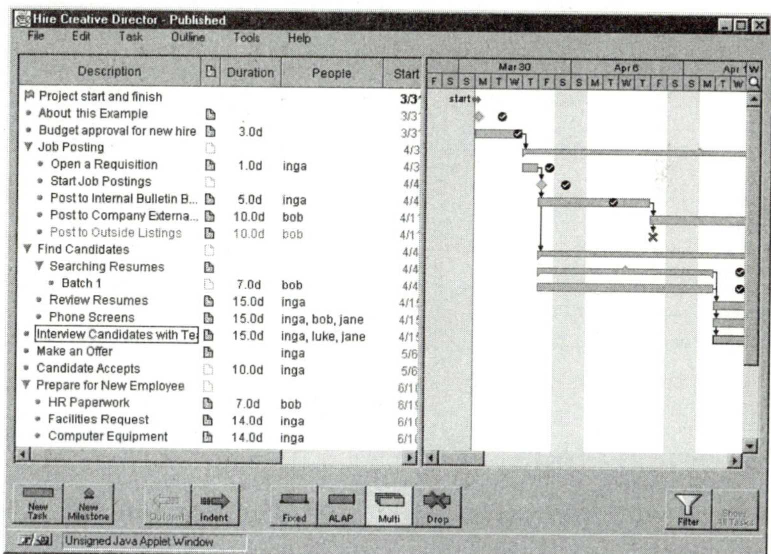

FIG. 12.12
Sample screen from Netmosphere's ActionPlan application.

ActionPlan is a Java-based thin-client application using a three-tier client/server model that installs easily using either a Web server or a Castanet Transmitter.

Digerati superMail

Company: Digerati Corporation

http://www.digerati.net/

Digerati's superMail product is a pure Java mail client written using IFC, and is based on standards such as IMAP4, POP3, MIME, and SMTP. Different mail systems are handled transparently, and preferences are stored locally or remotely. An address book, context-sensitive help, and network printing support are built in. Figure 12.13 shows a sample screen from superMail.

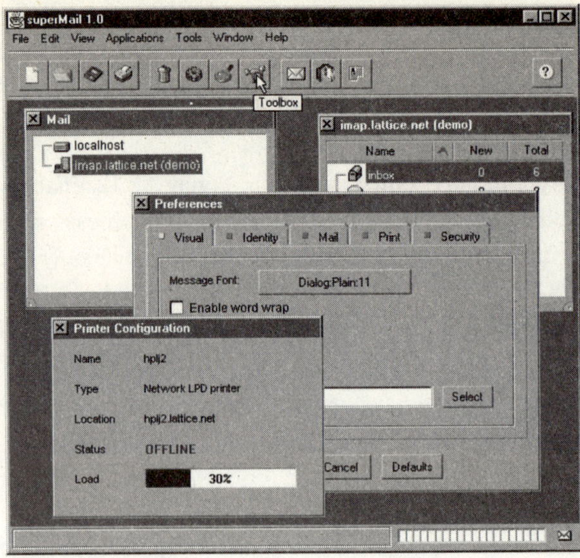

FIG. 12.13
superMail e-mail client from Digerati.

By extending many classes from IFC, superMail provides an advanced windowing system with embedded events, and implements most user-level operations using the drag-and-drop paradigm.

Sarrus Pencil-Me-In

Company: Sarrus Software, Inc.

http://www.sarrus.com/

Sarrus Pencil-Me-In is a Java-based calendaring solution that provides benefits to both end-users and the organizations in which they work. It is based on a new paradigm of open, standards-based Internet Calendaring Services. A sample screen shot is shown in Figure 12.14.

Pencil-Me-In has a typical calendar view, and you can arrange personal, group, and shared resource meetings. You can invite people to meetings and determine the best time for a particular meeting.

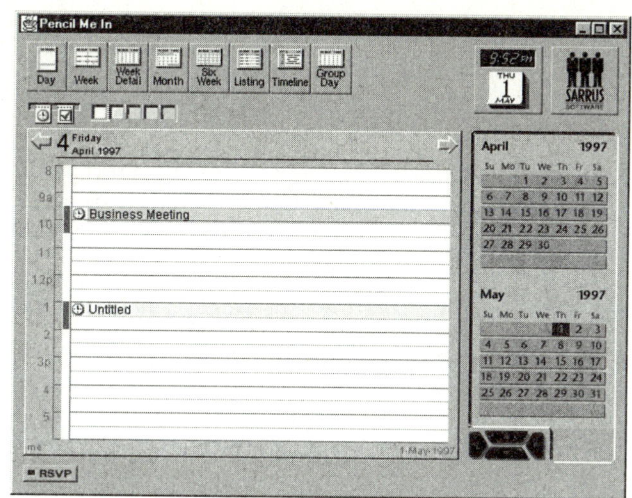

FIG. 12.14
The Pencil-Me-In calendaring package from Sarrus.

APPENDIX A

The Future

IFC has played a pioneering role in the field of foundation class programming on the Java platform. It has been used to develop powerful and robust applications in recent months.

To create an industry-standard user interface framework, Netscape has teamed up with Sun and IBM to create the Java Foundation Classes (JFC), which is going to be part of the core Java API, ensuring that it is present in every valid Java environment.

NOTE This information is based solely on press announcements made by Javasoft, Netscape, and IBM regarding the future of IFC. For the latest information, please check the Web sites of the preceding companies.

Java Foundation Classes (JFC)

At the JavaOne Conference at San Francisco in 1997, Javasoft and Netscape announced the Java Foundation Classes (JFC), which would draw on the strengths of both AWT and IFC technologies. JFC would be part of the core Java API, ensuring that it will be present on every Java installation.

The Java Foundation Classes is being developed jointly by Sun, Netscape, and IBM, and one of the primary goals is to provide a pluggable look and feel for Java applications that empowers users and developers to select the graphical user interface of their choice for each application. An example of such a pluggable look and feel is given in Figure A.1.

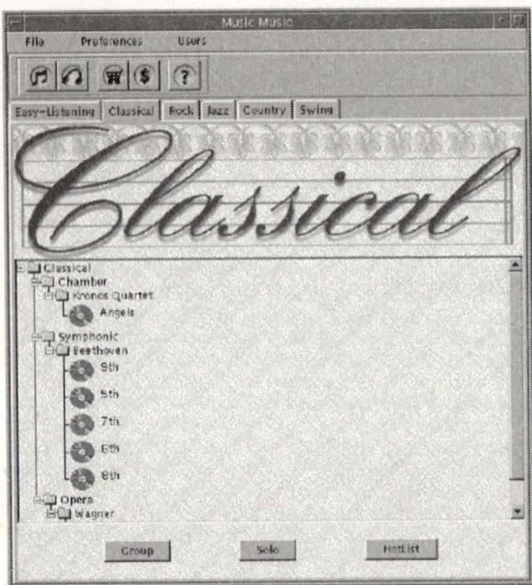

FIG. A.1
Win95 customized look and feel.

Some of the technical details known at this time are:

- All major IFC features supported, including lightweight user interface components, and the basic application framework.
- A straightforward migration path will be provided to quickly get both IFC and AWT developers upgraded to the new framework as quickly as possible.
- A complete application framework is provided to write pure Java applications.
- A robust set of lightweight, pure Java user interface components, which will be easily customizable.

- A simpler application model, including the ability to create single-threaded applications.
- Complex, rich text handling will be supported.
- Drag and drop support is built into the system.
- Keyboard-driven user interface support.
- JFC will include technology from JavaSoft that will allow for multiple "pluggable" UI look and feel sets. Several UI looks will be possible, including "Windows 95," "Macintosh," and so on.
- The new API will be compatible with JavaSoft's Abstract Windowing Toolkit (AWT).

IFC 1.1

In May, Netscape will ship version 1.1 of the IFC, which will be the last version of the IFC. Netscape will continue to provide technical support for the IFC well into the future, and the IFC will continue to be bundled in future Netscape products.

Netscape Constructor will continue to be available from Netscape as a free utility application for working with pure IFC controls and UIs. Constructor will be shipped in final form in the second quarter of this year. As with IFC 1.1, Netscape will continue to provide support for Constructor while also making Constructor available to third-party Java tools vendors for bundling in their products, in both source and object form.

IFC developers have been assured that they will have an upgrade path to the new JFC framework, which will become part of the core Java standard. Current IFC programs will continue to run unmodified in all future Java environments.

APPENDIX B

Frequently Asked Questions

Maintained for the IFC newsgroup by Jim White (jim@pagesmiths.com).

This appendix presents a list of some of the most frequently asked questions (FAQs) by IFC programmers. The latest list can be found at the official IFC site:

```
http://developer.netscape.com/library/ifc/
index.html
```

1. **Can anybody explain what all of the ALT stuff is about for buttons?**

   The `altImage()` and `altTitle()` methods are used to display the image and label, respectively, while the Button is in its depressed (or set) state.

2. **How can I convert a `java.awt.image` to `netscape.application.Bitmap`?**

   Use `AWTCompatibility.bitmapForAWTImage(java.awt.Image)`.

3. **How do I add a separator to an IFC menu?**

   IFC 1.1 has provided `Menu.addSeparator()` for this purpose.

4. **How do I create a popup menu in IFC?**

   Check out the aptly named `Popup` class.

5. **How do I embed an arbitrary applet inside an IFC view?**

   Take a look at `AWTComponentView`. It supports the embedding of any AWT component.

   Basically:

   ```
   AWTComponentView componentView = new AWTComponentView(x, y, w, h);
   componentView.setAWTComponent(anApplet);
   myView.addSubview(componentView);
   ```

   The component will be sized and positioned to be the same as the `AWTComponentView`. Overlapping IFC views will not clip the AWT component, causing the AWT component to always be drawn on top of IFC components, but events and redraws will happen at the right time.

6. **How do I implement drag-and-drop between my application's external windows?**

   Unfortunately, this is not possible. There is no provision in Java for drag-and-drop between external windows. You can, however, use IFC to implement drag-and-drop between internal windows with a minimal amount of effort by using the `DragSource` and `DragDestination` classes.

7. **How do I implement a password field?**

   Check out the `Password` field example in the IFC Examples available for download from the IFC site. It provides `PasswordField`, which extends `TextField` to echo the user's input, with each position filled with the same character that you specify.

NOTE IFC 1.1 has built-in support for implementing password fields with the `TextField.SetDrawableCharacter()` method.

8. **How do I tab between fields?**

   Use `TextField.setTabField()` and `TextField.setBacktabField()` to set the sequence/order between fields. Backtab is Shift+Tab.

9. **Drawing seems slow. How do I make it go faster?**

   There are a few standard things you can do to improve performance. Not all of them may apply to your particular case. They are as follows:

   - Make sure `View.isTransparent()` returns false for all completely opaque views.
   - Make sure the transparent flag is set properly on all Images and Bitmaps. Make it false whenever possible.
   - Make the View buffered (`View.setBuffered(true)`). This eliminates flicker at the cost of memory and CPU. IFC creates a single buffer for a view and all of its subviews, so it may be convenient to simply make the root view buffered.

10 **I'm creating a lot of external windows using IFC. I've noticed flickering when dragging windows from one location to another. Is there something that I can do to correct this problem?**

   Enable buffering in those windows. Use `myExternalWindow.rootView().setBuffered(true)`.

11. **How do I capture the "Window Close" (as with `Event.WINDOW_DESTROY` in AWT) event?**

   Use `WindowOwner`. Once you've created your window (whether internal or external), set the owner with `Window.setOwner`. You will get `WindowOwner.windowWillHide` and then `WindowOwner.windowDidHide` (if `windowWillHide` returned true) when the window is closed (as in AWT's `Event.WINDOW_DESTROY`).

   To close the window, use `Window.hide()`. In IFC, *hide* is synonymous with *close*. To detect the gain or loss of keyboard focus, use `WindowOwner.windowDidBecomeMain` and `WindowOwner.windowDidResignMain`.

12. **We want to set the override cursor so that a wait cursor is displayed during a long operation, so we execute `setOverrideCursor(WAIT_CURSOR)`. However, the wait cursor does not show up until the user moves the mouse. How do I force the override cursor to display?**

   Use `RootView.updateCursor()`, as in:

   ```
   myView.rootView().updateCursor();
   ```

   There is also `RootView.updateCursorLater()`, which will update the displayed cursor at the completion of the current event, along with the rest of the view updates.

13. **How can I make my `TextView` grow horizontally based on what's in it?**

    `TextView` does not grow horizontally; instead, it wraps lines. If you need this feature on a single line, you can use `TextField`.

14. **How can I make my `TextView` resize with its parent window or view?**

    To make a `TextView` or any other view resize with its parent view, you can use:

    ```
    // Where viewParent is the superview of view.
    viewParent.setAutoResizeSubviews(true);
    view.setHorizResizeInstruction(View.WIDTH_CAN_CHANGE);
    view.setVertResizeInstruction(View.HEIGHT_CAN_CHANGE);
    ```

15. **How do I get at the `EventLoop` for my application? Currently, I am passing a reference of the main class that extends `Application` to many subviews so that they can use the `Application.eventLoop()` method to get the eventloop for the application. This just seems like the long way around, especially when things like the `Button` class are able to get at the `Eventloop`.**

    Use the static method `application()` in the `Application` class to get a reference to the `Application` object.

    You can do this from any class without passing a reference. For example:

    ```
    Application.application().eventLoop().addEvent(anEvent);
    ```

    This is also a way to call any method in your `Application` subclass from any other class, except you need a cast:

    ```
    ((MyAppClass) Application.application()).myAppMethod();
    ```

16. **In my `View.mouseDown(MouseEvent)` method, the `event.clickCount()` is 1 no matter how fast I click. How do I get `clickCount` to be >1 for multiple clicks?**

    In order to detect multiple clicks, you must return true from `View.mouseDown(MouseEvent)`. Clicks must occur within 250 milliseconds (1/4 second) to be counted as multiple clicks. This is also true for receiving `View.mouseUp(MouseEvent)` and `View.mouseDragged(MouseEvent)` messages.

17. **I set the background color of my `TextView` to white with `TextView.setBackgroundColor(Color.white)`, but I only see the first line with background white. The rest is gray, and as I progress down, each line becomes white. How do I make the whole area white?**

    You also must set the color of the view that contains the `TextView`. The gray you see is not in the `TextView` itself but in the view behind the `TextView`, because the `TextView` does a `sizeToMinSize` whenever you add something to it.

    You need to do a `setBackgroundColor` for both the `TextView` and the `ContainerView`, `ScrollView`, or `ScrollGroup` that contains it, as appropriate to your application.

18. **It's nice how the `TextView` reads and displays HTML. Can I subclass the `TextView` to add my own tags/functionality? What's the API?**

    IFC 1.1 has added extensible HTML parsing to `TextView`. You can obtain the default rules from `TextView.htmlParsingRules()`. After defining the appropriate behavior for your tag(s) by using the `TextViewHTMLElement` subclasses, add them with `HTMLParsingRules.setRuleForMarker`.

19. **I'm using `PackLayout` to lay out buttons but the buttons don't appear. Why not?**

    Call `View.layoutView(0, 0)` after you have added all of your subviews (buttons). This is needed because `layoutView` is not called after each subview is added.

20. **`Unarchiver` has an `unarchiveIdentifier()` method, but I don't see how to get the identifier for a specific object. I can get the entire array of identifiers with the archive's `rootIdentifiers()`, but I don't know which identifier corresponds to what object until I unarchive them. In other words, my archive contains 50 objects and I want just one. How do I figure out which root identifier to unarchive from my archive?**

    The objects that you add to the archive are stored in the order you add them in the `rootIdentifiers` array. So, the identifier of the first root object you put into the archive is [0], the second is [1], and so on. If you don't like indexing by position, create a `Hashtable` of object names and root identifiers and then add that as the last root object. Unarchive the hashtable first, and then you can do all the name-based fetching you want. You could use that same `Hashtable` as a cache by replacing the `Integer` that was the root identifier with the unarchived object.

21. **I have a `TextView` that is having data from both the keyboard and the Net constantly appended to it. I want the keyboard data and the net data to be appended in different fonts. Since most of the data is from the Net, I executed `addDefaultAttribute(TextView.FONT_KEY, netfont)` for the Net and `addAttributeForRange(TextView.FONT_KEY, kbdfont, r)` for the keyboard data. But once I change the font to `kbdfont`, it changes for all subsequent `appendString()`. How do I set the attribute for characters or text appended to my `TextView`?**

    When you type a character in the `TextView`, the character attribute will not be the default attribute. It will be the attribute of the character near where you type. The exact rule is in the documentation.

    When one or more characters are inserted into the `TextView` by typing or by using the insertion methods, the following rules apply to determine how attributes apply to the new ranges:

- If there is a run after the inserted range, the inserted characters' attributes will be `defaultAttributes()` `UNION` the following run's attributes.
- If a run appears before the inserted range, the inserted characters' attributes will be `defaultAttributes()` `UNION` the previous run's attributes.
- If the previous two conditions don't apply, the inserted characters' attributes will be `defaultAttributes()`.

`TextView` in the future releases will provide a new API to set some "typing attributes." These attributes will be added for the typed character.

`TextView` provides both `addAttributesForRange()` and `setAttributesForRange()`. In your case, using `setAttributesForRange` is probably better.

22. **If I want to access an IFC applet called "myApplet" in an HTML page, should I use `AppletContext.getApplet("NetscapeApplet")` or `AppletContext.getApplet("myApplet")`?**

    Well, IFC doesn't have applets, it has `netscape.application.Application`. An applet is really `java.applet.Applet`. So, the answer to your question is `NetscapeApplet` (which extends `FoundationApplet`, which extends `java.applet.Applet`). You could, of course, change the name of the sample `NetscapeApplet` to be whatever you want, though.

    When using JavaScript you may use a name given by the `NAME` parameter of the `APPLET` tag. See the `JavaScriptLab` example, which is available as part of the IFC examples package, for more details.

23. **Since all IFC applets are launched by `NetscapeApplet` and are extensions of `Application`, how do I get to the applet's context?**

    Use `AWTCompatibility.getApplet().getAppletContext()`, which returns the applet for the application in the current thread group. Each instance of `netscape.application.Application` will be in its own thread group.

24. **Do I need to do anything to enable the small circle button on the top left title bar for the internal window? It is supposed to close the internal window, but it does nothing when I click it. Do I need to call an API to enable it?**

    Normally this problem crops up if you override `InternalWindow.performCommand` and do not call `super.performCommand()`. The `HIDE` command goes through `performCommand` to hide the window.

25. **Has anybody else noticed that when a drag session completes, the `mouseUp` event is never generated?**

    That is correct. The `mouseUp` event goes to the internal `DragView`. `DragSource` will tell you when the drag is done.

26. **Does `Bitmap.bitmapNamed()` wait until the image is loaded?**

    No, the `Bitmap` loads asynchronously. To start it loading and wait for it to finish, use `Bitmap.loadData()`.

27. **Why does using `Archive` to store and retrieve data seem very slow when I have lots of data?**

    This is very likely because the `String` names for your field keys in decode and encode are not identical (==) to the `String` names you used in `describeClassInfo`. To make these equal, define "final static String" constants for the field key names. You should also describe, encode, and decode the fields in the same order for fastest performance.

28. **When I remove a subview, drawing is messed up. What's wrong?**

    Do not use `View.removeSubview`, use `View.removeFromSuperview`. `View.removeSubview` is a protected method intended for `View` subclasses, which extend view functionality. `View.removeFromSuperview` is a public method intended for application interfaces.

29. **I have an applet that is displayed as an `AWTComponentView`. When I remove it, I only get a white rectangle where it used to be. What's wrong?**

    You may have a badly behaved applet that is not properly cleaning up after itself. Try using a simple applet that is known to be good to see if the problem is within your IFC application or in the AWT applet.

30. **What are text attributes?**

    Text attributes are a `netscape.util.Hashtable` of settings with a `TextView.XXX_KEY` key and a value whose type is a dependent key. Some commonly used text attributes are:

    - `PARAGRAPH_FORMAT_KEY`

      The value is a `netscape.application.TextParagraphFormat` instance. This is where you handle line spacing, justification, margins, and so on.

    - `FONT_KEY`

      Attribute that determines the font. The value is a `netscape.application.Font` instance.

    - `TEXT_COLOR_KEY`

      Attribute that determines the color of text. Value is a `netscape.application.a Color` instance.

31. **I add several `ListItems` to my `ListView`, but they don't show up. What's going on?**

    Call `ListView.sizeToMinSize()` to force the `ListView` to adjust to its new contents.

32. **After closing the IFC application, the Java command does not return. Why is this and how can I change that?**

    Closing your application's window(s) does not cause the application to quit. If you want the closing of your "main window" to quit your application, implement the `WindowOwner` interface in your `Application` subclass. In `windowDidHide()`, add `stopRunning()`. Before `app.run()` in `main()`, add `mainWindow.setOwner(app)`. After `app.run()`, add `System.exit(0)`.

33. Some of my `ExternalWindows` don't get positioned where I expect. Why not?

    There is a bug in the Windows implementation of AWT that prevents the correct bounds from being returned. It is supposed to be fixed under 1.1. It also currently should work correctly under Navigator.

34. **I've got a `TextFieldOwner` (call it "owner") and its owned text field (call it "field"). If I type into field and hit the enter key, owner gets a `textEditingDidEnd` call with the `<contentsChanged>` parameter correctly set to true if I made any changes, and set to false otherwise. However, if field loses typing focus because my code calls `field.completeEditing()`, owner gets a `textEditingDidEnd` call with the `<contentsChanged>` parameter set to false, regardless of whether or not the text has actually changed. Is this simply a bug in `TextField.completeEditing()`?**

    This was a bug in IFC 1.0 that is fixed in IFC 1.1.

35. **I am having a weird problem and I think it is a bug in the `upperCaseString()` method of the `Sort` class. I am trying to sort an array of strings that are all uppercase but that contain "dots" inside. Is there a problem with `Sort`?**

    There was a bug in IFC 1.0 that is fixed in IFC 1.1.

36. **`PackLayout` is not doing what I expect with my `ContainerView`. I'm using a `ContainerView` nested within a `ContainerView`, both managed by `PackLayout`. I'm expecting the red, inner view to be placed within the black, outer view, with a margin of 5. Instead, the inner `containerView` is placed as a small rectangle at the top, centered. Changing `SIDE_TOP` to `SIDE_BOTTOM`, for instance, has no effect on the placement of the red subview. Why?**

    This was a problem in IFC 1.0 caused by the `ContainerView` not respecting the `minSize` of its subviews.

The IFC 1.1 implementation now digs through its subviews and determines the current bounding box of all subviews. It then returns that size as its `minSize()`; an empty `ContainerView` would then have a `minSize()` of 0,0.

37. **Is there a problem with ASCII archives? `Archive.writeASCII` produces output that makes sense, but `Archive.readASCII` hangs somewhere. If I use binary `Archive.read` and `Archive.write` instead, things work okay.**

    This was a bug in IFC 1.0 that is fixed in IFC 1.1. The problem was that strings with "@" weren't getting quoted in ASCII serializations. Binary archiving never had this problem.

38. **In `TextView`'s definition of `LINK_KEY`, I read, "A range that has this attribute will tell the `TextViewLinkObserver` to follow the link when the user clicks the region." I've set the `LINK_KEY` attribute on some text in an applet, and sure enough, it highlights the text, changes color when clicked, and so on, but the HTML Browser does not follow the link. How do I implement links for TextView's HTML?**

    There is a problem in the documentation for `LINK_KEY`. You should read `TextViewOwner`, not `TextViewLinkObserver`.

    The idea is that when a link is clicked, the `TextViewOwner` receives the message `linkWasSelected(TextView sender, Range linkRange, String stringURL)`. In your implementation of `linkWasSelected()`, you can ask the current browser to load the page corresponding to the URL or you can ask `TextView` to load the URL (see the description of `TextView.importHTMLFromURLString(String urlString)` in the IFC documentation).

    The following example asks the current browser to load the page:

```
            public void linkWasSelected(TextView sender, Range linkRange,
String stringURL) {
                  java.applet.Applet jApplet = AWTCompatibility.awtApplet();
                  if ( jApplet != null ) {
                        java.applet.AppletContext ctxt =
jApplet.getAppletContext();
                        if ( ctxt != null ) {
                              try {
                                    ctxt.showDocument(new
URL(null,stringURL),"_self");
                              } catch (MalformedURLException e) {
                           Alert.runAlertInternally(Alert.warningImage(),"Bad
URL "+
                                    + stringURL + " is
invalid","OK",null,null);
                              }
                        }
                  }
            }
```

39. **I'm having trouble with Microsoft Visual J++. I am trying to compile the AddressBook Example from the IFC archive under Microsoft Visual J++ but I get the error "Need argument list for call to member 'Rect bounds()'." What's going on?**

    This is a bug in the MSVJ++ 1.0 compiler; you cannot have a data member and a function member of the same name.

40. **Is the ifc_10.zip file truly just a set of Java classes?**

    Yes.

41. **Why do I need to use an installer?**

    To bypass the performance problems of always having to download an applet from the Net each time you run it. An installer can overcome this problem by caching the relevant applet classes.

42. **Isn't there some better way to distribute the IFC classes than using the installers? And what about future updates?**

    This is being worked on for the next rev of the Navigator. We did the install stuff so that you didn't have to wait until then to deploy IFC applications. IFC also will be distributed as part of future releases of Navigator/Communicator.

Index

A

D

F

G

J

K

L

M

N

O

P-Q

R

T

W-X-Y-Z